The Spanish Pyrenees

The *Spanish Pyrenees*

Henry Myhill

FABER AND FABER LTD
24 Russell Square
London

First published in mcmlxvi
by Faber and Faber Limited
24 Russell Square London WC1
Printed in Great Britain by
The Bowering Press Plymouth
all rights reserved

To
GERALD BRENAN
To whom all who love Spain
owe so much

Acknowledgements

I wish to thank Mr. J. B. Morton for his permission to publish an extract from his book *Pyrenean*: Dr. Enrique Balcells for allowing me to attend the first course organized by his Pyrenean Centre for Experimental Biology; Dr. Antonio Casayús of the University of Zaragoza for arranging this and much else; Dr. Alfredo Floristán of the Catholic University of Navarre for reading suggestions; Doctora Carmen Virgili of the University of Oviedo for explaining *in situ* the structure of the central Pyrenees; and, for other help, Don Luis Bisquer and Don Veremundo Méndez of Hecho; the Secretario of Arano; the Secretario of Cadaqués; Señor Marcos of the Banco de Aragon in Jaca; and last but not least, the 'Alcalde' of Cabo Higuer.

I am grateful to the following people and agencies for permission to use their photographs:

Numbers 1, 3, 9, 12, 19, 21, 22, 23, 24, 25, 26, 27: Spanish National Tourist Office, London, S.W.1.

Number 2: Sr. Rafael, Zapatería 38, Pamplona.

Numbers 4, 5, 6, 8, 10: Ediciones Sicilia, Jesús 2, Zaragoza.

Numbers 7, 11: Ediciones Peñarroya, Mayor 30, Jaca (Huesca).

Numbers 13, 14, 15, 16: Sr. Porras, Viella (Lérida).

Numbers 17, 18, 20: Oficina de Turismo, Pobla de Segur (Lérida).

Contents

9

Contents

Part Three: THE CATALAN PYRENEES

MAPS

Illustrations

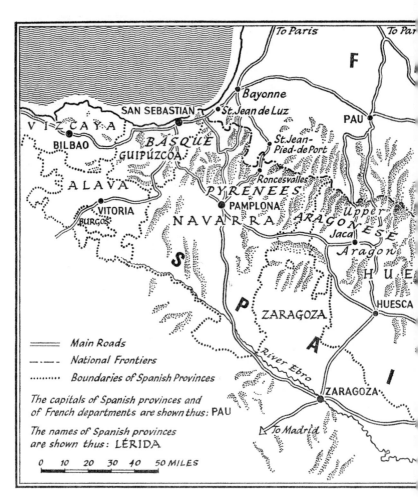

I GENERAL MAP

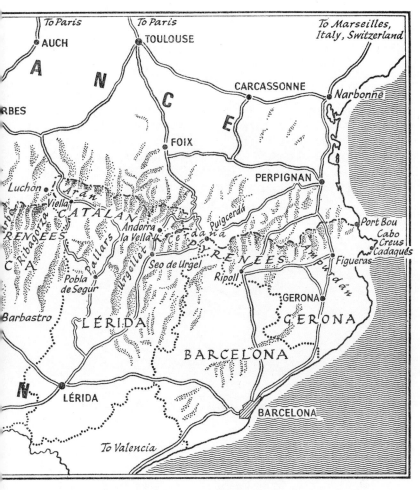

Neither this general map, nor any of the more detailed maps which follow, make any attempt to show everything, or even everything of interest. Nor should the fact that no road is marked between two places necessarily be taken to mean that no road of any sort exists

NOTE

Individual Spanish words have all been placed in italics, with the exceptions of fiesta, sierra, siesta, and pelota, which the author, following the Concise Oxford Dictionary (1949), took to be already integrated into English. Place names are spelt as in Spanish, except where there exists a generally used English equivalent, such as Navarre (instead of Navarra), or Saragossa (instead of Zaragoza). For the same reason an accent has sometimes been dropped. We know Henry VIII's first Queen as Catherine of Aragon, not as Catherine of Aragón.

Prologue at Cabo Higuer

'Desde el cabo Higuer, en el golfo de Vizcaya, hasta el cabo de Creus, en el Mediterraneo, en una longitud de 435 kilometros, forman los Pirineos una muralla rigida y apenas franqueable entre España y Francia.' (Luis Solé Sabaris, in *Los Pirineos*.)

The Pyrenees come into view as the train draws into the station of St. Jean-de-Luz. The traveller by road is conscious of them much earlier: on a clear day, indeed, they are said to be discernible as far away as Agen. It is the approach by train, however, that I have come to know the best. For every Monday morning for seven summers that view promised me rest and leisure after a long, long journey.

My work was to accompany the clients of eight of the largest British travel agencies between the Basque coast and the English Channel. Every Saturday evening between April and October I left northern Spain with the returning holidaymakers. When we reached Dieppe at midday on Sunday I saw them safely on to the ferry boat, and then travelled back with a newly arrived party by the same route, across Paris and down through Tours and Bordeaux. The parties were sometimes very large. The weather was sometimes very hot. There was much to do, and little time for rest. By the time that the train reached St. Jean-de-Luz, early on Monday morning, I was always very tired.

The sight of those familiar and well-loved mountains never failed to refresh me. I knew that I was back in my homeland, the wide and lovely belt of country across which I would soon be free to wander. For once the holidaymakers had reached their hotels my '40 hour week', accomplished all at one stretch, was over. From Monday morning until Saturday evening my time was my own, with the French department of the Basses-Pyrénées, and the Spanish provinces of Guipuzcoa and Navarre, waiting to be explored.

Prologue

Of those seven glorious summers which I spent on the Basque coast, working all weekend, but having the entire week at leisure, I suppose that the seventh was the best. This was really inevitable, for with every year that passed I adapted myself to make better use of the opportunities which my unusual occupation offered me. Instead of staying in hotels I began to take furnished flats. Instead of travelling by buses and trains I purchased a small car. And finally I succeeded in merging these twin concepts of independence and mobility. For at the beginning of my seventh summer I drove down through France in a motor caravan.

This gave me the freedom of the entire Basque country. Each Monday morning, as I added the cheeses which I had purchased the day before in Normandy to the wine and brandy of Spain, honey from Jaca, and tea and coffee which I had brought out from England, I tried to make up my mind where to drive for my five days of freedom.

There was a surfeit of choice. The sophistication of St. Jean-de-Luz and Biarritz, with tasty *pâtés* and fine bathing. The other-worldly atmosphere of Arano, a mountain village in Navarre, where the great mushrooms were just coming into season. Louhossoa, again over in France, deep in the valley of the Nive, where a luxurious but little-frequented camping site had been developed around an old hunting lodge of the Counts of Macaye. Or I could stay in San Sebastian itself, and enjoy my many long-standing friendships, and the programme of cultural events which unwound from June to September in Spain's summer capital. There were many other possibilities besides.

But more and more frequently, as that seventh summer wore on, I found myself, loaded with strawberries and cherries and green peas and whatever else was in season, driving out alongside the estuary of the Bidassoa, the river which forms the frontier between France and Spain. Over on the French side, the coast soon turns away north, but on the Spanish side it is continued by a single mountain, Jaizquibel, the last height of the Pyrenees. This in its turn is prolonged by a rocky cape, surrounded on three sides by the sea.

A lighthouse dominates Cabo Higuer, as this promontory is known (though no fig tree, or *higuera*, has ever been known to grow there). There are two other buildings nearby, a barracks of the Civil Guard, and a huge villa, with grounds surrounded on three sides by a high wall, and on the fourth side by the sea. There is also an open-air bar, operated during the summer by a man with a restaurant in the fishing town of Fuenterrabía, a couple of miles up the estuary.

I had already been aware for some years of the attractions of this lonely spot. However, I was uncertain whether the Civil Guards – Spain's helpful but efficient police – would take kindly to the idea of a foreign motor caravan parking there for days on end. But the very first time that I drove it out there, it excited the interest of a handsome dark-eyed man who emerged from the grounds of the big villa.

He proved to be not only the caretaker of the villa, which was the summer home of Spain's senior government architect, but also a retired Civil Guard. Over a glass of red wine at the bar – where we were to drink so many bottles of red wine in company that summer – he invited me to stay at Cabo Higuer for as long as I wished, assuring me not only of the tolerance of the Civil Guards, but of their active vigilance in protecting me when asleep, and my mobile home when I was absent. His invitation was issued with authority, and I was soon to learn that this authority was that of a mayor.

'If the *alcalde* says that you can park here,' said Juanito, the owner of the bar, 'Then there's no more to be said. Enrique' – he pointed to my new friend – 'is the *alcalde* of Cabo Higuer, and what he decrees in the *ayuntamiento*, or town hall, which is where we are now, has all the force of law.'

And thus I was initiated into the great charade, in which I was to play a part all summer long. That very evening Enrique, the *alcalde*, appointed me as one of the *concejales*, or town councillors of Cabo Higuer (with special responsibilities, in view of my nationality, for foreign affairs!), and I attended the first meeting, under his firm chairmanship, of the 'town council' in the 'town hall'.

One by one I met my fellow-councillors, as they arrived at the bar. There was Juanito himself, who was *secretario*, or town clerk, in view of his all-important function of keeping the councillors' glasses topped up. There was Paco, a Basque bachelor in his mid-sixties, who walked every day from the farm where he had been born, beret on his head, and thick umbrella in his hand, to assist Enrique in keeping the grounds of the villa in order. His life had settled into an even pattern since he had done his military service in Morocco back in 1922. Only once had he crossed over to France, which we could see a couple of miles away from where we stood at the bar. That had been in 1924, when he had purchased, for ten pesetas, a heavy pocket watch which he still pulled out from a leather case whenever he wanted to know the time. He was a living example of the conservatism and tenacity which form one side of the Basque character. For although he lived within sight of France, and in a village which every summer filled with *veraneantes* from Madrid, he spoken Castilian only with difficulty.

Two other councillors who attended the meetings at the *ayuntamiento* with fair regularity were his nephews. Pascual and Ignacio, in their thirties, were joint owners of a fishing boat. Self-employed and independent, they typified another side of the Basque character: the seafaring, adventurous spirit which had made a Basque the first man to sail right round the world. Indeed, Ignacio's *novia*, or fiancée, was from Guetaria, the home village of El Cano (who took over command from Magellan on the latter's death in the Philippines); and it was not surprising that their fishing trips often took them west, to where the 'Mouse' rock of Guetaria stands out to sea.

They had often been farther afield. Two years previously, a syndicate in Fuenterrabía had fitted out a boat which had spent several months fishing off West Africa. It was interesting to hear their account of the then British colony of Sierra Leone, with 'the black men who spoke English', as it appeared to Spanish eyes. From out at sea Pascual and Ignacio could see my motor caravan, and knew when I had arrived at Cabo Higuer. 'Ha llegado el inglés!' and they would make for the shore, and for the *ayuntamiento*.

A more occasional attender at council meetings was Pedro, the chauffeur of the family who owned the villa. He was a rather taciturn character, and of much fairer hair and complexion than the average Spaniard, but with a deep sense of humour.

Then there were the Civil Guards, who would walk up from their barracks in mufti, or who would join us for a drink as they set off, always two at a time, on a tour of duty. They were on the watch not only for smugglers from France, but also for Spanish citizens attempting to leave their national territory without a passport, and for illegal conducted tours. These last were groups of

Portuguese whom self-appointed couriers had volunteered – for a consideration – to spirit out of Portugal, across Spain, and into the promised land of France.

These *parejas* or pairs of Civil Guards, off on a long and sometimes a cold night's vigil, were always welcomed to our meetings by Enrique, who only a few years before had been one of them himself. Born in Seville, he had early in his career been 'destined', as the Castilian so appropriately phrases it, to this corner of the frontier. But neither his long residence in Guipuzcoa, nor the fact that he had married a Basque girl, had changed in the slightest degree his Andalusian temperament and manner. It was with a superb panache that he used to preside over our meetings at the *ayuntamiento*.

And what meetings those were, of the town council of Cabo Higuer! While the evening was still young, we would sit quietly in a corner apart, or stand at one end of the bar. From a distance we would eye with interest the *juventud dorada*, the bright young things down from Madrid, infinitely agreeable young men in various shades of beige accompanying infinitely appealing girls in pale blue jeans and darker tops, with even darker eyes. Then, when the last of these had returned to dinner at the villas or apartments in Fuenterrabía where they were spending the summer, the corporation of Cabo Higuer, left to itself, moved into the centre of the stage. Our laughs grew louder, and our conversation more uninhibited.

There was a more than alcoholic intoxication about those summer nights. As the beam of the lighthouse swung regularly round, we felt ourselves a little oasis of life, alone between the ocean which we could hear breaking all around us, and the clear starlit sky above. Alone, too, between two nations, for the lights of the French coast winked away at us from Hendaye to Biarritz, until the horizon hid the flat shore beyond the mouth of the Adour.

There was a further element in the landscape, which at once heightened and tempered our exhilaration. When the moon was not shining this was an element which we could not see, yet even then I think that we were each conscious of its presence, like an invisible guest at our gatherings.

Perhaps it was for this reason that our conversation – or rather, 'the deliberations of the town councillors of Cabo Higuer' as

Enrique would correct me – so often turned in the same direction. For the whole world was ours, on our rock in the ocean, and it can only have been the mountains themselves which brought our thoughts and our talk again and again back to the Pyrenees.

The pairs of Civil Guards, stopping for a drink as they went on duty, would talk of their winter life cut off in the Casa Blanca, another of their barracks high up on the face of Jaizquibel. Enrique would reminisce about the German occupation of France, when especial vigilance was required along the frontier, and would describe duties which had taken him up the Peña de Aya, the Mountain of the Three Crowns. Pascuel and Ignacio would explain how even when they had missed the weather forecast on the radio, they knew what to expect from the appearance of the mountains out at sea.

Inevitably, in view of the generation to which Enrique and Pedro belonged, our talk often wandered to the Civil War. But in doing so, it did not leave the mountains. For although there were so many fronts on which they might have fought – Estremadura, Madrid, Guadalajara, or the Ebro, to give only four of the best known – it so happened that both had spent almost the entire war on one of the least known of all: the front in upper Aragon, which ran from the besieged city of Huesca into the very heart of the Pyrenees.

It had been one of the least active fronts in Spain. The great battles which had decided the war had been fought elsewhere. But life had been far from dull. Both sides were alert in the keen mountain air. The Republican lines lay only a few hundred yards to the east of the main road from Jaca to Huesca, and it had been Pedro's nightly task to drive along this road bearing dispatches and supplies. He had found that the one infallible method of avoiding fire had been to keep up such a speed that he was past any particular group before they had time to train their sights on him. But this very speed had its own dangers. For he recalled one particularly dark night when he took a wrong turning, and was almost across the enemy lines before he had realized his mistake.

Enrique, too, would talk of the long distances across which one could see in the still hot air of the long summer days, and of the long distances across which sounds would carry in the still cold air of the long winter nights. Listening, I was carried back to the peaceful, but equally still and stimulating upper Aragon which I had known twelve years after the Civil War had ended. They were very male gatherings, those meetings of the councillors of Cabo Higuer. Juanito had two female assistants, but both accepted that when the *ayuntamiento* was in session, they were there merely in order to replace each bottle of red wine as it was emptied by another full one, and to act as the cheerful butts of our unmalicious but blunt humour. This they were well qualified to do. The younger, a handsome Basque girl from Vizcaya, the next province. was what is known as *salada*. This meant that she was 'salted', or witty, and knew how to answer back, smartly and pertly, to the various sallies which were constantly thrown at her across the bar.

The older woman was the wife of the lighthouse keeper. She spoke little, for she belonged to one of Spain's less exuberant races. She was that *rara avis*, a *catalana* amongst the Basques. Nor was she from Barcelona, nor from one of the interior capitals such as Gerona or Lerida. She was from the coast, and from the very village, Cadaqués, which stands in an almost antipodean position in the Mediterranean to that of Cabo Higuer in the Atlantic. For whereas Jaizquibel, the last height of the Pyrenees in the west, falls into the Atlantic in Cabo Higuer, so the Sierra de Rosas, the last height of the Pyrenees in the east, throws one last promontory into the Mediterranean, Cabo Creus, on which stand the fishing village of Cadaqués.

The eyes of the *farista*'s wife more than made up for the few words which left her mouth. Anyone who knew a great deal about eyes and about women could have read worlds into the flash of her pupils and the lowering of her eyelashes. Even I, in my inexperience, felt one day that I had been given a full, perfect, and sufficient answer when in reply to my remark 'There are many mountains between your birthplace and where you live now', she had merely nodded her head.

For watching her eyes, I could sense her mind measuring the mountains and the distances which lay between Cabo Creus and Cabo Higuer, 270 miles and several worlds apart. My own eyes must have taken on much the same look as hers, for I, too, knew something of the country in between. The olive-covered hills near her home. The lost valleys of Aragon. The proud communities of Navarre. And there was so much more that I wanted to know.

21

Prologue

The hidden villages within sight of Canigou. The ski slopes and spas beloved of the Barcelona *bourgeoisie*. The great peaks clustered where Catalonia meets Aragon. The Swiss quality of the Valley of Arán. It seemed more than mere chance which had brought a native of Cadaqués to Cabo Higuer, to live beside another sea but under the spell of the same range of mountains.

It is not only the nights, gathered in the *ayuntamiento*, which have left me with fond memories of Cabo Higuer. My days, too, were golden days, undeserved by anyone over the age of twelve. Mount Jaizquibel, sloping steeply into the sea, provided me with an unspoilt playground some ten miles long by two miles wide, with only footpaths leading from freshwater springs down lonely combes, or from shepherds' huts amongst the bracken to the occasional deep creek made by the sea. Day after day I set off amongst the pinewoods wearing only swimming trunks and rope-soled sandals, to spend hours on end in the shade of a rock beside a calm inlet, with a book and a *bocadillo* and a cool half-litre of wine.

It may be wondered what view the police took of a lone Englishman wandering half naked along a Spanish mountainside within sight of France. But the police were my friends. They were the same Civil Guards with whom I had been drinking the previous night at the *ayuntamiento*. A black three-cornered hat would dissociate itself from the rocks high above my inlet, and a gun would be raised in greeting. Or a *pareja*, on their tour of duty together, would halt for a few minutes' chat when our paths happened to cross. Occasionally I would pass a single Civil Guard, travelling to or from the Casa Blanca, the white barracks far up the mountain which was the last human habitation for eight miles. It was at such moments, alone with a foreigner amidst the pine and the bracken, that a man might sometimes give voice to deep feelings, too poetic for expression to his fellows.

I remember in particular one lovely morning. My haversack contained bread and wine, cheese and tomatoes, peaches and grapes, with a copy of the *Observer* to digest when the swimming and the eating were over. My body was already that deep brown which comes only from a long summer of Latin sunshine. The sea sparkled as it broke against the rocks far below. And I could almost feel the resin-scented air of the pinewoods building up a protection within me against the ills of an English winter. As I turned a corner I came face to face with an old friend, a sergeant in his forties.

'Yes, it is a lovely day,' he said, in answer to my opening remark. 'And this is a pretty spot, too, as you say. But it's not the real thing, you know.'

I looked at him, a little puzzled. Real or not, I found it hard to believe that there could be a more beautiful place than where we were.

'These mountains are just toys,' he continued. 'And this air is soft and sweet, but it's not the true mountain air. It's not like Salvatierra.'

'Which Salvatierra?' I enquired, for there are almost as many Salvatierras in Spain as there are Newtowns in England. I imagined some hamlet of the Sierra de Gredos, or of the Maestrazgo.

'Salvatierra de Esca, in the province of Saragossa,' he replied. At first I could recall no mountains near that city of the flat Ebro plain. And then the name itself rang a bell. I remembered how a thin tongue of Saragossa province licks up, over the Canal de Berdún, to the very gateway of the Valley of Roncal.

'Salvatierra is my wife's *pueblo*,' he went on. 'There you can see for kilometres in the clear mountain air of Navarre and of Aragon. At night, after dinner, my brothers-in-law leave the house and in sheer joy burst into song, echoing across the valley. And when I am there, I sing with them. And the whole silent world is ours.'

And beautiful as is the coast near Cabo Higuer, I knew enough of the mountains in the interior to understand what he meant, and to feel a nostalgic yearning for the dry air, for the small stone villages, and for the climbing dusty roads. If the following year I gave up an impossibly good job, it was not only because my discovery of the motor caravanning life had made it possible for me to explore Italy, and Austria, and Scandinavia, and so much else. Nor was it only because seven summers of simple living in the Basque country had enabled me, squirrel-like, to accumulate sufficient acorns for many winters. It was also because I wished to deepen into friendship my acquaintance with the Spanish Pyrenees.

Part One

The Basque Pyrenees

1. West of The Pic D'Anie

The Pyrenees form the western half of the longest of the various ranges which run from west to east across the Iberian peninsula. Rising in Galicia, this range runs parallel with and close to the coast. In Asturias it throws up a series of peaks approaching 8,000 feet known as the Picos de Europa. It then passes through the most northerly province of Old Castile, Santander, which is so hilly that it is commonly known simply as *la Montaña*, the Mountain. The range descends to lower altitudes in the Basque country, and only where it leaves the coast to form the frontier between France and Spain does it become the Pyrenees. This first part of the book will therefore only mention one of the three traditionally Basque provinces: Guipuzcoa. For Guipuzcoa alone has a frontier – albeit a short one – with France.

With one small exception, indeed, all the places described in this book are situated in the five northern frontier provinces, so that the area covered may be defined as the Pyrenean regions of the provinces of Guipuzcoa, Navarre, Huesca, Lerida, and Gerona. I am aware that the great sierras around Berga may be regarded as essentially Pyrenean; but I am sure that any Catalan would agree with me that the mountains of Barcelona province deserve a book all to themselves, and because Barcelona province just fails to reach the frontier at Puigcerdá, I have chosen a definition which will allow the Sierra del Cadí to act metaphorically as the wall which anyone who sees it will recognize it to be.

Guipuzcoa, as noted, has only a short frontier, and most of this section will be devoted to Navarre. Yet I have given it the title 'The Basque Pyrenees'. This is because Navarre is just as Basque as the three traditionally Basque provinces, but has enjoyed a different political development. Once Basque was spoken in every corner of Navarre, and within living memory* it was

* See Part One–8, 'The Dying Tongue'.

still in use throughout the Pyrenean belt of the province. Even today it is the everyday language of most of this belt, so that there is no need to adopt the cumbrous adjective *vasco-navarro* used by Spanish geographers. 'The Basque Pyrenees' will cover everything from Jaizquibel to Roncal.

There are good reasons why this area should form a unity. The tendency in England is to sniff at both France's departments and Spain's provinces, as being artificial creations of the Age of Reason, of the French Revolution or of that enlightened despot, Charles III. Even University lecturers will compare them unfavourably with our own counties and shires. Yet the English shires, except when they directly correspond with the ancient kingdoms of the heptarchy (Yorkshire, Kent, Essex, and so on), were purely artificial creations of King Alfred and his successors.

The French departments and the Spanish provinces, on the other hand, were subdivisions of ancient kingdoms and duchies, and these subdivisions themselves often followed well-established frontiers of ethnic, geographical, or political origin. Bedfordshire, Northamptonshire, or Leicestershire may have been administrative divisions since the turn of the tenth century, but they remain artificial creations beside such departments as Aveyron, with its pre-Roman tribal origins, or beside such provinces as Huesca or Navarre.

For the truest frontiers, sad to relate, are frontiers which have been fought over. No battles determined that the Welland should divide Leicestershire from Northamptonshire. But blood was spilt on the Tamar or in the Weald, before it was decided where Cornwall or Sussex should end, and where Devon or Kent should begin. And blood was spilt, too, on the arid marches between Javier, the outpost of Navarre, and Sos del Ray Católico, the birthplace of Ferdinand of Aragon.

Javier is a name with little significance for English ears. But just as Don Quijote becomes more familiar in his sixteenth-century form of Don Quixote, Javier too becomes more recognizable as it was spelt in 1506, when a son newly born to the house of Xavier was christened Francisco.

We shall have more to say about St. Francis Xavier later on. Many have wondered at his success in communicating with the peoples of the Far East, in an age when there were no chairs of Oriental languages in the universities of Europe. He may have owed something of this success to the fact that the first language he ever learnt was probably the most difficult language of all: Basque.

For there have survived letters of St. Francis Xavier written in Basque, and it is almost inconceivable that he should have acquired a knowledge of it in later life. Not only would there have been no point in his learning it after childhood, but the proved cases where this has been achieved can be counted on the fingers of two hands. M. Pierre Lamarre has repeated the remark which one so often hears in the Basque country. 'Isn't it said on the spot that it is necessary to have learnt it [the Basque language] at a mother's breasts?' And to emphasize its difficulty he goes on: 'It is true the mothers there used to breast feed for as long as they had any milk.'

So in the early-sixteenth century Basque was almost certainly the everyday language of all classes in most of Navarre, even on the extreme eastern frontier at Javier. But even without the evidence of St. Francis's letters we would know that Basque had been spoken there at some moment in the past. We would know this because of the name Javier itself, which is a typically Basque place-name.

Anyone getting out a map to search for similar place-names would soon be rewarded in stumbling across villages named Javerregay and Javierrelatre. But he might feel confused when he found that these were situated not in Navarre, but well across the border of Aragon. The answer to this paradox is that just as within historic times Basque was spoken throughout Navarre, so in prehistoric times it was spoken over a far wider area still. We shall still be noticing Basque place-names deep in the Catalan Pyrenees*, when we are nearer to the Mediterranean than to the Atlantic.

Exactly who the Basques were, and exactly how wide the areas where they once lived, are questions over which the experts themselves disagree, about which such evidence as exists is often confusing, and about which much research remains to be done. They are not, in any case, questions which it is necessary to try to answer in a general guide to the Spanish Pyrenees. Here it is sufficient to say, as non-committally as possible, that the Basques are an ancient race, probably of pre-Indo-European origin, and

* See Pierre Lamarre's article in *Pirineos*, Año XII, 1956.

that their lands may once have included most of the Pyrenees, and wide regions to north and south, at least as far as Bordeaux in France and Soria in Spain.

They probably, therefore, occupied a cardinal place in the Pyrenean past. And there is no doubt that even in their present restricted homelands they play a major role in the Pyrenean present, as the title of this section shows. And the question to which this book ought to suggest an answer is why the Basque Pyrenees are situated where they are. Or, to put it another way, what qualities are possessed by the lands described in this section which have enabled an ancient race speaking a strange tongue to survive there intact – and there only – until the present day?

Thinking of the Romanche of Switzerland, of the Albanians, or of the Lapps, many might at once suggest distance from the main lines of communication, and mountains. But the Basque country lies directly across the main route from France into Spain: from Paris to Madrid. Here, along the Bidassoa, and nowhere else on the frontier, have the customs authorities thought it worthwhile to establish two entry points within a couple of miles of each other. And the outstanding quality of the Basque Pyrenees as mountains, by comparison with the rest of the range, is that they are low, rounded, and crossed by many easy passes. It is with good reason that the French have called their department which runs parallel to Guipuzcoa and Navarre the Basses-Pyrénées. If the Basques once occupied the difficult highlands of the Central Pyrenees, then why have they not survived there, rather than amongst these coastal hills?

Yet the first, obvious answer may be the right one, although not for the obvious reasons. It is true that today even more tourists pour across the Bidassoa and through Irún than across the Perthus Pass and through La Junquera. Yet in Hannibal's time, and for almost two thousand years afterwards, it was this latter, Mediterranean route which carried most traffic, and all the great invasions in both directions. This was not only because the countries of northern Europe were then relatively less important than those around the Mediterranean. It was due also to the very structure of the Basque Pyrenees.

The reader may have wondered whether I have forgotten Roncesvalles and Charlemagne, in declaring that none of the great invasions passed this way. But this was a raid rather than an invasion. The enduring legacy of the Carolingians south of the Pyrenees was elsewhere, in the stimulus given to early Aragon, and in the Spanish March which from Narbonne to Barcelona straddled the old *Via Domitia* through the Perthus.

Viewed even as a raid, the Roncevalles episode was successful only as an inspiration to later poets. For Charlemagne's rearguard under Count Roland was destroyed as it made its way through the pass. And its attackers were not the Moslems, but, as Charlemagne's first biographer Einhard tells us – in perhaps the first literary reference to the Basques – the *Wascones*.

Roland died in 778, just four years less than a millenium after Hannibal had marched north from Sagunto; and after yet another millenium another battle illustrated the dangers of crossing the Pyrenees at the Atlantic end instead of by the Carthaginian's Mediterranean route. For on 21st June, 1813, near Vitoria, the capital of the Basque province of Alava, Wellington routed the French under Napoleon's brother King Joseph. The French army was lucky to escape to Pamplona by the one narrow road left open, and had to abandon all but one of their 152 guns, and their whole vast baggage train, loaded with the spoils of five years' occupation of Spain.

It is true that west of the Pic d'Anie – which is both the last peak over 8,000 feet, and the beginning of the Basque lands – the Pyrenees are lower; but the country is anything but a level plain. The population centres lie in fragments of old valleys, with no natural lines of communication to the interior. Such natural routes as do exist are along the short rivers which run north into the Atlantic. These not only lie across the main road from France into Spain, but they have led the inhabitants to look away from the rest of Spain, and towards the sea.

Simple, by comparison, are the massive lines on which are built the Central Pyrenees. From the high peaks long wide valleys have been ploughed through the pre-Pyrenean sierras by the glaciers of the Ice Ages. Up these have slowly penetrated the culture and the language of the plains. For the peoples of these valleys are not only fewer on the ground than in the Basque country, but have not had the sea to turn them away from the interior.

The Basques were therefore at once left to themselves and drawn together by the absence of natural land routes. They were also protected to the north, until two centuries ago, by the inhospitable nature of the Landes, before the government of Louis XVI began the work of afforestation. Everything combined to make them develop on their own, preserving amongst themselves the language and the way of life which already made them unique.

2. The Basques

The wrath of all the experts has already been invited by a mere suggestion of the possible origins and extension of the Basques. So we shall not refer to these problems again, except to repeat that they exist, and that they are amongst the most fascinating problems of ethnology.

Whatever areas they once occupied, and wherever they came from, where do the Basques live now, and what are they like?

They live where the Pyrenees meet the Atlantic, in an area unequally divided into two by the frontier between France and Spain. Of the seven Basque provinces, three are situated in France: Labourd, which means, as it sounds, the border of the sea, and includes all the well-known resorts of the *Côte Basque* – Biarritz, St. Jean-de-Luz, and Hendaye; Basse-Navarre, the trans-Pyrenean territory of the old kingdom of Navarre, centred on St. Jean-Pied-de-Port; and Soule, the hilly country around Tardets and Mauléon.

But these are all small. All three are included in the department of the Basses-Pyrénées, two-thirds of which is occupied by the old county of Béarn. Not one of them is as large as any of the four Spanish Basque provinces. These are Guipuzcoa and Navarre which we have already mentioned, and Vizcaya and Alava farther away from the frontier.

History has not only separated the Spanish Basques from their kinsmen over in France. It has also tended to divide them amongst themselves. A significant date was 1200, when King Sancho the Strong of Navarre was forced to cede the overlordship of Alava, Vizcaya, and Guipuzcoa to Castile. Without a coastline, Navarre thenceforward had few commercial contacts. And after her glorious part in the battle of Las Navas de Tolosa in 1212, she had no further role to play in the reconquest of the peninsula from the Moslems, the *Reconquista*, which swept on far beyond her own southern frontier on the upper Ebro.

So Navarre, which should have been the natural political expression of all the Basques, developed the traditional and conservative attitudes of a pastoral and agricultural people, in marked contrast to the thrusting, adventurous spirit of the coastal towns. The Carlists, during both the civil wars of the mid-nineteenth century, found their main support in Navarre, and there established their headquarters – in Estella the younger Don Carlos even held court for a time – but they never succeeded in taking Bilbao or San Sebastian.

During the following years the contrast between the two regions grew, as industry came to the coast. *Los Altos Hornos de Vizcaya* became Spain's safest blue-chip investment, and the *Banco de Bilbao* the doyen of her commercial banking system. But up in Lecumberri and in Elizondo they were still dreaming of a medieval never-never land of 'one monarch, one empire, and one sword'.

The last act in this story was perhaps the saddest of all. With whichever side one has most sympathy, the Civil War of 1936 to 1939 was a tragedy. It divided many families, and unhappily it divided the Basque family. A movement for home rule had been slowly growing amongst the coastal Basques, and home rule was actually granted in a last-minute bid for support by the Republican government. The bombing of Guernica (the old capital of the three traditionally Basque provinces) by the Germans, and the boatloads of children evacuated to Britain from Bilbao, are still amongst the most vivid memories of that war in English minds.

On the Nationalist side, on the other hand no troops were more dedicated than the Carlist *requetés* of Navarre. They formed the extreme right wing of the various sections of Spanish society which rose in the National Movement of 18th July, 1936; and one of the cleverest steps ever taken by Europe's cleverest statesman, Francisco Franco, was when he persuaded the Carlist organization to merge with that of the national socialist *Falange*, the least conservative of his supporters, in April, 1937.

The paradoxical result of the war was that the coastal Basques lost not only the complete home rule for which they had been fighting, but also the very real measure of autonomy which Vizcaya and Guipuzcoa had always enjoyed; whereas Navarre, fighting for a centralizing government, retained her ancient autonomy intact. (A few *fueros* were also retained by the other inland Basque province, Alava). Most of what happens in Navarre is still decided not in Madrid, but in Pamplona.

The key to any such independence is necessarily financial. Certain taxes are locally raised and locally spent, instead of being handed out in grants from the central government. As a result, matters which Navarre regards as important get prior attention. The roads of Navarre are recognized as good throughout Spain, and although they seem little different to the motorist driving up from Guipuzcoa, it must be remembered that the latter is one of the most densely populated provinces of Spain. Entering from Logroño or from Huesca, the improvement in surface can be startling. The tourist will also be pleased to find that the historic monuments of Navarre are meticulously cared for by the *Instituto Principe de Viana*, which combines the functions of Ministry of Works and Archives Department (Prince of Viana was the title given to the Crown Prince of Navarre).

This little self-sufficient world of Navarre has recently been provided with the one institution which it lacked. For, like York or Norwich, Pamplona was almost tailor-made to become a seat of higher learning. In Navarre, however, as we see, everything is a little different. And when a University came to Navarre, it was not founded by the government, and lies right outside the State system.

The Catholic University of Navarre is a free University, using 'free' in exactly the same sense as it is used of the 'free' University of Louvain, in Belgium, or of the *écoles libres* of France. For freedom can be used to turn to the right, as well as to the left. The Opus Dei, that benevolent and powerful body of Catholic laymen, who number two ministers in Madrid as declared members, felt that the Carlist traditions of Navarre would be as healthy for young minds as the pure air of the Pyrenees for young bodies. And the University which has been founded with their backing, because it is a Catholic University, outside the State system, but with ample funds, has been able to bid for the best academic talent in Spain.

The presence of this talent has in itself attracted brilliant students both from Spain and abroad. Moreover, hundreds of scholarships have been given to students from 'Black' Africa, with the deliberate intention that Pamplona should become the West's answer to the Patrice Lumumba University outside

Moscow. Whatever the reader's political leanings, he can only admire Spain's pluck in providing, from slender resources, this direct and practical reply to the Communists' challenge.

This pluck may be rewarded. 'We like the ones from Kenya even more than the ones from Katanga,' a farmer near Pamplona told me. There is no colour bar in Spain, and those who have studied in the homeland of St. Francis Xavier, the Apostle of India, are likely to return to the non-aligned world with happier memories than their contemporaries who have studied in the unsympathetic atmosphere behind the Iron Curtain.

Despite the tragedy of history, which has not only separated the Spanish Basques from their kinsmen over in France, but has also divided them against themselves, they retain much in common.

They retain, above all, their language. Like any language, Basque has its dialects, and these are more pronounced in the case of a tongue in which nothing was written before the sixteenth century, and in which the work of creating a 'literary language' is even now uncompleted. But although there are wide variations both of accent and of vocabulary between, for example, *souletin* and *vizcaino*, it is untrue to suggest that the Basques from different regions cannot understand each other, and have to communicate in French or Spanish. Given a little patience to accustom their ear to another way of speaking, they can follow each other without much difficulty.

There are two merely local accents which other Basques find incomprehensible. These are the accent of Fuenterrabía, the fishing town on the Franco-Spanish frontier, and the accent of Bermeo, another fishing port, over in Vizcaya. At seven o'clock one morning on Fuenterrabía beach I was given a possible explanation for this by a friendly Jesuit, who emerged from his early morning swim at the same moment as myself, and whom I found to be a *vascófilo* (devoted to Basque). He said that it was thought that contact with other countries by sea may have influenced the vocabularies of the people of these two ports; and also that the necessity for shouting from one ship to another over long distances may have contributed to their strange accents.

'But even without those influences, the dialect of Fuenterrabía would still differ from that of the villages to east and west along the coast', he went on. 'You see, just as the Guipuzcoan dialect is spoken in many villages of northern Navarre; so a thin tongue of the Navarrese dialect runs right down the Bidassoa, cutting across Guipuzcoa to meet the sea at Fuenterrabía.'

As he was speaking, he had set to work with the big toe of his right foot, to draw a map illustrating these points, and others which followed. At an unusual hour, and in unusual circumstances, I was receiving my first lecture in Basque philology.

I learnt that the boundaries of the eight linguistic regions of Basque often differ widely from the boundaries of the seven provinces. I heard of the mystery of Alsasua, an island of Vizcayan speech between Guipuzcoa and Navarre – explained by the fact that the 'bridge of speech' which once linked it to Vizcaya had been 'worn away' by the spread of Castilian. And I heard for the first time the name of the geatest *vascófilo* of all, Prince Lucien Bonaparte, who, when other members of his family still dreamt of imperial greatness, found his life's work in the study of a tongue which had been spoken before Europe had known an empire.

The central Basque province, surrounded on every side by other Basque provinces, is Guipuzcoa; and the Guipuzcoan dialect is widely regarded as the 'best Basque'. It is the rather depressing little industrial town of Tolosa, where Basque berets are made, and once the capital of the province, which provides in its speech the model for Basque which Tours provides for French, Siena for Italian, and Valladolid for Spanish. No large town can be properly described as Basque speaking today. Bayonne never has been. Centuries have passed since Pamplona or Vitoria were. And Bilbao has in this century endured an emigration from Estremadura and Andalusia which has diluted its Basque character.

San Sebastian, since 1835 the capital of Guipuzcoa, is in appearance even less typically Basque than any of these cities. Its old quarter had to be rebuilt after the French and British had combined to destroy it in 1813. And it owes its fine new districts to its growth during the last hundred years as Spain's most fashionable seaside resort, which has brought the language not only of Madrid, but of all Europe to the beaches of La Concha and Ondarreta. But from those very beaches can be seen all around green hills dotted with white farm houses; and from the big families of those farmhouses come the young men and girls who staff the hotels and restaurants and shops of Spain's summer capital. They talk Basque amongst themselves, and if their *novio* or *novia* happens to be Basque as well, they will continue to speak it after marriage.

The Basque Pyrenees

Without being able to claim San Sebastian as a Basque-speaking city, one can say that a great deal of Basque is still spoken there.

It is an agglutinative language, with strange word orders, and extraordinary verbal constructions. The plural is formed by adding the suffix *-k*, and is almost as bewildering at first as the Hebraic plural in *-im*. To form phrases, or still more, to think in Basque, requires a different mental approach from that demanded by Indo-European languages. But the ability to bring out even half a dozen odd words will create enormous pleasure in a bar or village square: it is a discreet but very real compliment to the continent's oldest race. So the traveller in the Basque Pyrenees may care to note:

egunon, good day.
aratzalde-on, good afternoon.
gabon, good night.
bai, yes.
ez, no.
eskañkasco, thank you.
ardua beltza, red wine.

And he must be warned that when the chambermaid in his hotel tells him to say '*Neska polita, ekatzu musu bat*' to the waitress downstairs, he will not, in spite of her assurances, be making a bright comment on the weather. For the phrase means 'Pretty girl, give me a kiss'.

Associated with, and even reflecting the language, is Basque folklore. Some of its best-known manifestations, such as the *Pastorales* of Soule, are from over the frontier. Others, once widespread, have only survived in odd corners. For example, a variant of the cruel *Antzar-joko**, or goose-game only survives, so far as I am aware, at Lequeitio on the Vizcayan coast. The two aspects of folklore which the visitor to the Basque Pyrenees is most likely to encounter are dance and costume.

The easiest way for him to get a good general impression of both is to visit San Sebastian during its annual Basque week at the beginning of September, which includes performances by leading teams of Basque dances in costume every evening in front of the town hall. The most interesting, and the most typically

* A goose is suspended by its legs on a line stretched over the water, and a team of oarsmen strive to obtain sufficient speed to enable one of their number, as their boat passes beneath, to decapitate the living bird with his bare hand.

Basque of these are the Sword dances, performed by men only, who wear white shirts, white trousers, red sashes round their waists, rope-soled sandals, and red berets.

In describing the Sword dances as the most typically Basque, I am aware that I am implying that the round dances in which both sexes take part are rather less typically Basque. Rodney Gallop, that authority on the Basques, regards these – the *farandole*, the *fandango*, the *aúresku*, and the *arin-arin* – as all derived to a greater or less extent from country dances in other parts of France and Spain, and more especially from the Aragonese *jota*. This seems probable. But in being thus transplanted, the *jota* has been re-newed. For whereas in the fiestas of Hecho in Aragon, the jota was danced on only one evening, by a company of dancers speci-ally hired from Saragossa, at Arano in Navarre I came across all the seven- and eight-year-olds at the bottom of the village street one evening, learning the steps of the Basque dances from a 'big' girl of twelve.

As regards costume, however, it is the Aragonese who have preserved a more living tradition, as we shall see when we reach Ansó. Full Basque costumes have for long only been worn on special occasions.

Yet one can always recognize a Basque when one sees one. And this is not only because of his characteristic physiognomy: a long head, dark hair, and a long, sometimes hooked, nose. (No ethnic group in Europe is more homogeneous in appearance). Even when he is too far away for one to make out his features, one can tell a Basque by what he wears and by how he wears it.

The countryman's dress will consist of rope-soled sandals, a dark pair of trousers, a freshly laundered white shirt, and a beret. The jacket, if worn, is often draped round the shoulders, without slipping the arms into the sleeves.

His cousin in Bilbao or San Sebastian will wear a suit, and well-polished black shoes, but his white shirt and his beret will be un-changed. And if it is raining – as quite often it is – his raincoat (the Basques, like the British, make very good raincoats) will probably be draped loosely over his shoulders in just the same way as the countryman's jacket.

I have given prominence in this description to the beret and to the rope-soled sandals, or *alpargatas*. It might be objected that although they may be part of the typical Basque's dress, there is nothing particularly Basque about them, as they are each worn in several other parts of Europe. But the beret may well have originated amongst the Basques: it is significant that they have their own word to describe it, borrowed from neither French nor Spanish. Their beret is normally black, or very dark navy blue; but a pleasing touch of fantasy survives in the red 'Carlist' beret, sported by the *Falange*, and by all public work employees in Navarre. Although a distinction is made in France between the wide, floppy *beret alpin*, and the smaller *beret basque*, which sits on the head like a button, one in fact sees all sizes and shapes of berets on Basque heads.

There is, however, a difference between the *alpargatas* worn in the Basque country, and those worn in other regions. (The *alpargata* is the French *espadrille*.) The Basque sandal has a sole of simple hemp, softer but quicker drying than the hard-wearing esparto grass of the Catalan sandal, and therefore better adapted to the damper Basque climate. Its upper is of plain blue canvas, with or without tapes to secure it. This is in marked contrast to the Catalan, which at first sight seems to consist mainly of tapes, half a dozen of which fan out from the toe to wrap themselves round the ankle, and which help to make the *alpargatas catalanas* the most classical-looking footwear in Europe. It will always be disputed whether the *sardana* of Catalonia owes anything to ancient Greek dancing; but the inhabitants of Ampurias must surely have been shod almost exactly as the present villagers of La Escala.*

Equally typical as the Basque's dress is the house which he lives in. And just as the essentials of his dress can be adapted to modern life, so the best aspects of Basque traditional architecture have been successfully incorporated into many homes of recent construction. The *villa basque* is now one of the favourite designs of Frenchmen building a weekend chalet or a country home, and glossy publications detail one lovely example of the other from St. Jean-de-Luz or Guétary.

The French, of course, have a flair for producing high-quality merchandise at once small and individual, whether perfumes, sports clothes, or villas; and it must be admitted that some modern Spanish examples of Basque villas, in the San Sebastian suburbs, or built for the homecoming Nevada *ricos* in Elizondo, unhappily

* There also exists – though seen only rarely – an Aragonese *alpargata*, resembling the Catalan, but with fewer tapes in evidence.

remind the English visitor of our own mock-Tudor. But it is easy to see why the Basque farmhouse has lent itself so well to modern needs, at a time when so many regional styles survive only in the buildings of past centuries.

For the Basque, however remote his origins, has always been a modern in his emphasis on the private life. Not for him the nucleated village and common fields of old England: still less the 'rural towns' of fifteen and twenty thousand souls which supply the labour reservoirs of the Andalusian *latifundia*. He allows the public life of society its part, but a set, limited part: the pelota court, the village fiesta, the market, and – most important of all – the gathering at Mass on Sunday morning, and the gossip afterwards in the square and at the bar. But this public life is a permitted intrusion on his main, private world, in contrast to Mediterranean man, for whom his private life, today as in classical times, is no more than an afterthought to a mainly gregarious existence.

The Basque farm, therefore, standing by itself, its bright whitewashed walls gaily reflecting the sun, is easily adapted to modern needs. It is neither too large, like so many country homes of the past, nor too small, like the terraced cottages of French and Spanish villages. There are stables to provide garage room; there is ample space for the pursuit of 'leisure activities'; and there is a bedroom for the odd girl who has come in to help from the farm next door – but there are not entire wings given over to servants' quarters. From the cosy kitchen of such a home the individual can venture out into society or retreat from it when he chooses.

Rodney Gallop has noted that whereas Soule, which has the strongest Basque traditions of the three French Basque provinces, is the least Basque in appearance – its villages almost indistinguishable from those of the neighbouring Béarn – Alava, where the Basque language has almost died out, is typically Basque in architecture and atmosphere. It is thirty-five years since Gallop's wonderful *A Book of the Basques* was published, and he already noted the fading of Basque not only in Alava, but in the eastern Pyrenean valleys of Navarre. He could speak of 'the almost extinct Roncal', and, as I shall show later on*, Castilian has since then gained the ascendancy over an even wider area of the Pyrenees. But these eastern valleys, though they have forgotten their language, have not forgotten their race, which they pro-

* See Part One–8. 'The Dying Tongue'.

claim just as loud as Alava. Miles Walker, the protagonist of J. B. Morton's *Pyrenean*, on his heroic trek from the Mediterranean some forty years ago, crossed from Aragon into Navarre without at first being aware that he had done so.

'I went up a slaty slope to the baby Col, and down into a gorge that was filled with the noise of water. The path was clear here, though it was rough going, and presently the gorge opened out, and I had before me an upland pasture, with cows, and a man watching them. This man stood still, with his hand shading his eyes, looking up at me, and I knew I had crossed into the Basque country. . . . He wore a blue smock to his knees, and carried a pronged stick, but what stamped him was the large and floppy béret which the Basques on the Spanish side of the mountains affect. On the French side they wear the smaller béret, and they wear it straight, without any of the jauntiness of their neighbours. In the Soule or the Labourd everyone would have known this man for a Spaniard.

'He stood motionless as I descended, and when I came near I saw that his face was the face of an old man. It was the colour of walnut and deeply lined round the eyes and the mouth. He saluted me in silence, and I respected his silence and passed on my way, climbing small knolls, plunging into small ravines, skirting coppices, until I saw before me a neat village, and a stream flowing through it. Like the man, the village was unmistakable. There were the barns with the great segmental arches, and the traditional way of building which the Basques have refused to abandon. . . . And about it all was that air of prosperity and security and self-respect which is so eminently Basque. There was the solid little church of sombre stone, and the pelota-court, and over a house-door here and there the name of the man and woman who had built the house, and the date of the building.'

Mr. Morton never mentions the name of the village, but from his description it must have been Isaba. And as the old man saluted in silence, we shall never know whether his greeting would have been 'Buenos dias' or 'Egunon'. For an old man in Isaba forty years ago probably spoke Basque.

A knowledge of Basque would be of no use today to a traveller following that path from the valley of Ansó into that of Roncal. But he would know, just as unmistakeably as J. B. Morton's traveller knew, that he had crossed into the Basque country.

3. The Bidassoa Valley

Two valleys run up from the coast of Guipuzcoa into the mountains of Navarre. That of the Urumea, the river of San Sebastian, is the shorter. But it is little used. The main road to Madrid and Pamplona runs farther west, along the valley of the Oria. In any case, it will be dealt with during out interlude at Arano, a village which lies above it.

The valley of the Bidassoa, on the other hand, is of cardinal importance. During its last ten miles, when it is flowing alongside Guipuzcoa to the sea, it serves as the frontier, and throughout its length it bears one or other of the two main roads from the French coast towards Pamplona. And its upper part, where it is known as the Baztán, is the first, and not the least typical, of those valleys of the Spanish Pyrenees which have at all times enjoyed a certain measure of autonomy.

Following it upstream, we must start inevitably at Cabo Higuer, which has already served as the background of our prologue. Two roads lead there: one alongside the estuary, and one *en corniche* a couple of hundred feet above, and at the tiny fishing harbour at the end of the lower road they are connected by a steep narrow climb. But this connection is 'one way only': no vehicle is allowed to descend it. So in order to see both roads, it is necessary to take the lower one on the way to the lighthouse, and to return by the upper road, with its magnificent views of the French coast.

A signpost near where the upper road leaves Fuenterrabía beach provides the easiest way of finding a road with even more extensive views. This is the road built since the end of the Civil War which runs on the seaward side of Mount Jaizquibel, only a little distance below the crest. Although the unprotected slope down to the sea twelve hundred feet below falls away at a gradient of one in three, this road is less terrifying for the nervous than the corresponding one between Cerbère and Colera at the Mediter-

43

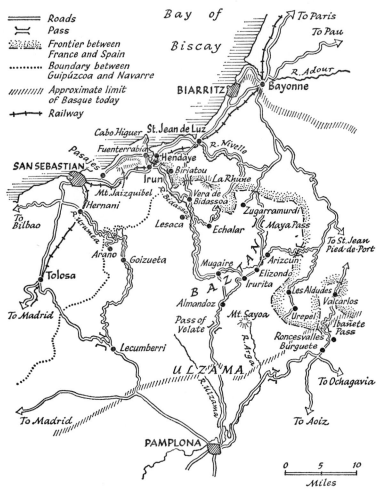

II Basque Pyrenees—West

ranean end of the range. This is partly because the actual climb up
from sea-level at Fuenterrabía, and down again to Pasajes San
Juan eleven miles farther on, takes place out of sight of the sea, on
the side of Jaizquibel facing south. And once on top, the road
runs for several miles on a level, with no hairpin bends or dizzy
precipices to distract attention from the pinewoods, the watch
towers, and above all, the unending waves.

Immediately above Fuenterrabía, where the crest comes to an
end, there is a greater variety in the view. For from here the
observer dominates not only the uninhabited northern slopes of
Jaizquibel, but the estuary of the Bidassoa, the French coast as
far as the eye can see, and to the south-east range after range of
the Basque Pyrenees.

A few yards from the old watch tower has been placed a *table
d'orientation* showing in detail where all these features can be found
on the living map below. For the scene beneath, with sea, river,
towns, villages, roads, railways, plains and mountains, is a geography lesson come to life. And to enjoy the lesson to the full the
visitor can have a drink or a meal on the terrace of the nearby
parador. This is one of two hotels built by the province of Guipuzcoa, which offer the same high standard of food and accommoda-
tion as the state *paradores* in the more deserted parts of Spain. It
has been necessary for the provincial government to step in,
because Madrid's wise policy has been to provide these hotels only
in underpopulated areas which lack the capital and private initia-
tive which are so abundant amongst the Basques. Seated on the
terrace of the *parador*, the visitor can follow the valley of the
Bidassoa up to the point where it is lost in the hills on crossing
into Navarre.

Half-way up Jaizquibel, on the road from Fuenterrabía, a low
spire beside a farm marks the sanctuary of Our Lady of Guadalupe.
The principal shrine of this particular manifestation of the Virgin
is of course at the great monastery of Guadalupe in Estremadura.
This so much smaller shrine is of no great antiquity, but in an
inconspicuous way it is all that a rural sanctuary ought to be.
There is the simple church, with its statue and the commemora-
tive plaques and discarded crutches of the worshippers whom the
Virgin has cured. Attached to it is the equally simple priest's
dwelling. And on the other side of the narrow road a grove of
trees has been planted around a cool spring, with stone tables and

benches for pilgrims – or for picnickers – with a view only a little less extensive than that from the *parador*. Guadalupe thus has all four of the qualities which have constituted the European sanctuary during the past five thousand years: a grove, a spring, a priest, and, for those who wish to acknowledge her, the presence of a goddess.

The town from which her worshippers climb in crowds to pay her homage on 8th September, the first day of their fiesta, is Fuenterrabía, which lies as far below the sanctuary as the *parador* lies above it. Places which are called by different names in different languages are generally both ancient and interesting, and Fuenterrabía, the Basque Ondarribia, is known to the French as Fontarabie. There even exists a bastard English form in Fontarabia, which sounds the most romantic of all, and has been incorporated with lyric success in more than one poem.

Fuenterrabía, moreover, demands this romantic treatment. For apart from Puigcerdá in the remote Cerdaña, it is the only Spanish town which the traveller from the west can see without crossing the frontier. And thus seen half a mile away across the Bidassoa estuary, it looks far more romantically Spanish than it really is. 'Fontarabia': the word perfectly evokes the almost mosque-like appearance of the parish church sitting above the old town, framed by the white houses of the Marina along the waterfront. Here, before the Pyrenees have really begun, the gazer at Hendaye-Plage already finds himself echoing the quarter-true platitude: 'Europe ends at the Pyrenees.' And the sense of remoteness is increased if we recall how inaccessible this Basque fishing town under the shadow of Jaizquibel seemed as recently as the German occupation of France, or even the post-war period when the French closed the frontier.

The frontier is now well and truly open. But there exists a little-known and quieter way of reaching Fuenterrabía for anyone who wishes to avoid the long queues which often build up at the International Bridge between Hendaye and Irún. (This was built as an International toll bridge in 1914. Inflation has rendered meaningless the fixed toll, but inflation has proceeded ten times as rapidly in France as in Spain. So the French never bother to collect their half, but an indeterminate Spanish official still spasmodically collects the due of 10 céntimos, or half a farthing, for every person crossing).

The Bidassoa Valley

This off-beat method of entering Spain is to be found by walking a couple of hundred yards along the road to Hendaye-Plage, and taking a cul-de-sac which leads down to the river and the *bac*, or ferry. Here an informal customs and passport clearance is carried out by a woman in a white nylon overall, before the dinghy pulls us gently away into midstream. The Civil Guards who await us near the Guadalupe Hotel are equally friendly, if rather less informal, and we are soon free to explore this little-used gateway of Spain.

In doing so we soon become aware that it was once a gateway of some importance, and that it has found a new role as one of the most exclusive and pleasant resorts in Spain. For the old town, still entirely surrounded by its wall, is full of solid houses, whose escutcheoned doorways already sheltered families in 1638, when Fuenterrabía defied the French army which laid siege to it under the Prince of Condé, and was granted the title of city by Philip IV in recognition. It had endured an earlier French attack in 1513, and was actually held by the French between 1521 and 1524. It must have been that disaster which caused the government to rebuild the fortress now known as the castle of Charles V in the vast central square at the top of the old town.

It may be asked why in the sixteenth and seventeenth centuries in particular Fuenterrabía should not merely have received such a fortress, but should have needed it. The reply must be that it was only in those two centuries that France and Spain were directly competing for the place of 'top nation'. Throughout most of the Middle Ages the neighbours along this part of the frontier were the small kingdom of Navarre and the autonomous Basques on one side, and the autonomous vassals of the English viceroys at Bordeaux on the other. These last became dependent upon the French crown after the defeat of the English in 1453. But it was only upon the conquest of Navarre by Ferdinand the Catholic in 1512, and the union of Aragon-cum-Navarre with Castile in the person of his grandson Charles V four years later that a Spanish state could be said to face a French state across the Bidassoa. It is with good reason that Fuenterrabía's castle is known as *el castillo de Carlos Quinto*.

The struggle which ensued went at first in favour of Spain: the French were defeated at Pamplona in 1521, and later Francis I became Charles's prisoner. When in 1588 Philip II gathered part

of his Invincible Armada at Pasajes, on the other side of Jaizquibel, a Spanish Empire in Europe, such as already existed in the
Americas, seemed very near.

But the very year after the defeat of that Armada the titular king
of Navarre, grandson of the little Henri d'Albret whom Ferdinand
had chased across the Pyrenees, became King Henry IV of France.
Hoping to unite France, he became a Caholic, and it was two
Cardinals who continued his work. The siege of Fuenterrabía in
1638 took place when Cardinal Richelieu was directing French
policy, and acknowledgement that Spain had decisively lost the
long struggle came under his successor, Cardinal Mazarin.

From the terrace of the *parador*, we can see the island in the
Bidassoa where that acknowledgement took place. The Pheasant's
Island, a few yards downstream from the second bridge across the
frontier, at Behobia, bears a plain monument recording the meeting there in 1659 of His Catholic Majesty Philip IV of Spain with
the Most Christian King Louis XIV of France, for the signing of
the Peace of the Pyrenees. This island was chosen because the two
kings were there able to face each other across the conference
table without either of them leaving his own dominions.

The quaint mechanics of such a confrontation appeal to any age,
but they had a particular charm for the seventeenth century. The
various pictures of the scene in the Museum of San Telmo in San
Sebastian, showing the two long cavalcades winding down towards Behobia from opposite sides of the river, and the arrangements on the island itself, remind the Englishman of the more
sombre colours, but equally puppet-like figures, in contemporary
engravings of the Long Parliament, or of the crowds at Dover
awaiting the restored Charles II.

The Peace was sealed by the marriage of the young French
King to the Infanta Maria Teresa, daughter of Philip IV, that unhappy ruler whose only successful role in life was as a model for
Velázquez. Here again, reasons of prestige required two separate
marriage ceremonies: the first in the church of Fuenterrabía, when
the bridegroom, so that he need not leave French soil, was represented by a proxy, and the second over at St. Jean-de-Luz when
the bride, now Queen of France, had crossed the frontier to
join her husband.

It was not an idyllically happy marriage, and the cynic might
argue that its main historical result was to lead directly to the

1. Fuenterrabía at the mouth of the Bidassoa estuary. On the right the last promontory of French soil. In the top left-hand corner Cabo Higuer

2. First view of the high Pyrenees from the Lazar Pass

3. House in Isaba, valley of Roncal

disastrous war of the Spanish Succession, from which the French
monarchy never fully recovered, and in which Spain, after knowing civil war, lost all her European possessions. But for the
Pyrenees themselves 1659 marked a lasting settlement. The Peace
of the Pyrenees was largely about the Pyrenees, and there have
since been only minor changes of the frontier, peacefully decided
upon by mutual agreement for common convenience.

The great frontier alterations of that year took place at the
other end of the range. Here, where the Peace was signed, it
brought no changes. Changes of another sort have come about,
however, during the intervening three centuries, as anyone can
see who compares one of the bird's-eye views of the Peace conference in the Museo San Telmo with the same view from the
parador of Jaizquibel today. And the greatest of these changes is
the development of Irún, then far smaller than Fuenterrabía, to a
busy commercial town of 30,000 inhabitants, today the third
largest town in the province of Guipuzcoa. Most of its shops and
apartment blocks are even more recent than this might suggest.
For much of Irún had to be rebuilt after the fierce fighting of
September 1936 which opposed Navarre's *requetés* to Basque
nationalists in a tragic fratricide of Basque against Basque. But old
customs have survived civil war, and survive too the new invasion
which brings millions of tourists through this northern gateway
of Spain each summer; and the annual pilgrimage to the chapel of
San Marcial overlooking the Bidassoa on 30th June, remains one
of the most popular fiestas of the province.

Some changes have been and gone since 1659, and amongst
them is the narrow-gauge railway which used to follow the
Bidassoa from Irún right up to Elizondo. Its closure is surprising
in the one country of western Europe which is still adding to its
mileage of railway track, and is perhaps a tribute to the more
advanced economic development of the Basque provinces. Since
its closure more people have in fact travelled between Irún and
Elizondo than ever before, for near Elizondo the Americans built
one of their two radar stations allowed for under the Spanish-
American Treaty of 1953. It was evidently thought that the
servicemen's wives would die of boredom up in the Baztán, so
quarters were found for them in Fuenterrabía, and the rota teams
going on and off duty drove up and down the valley by car. Even
the unmarried servicemen, to my amazement, often became bored;

D   49

and English girls working for travel agencies at the Basque resorts found their leisure hours fully booked once these young Americans had learnt that there were girls within reach 'who could speak English'.

In travelling up the Bidassoa by road, however, we shall see just as much as did the passengers in the quaint Emmet-like train. Only a couple of miles after leaving Behobia we shall see the village of Biriatou clinging to the steep slopes of the French side of the river. It is a microcosm of all that a Basque village, whether French or Spanish, ought to be, with tiny galleried church, and pelota court, or *frontón*. Only one narrow road, connecting with the main *Nationale Dix* a mere five yards inside the frontier, joins it to the rest of France. It is therefore ideally placed for smuggling; and a story, which the Anglican chaplain at St. Jean-de-Luz assured me was authentic, is worth retelling.

The Prefect of the department of the Basses-Pyrénées, paying a visit to Biriatou, sat down to lunch with the principal inhabitants. By the time they had reached the coffee and cognac stage, the atmosphere was relaxed, and tongues were loosened. The Prefect addressed himself to the mayor, who was sitting on his right.

'I have always heard, M. le Maire, that Biriatou is a great centre for smuggling.'

'Well, M. le Préfet, I would be the last to deny that there are no smugglers at all in Biriatou, situated as we are a mere stone's throw from Spain.'

'What you say intrigues me, M. le Maire. Tell me, in complete confidence, as man to man, without fearing any consequences, how many of the twenty people round this table are smugglers.'

The mayor did not even bother to look round at the shrewd smiling faces before replying: 'There are eighteen smugglers, M. le Préfet.'

The Prefect jumped, evidently surprised to find such a high proportion of his hosts involved in illicit traffic.

'But that leaves only you and me who are not smugglers, M. le Maire.'

'No, M. le Préfet, not you and me, but you and M. le Douanier.'

The road above the French bank stops at Biriatou, its passage barred by Mount Choldocogagna; and there is only just space for the road along the Spanish bank between the hills and the river. At the boundary of Guipuzcoa and Navarre it crosses the Bidassoa by a bridge, and at this point, too, the national frontier leaves the river, and veers away to the north-east. From here onwards, the Bidassoa flows entirely within Navarre.

The hills soon draw back to leave a small plain, in the centre of which lies the large village of Vera de Bidassoa. A feature of all parts of the Basque country are the balconies decorated with flowers in pots and window boxes, and Vera is particularly rich in these. It is also the point of departure for a road which crosses the first of the Pyrenean passes: the Col d'Ibardin. It is from Vera, too, that anyone would set out who proposed to climb from the Spanish side the 2,950 feet La Rhune. This belvedere of the Basque country, with its unmistakable silhouette when seen from the coast, stands astride the frontier, but those to whom 'sense is given, to follow in the train', will find it waiting for them over in France, half-way between Ascain and Sare, where stands the terminus of a ratchet railway which will carry them all the way to the summit.

Four miles beyond Vera, and just before the hills close in again on the river, another road leads off towards another pass, that of Lizarrieta. But man is not the only animal which has learnt its value. Every autumn tens upon thousands of pigeons sweep through the passes of the western Pyrenees, and so certain are their routes that from time immemorial it has been the custom to trap them, by hundreds at a time, in nets spread across the narrow valleys. Echalar, as the village on the road up the Col de Lizarrieta is called, is one of the biggest centres of the pigeon shoots, which are as well organized and as expensive as many better-known sports. Throughout the year, the traveller can see the nest-like platforms up in the trees near where the pigeons pass, from which are thrown the nets, or the various devices used for luring the birds towards the guns.

A mile farther on the road passes the Venta de Yanci, itself of little interest, but the first of many ventas which we shall encounter in the Basque Pyrenees. They are – or in many cases were – rough inns, providing refreshment and the occasional bed for travellers along the main roads. The village from which they took their name often stood some distance away, as does Yanci, whose inhabitants come down to the Venta to catch a bus up the valley to Elizondo or Pamplona, or down to Irún. Sometimes, as at Venta de Arraiz on the other side of the Velate pass, the venta itself becomes a little nucleus of population, forming a hamlet on its own.

The secondary road to Yanci continues on to Lesaca, and then by a track which passes through a tunnel under the 2,700-foot Peña de Aya at the border of Guipuzcoa, and on to San Sebastian.

It was along this track that the Duke of Wellington set out early on the afternoon of 25th July, 1813. After the battle of Vitoria, his troops had rapidly advanced towards the frontier, and he had established his own headquarters at Lesaca. It may seem an odd spot to have chosen, but in the particular circumstances of the campaign, it is hard to see how he could have chosen better. For French garrisons still held San Sebastian and Pamplona, and the British forces were widely extended. Some were besieging San Sebastian. Some were in positions along the Bidassoa. Others again were holding the Maya pass astride the main road from Bayonne to Pamplona. Lesaca was equidistant from, and connected by road to all three groups, although communications must have been rather strained with a fourth force, which defended Roncesvalles itself.

But Roncesvalles was easily defensible, and Wellington fully anticipated that any counter attack would be launched across the Bidassoa, with a view to raising the siege of San Sebastian. He therefore decided to wipe out this pocket of resistance at once, and the attack had begun at dawn on 25th July. The gunfire could be heard at Lesaca, and the experienced ear of the British commander told him that his troops on the coast were encountering fierce resistance. He set off to investigate the position for himself.

It was at this moment that his French opponent, Marshal Soult, chose to launch his counter attack. It came not across the Bidassoa, however, but against the passes of Maya and Roncesvalles, in order to relieve not San Sebastian, but Pamplona. The British held their well-chosen positions against their numerically superior assailants. But their commanding officers had little experience of taking their own decisions. They were worried by the distance which separated them from headquarters, and by the vulnerability of their lines of communication. During the night of July 25th to 26th they fell back from both passes towards Pamplona, surrendering the ground for which many members of the 92nd Highlanders had given their lives on the alien heather of Baztán.

On his return to Lesaca late in the evening, Wellington at last heard the news of the counter attack. It is his behaviour at such moments as this which makes us realize that the protagonists at Waterloo were evenly matched. The lean Irishman who left Lesaca at four o'clock on the morning of 26th July would require no handicap when he came face to face with the podgy Corsican who had once joined the Army of Italy over the snow-covered Alps. Past Venta de Yanci he rode with a small party of aides into the narrowing valley, with the stars overhead. Their horses' hooves would echo down the long street of Sumbilla. Dawn probably broke between Santesteban and Mugaire. And at Irurita, two miles before Elizondo, he came upon the troops which had retired from the Maya pass. He saw that they were placed in good defensive positions, well in advance of the main road to Pamplona, which then as now turns southward from the Bidassoa at Mugaire. He also learnt that the force which had retired from Roncesvalles was holding similar positions at Zubiri on the upper Arga, thus protecting the same vital road. His lifeline seemed secure, and he was able to pass a peaceful night at Almandoz, in the shadow of the pass of Velate, which lies between Irurita and Zubiri.

On the morning of July 27th he continued south, climbing steeply to the unexpected level plateau at the top of the pass, and descending through the beechwoods into the valley of Ulzama. It was at Ostiz – still a Basque-speaking village in 1813 – that he heard with dismay that his right wing had retreated from Zubiri to within sight of Pamplona. The advancing French might at any moment cut the main road.

Wellington therefore galloped ahead to Sorauren, and just before his lifeline was broken managed to send back orders for the forces in Baztán to join him. With himself in command, there was no more thought of retreat amongst the troops who blocked the road between the French garrison of Pamplona and the French relieving forces who had advanced through Roncesvalles. For they knew that it was not they who were caught between two fires, but the French, who might at any time find themselves attacked in the rear by the British regiments marching down from Baztán.

As at Waterloo, the thin red line held, and the great counter attack, which seems to come so often towards the end of a long war – as in March, 1918, or in December, 1944 – had failed. The French retired once more behind the frontier, and Wellington was able to proceed with the reduction of Pamplona and of San

Sebastian before following them across the Bidassoa and beyond the Pyrenees.

Much of the fascination of the Peninsular campaigns for us today lies in the contrast between the peaceful England of Constable's paintings from which the English soldiers came, and the alien landscapes where they fought. Thomas Hardy, who loved that pre-industrial England, saw this contrast, and brought it out in *The Trumpet Major*, the very last paragraph of which describes the farewell of a soldier about to leave quiet, rural Wessex for ever.

'The candle held by his father shed its waving light upon John's face and uniform as with a farewell smile he turned on the doorstone, backed by the black night; and in another moment he had plunged into the darkness, the ring of his smart step dying away upon the bridge as he joined his companions-in-arms, and went off to blow his trumpet till silenced for ever upon one of the bloody battlefields of Spain.'

In following Wellington's tracks we have already seen something of Baztán, as the upper valley of the Bidassoa is known. Travelling the same road from Venta de Yanci at greater speed than he did, but with more leisure, we shall notice the well-kept church at Navarte, its wall bearing a creeper trained in the form of a cross. At Mugaire a gate on the left is posted as a *camino particular*, or private road. But I have been told that permission is seldom withheld to visit the dense forests which form the wealth of this mountainous estate, the Señorío de Bertiz.

Irurita has a large Baroque church, and on a side road to the left is the college of Lecároz, whose charming *capuchino* fathers always furnish a chaplain for the summer university courses at Jaca. Wellington on that summer morning proceeded no farther up the valley, but it has been described for us by a more articulate traveller, who over a century after the Peninsular War had ended drove down towards us from the frontier, in what would now be a vintage car with long bonnet and 'dickey'.

'We crossed the Spanish frontier. . . . For a while the country was much as it had been; then, climbing all the time, we crossed the top of a col, the road winding back and forth on itself, and then it really was Spain. There were long brown mountains and a few pines and far-off forests of beech trees on some of the mountainsides. The road went along the summit of the col and then dropped down, and the driver had to honk, and slow up, and turn out to avoid running into two donkeys that were sleeping in the road. We came down out of the mountains and through an oak forest, and there were white cattle grazing in the forest. Down below there were grassy plains and clear streams, and then we crossed a stream and went through a gloomy little village, and started to climb again.'

The road does in fact cross the infant Bidassoa before entering Elizondo. And the first Spanish village after crossing from France always seemed gloomy by comparison. But the capital of Baztán deserves more than this passing reference which is all that Hemingway allows it in *The Sun also rises*.

To begin with, it is in every sense a capital: a true metropolis which has gathered to itself the government of the entire valley, from Maya to Sumbilla. Some commentators have spoken of Baztán as if there were something quite extraordinary about its autonomy, the self-consciousness of its inhabitants, and the treaties, called *facerías*, into which they have entered with their neighbours across the frontier. But we shall see as we proceed that almost every valley of the Spanish Pyrenees is autonomous to a greater or less extent, and throughout the range one finds villages which feel as much or more in common with the French mountain hamlets beyond the watershed as with the provincial capitals in the plains scores of miles and thousands of feet below them. It has only required the accident of disputed sovereignty to give one valley complete independence. (I refer, of course, to Andorra).

The valleys differ in their political organization as much as did the states of ancient Greece. It is even tempting to make comparisons. Thus, Andorra itself, in which Andorra la Vella is no more than the *primus inter pares* amongst the six parishes which make up the country, might be compared to Boeotia, where Thebes was no more than the head of a league of cities. Hecho and Ansó, on the other hand, are unitary states, as was Athens, which absorbed all the inhabitants of Attica as citizens of the one city.

There is a villain's role in this catalogue from ancient history: that of Sparta, which reduced to the level of subject communities the smaller towns of the Laconian vale. And it must sadly be recorded that the outlying hamlets of Baztán feel an almost helot-like resentment to the pretensions of Elizondo. *Tontos*, and *presumidos* are the two epithets bandied about when the traveller starts discussing the capital of the valley in a bar in Berroeta or Almandoz. But its *ayuntamiento* is a fine enough building to act as the administrative centre for the whole district. And by walking through the archway on the left of it, and across a bridge, one has a view of the backs of the houses giving on to the river which is not only picturesque but even gay.

Like Irurita, Elizondo has a huge Baroque church which must require a large attendance from its four thousand inhabitants if it is ever to be filled. But it is the twentieth century which is responsible for many buildings on the outskirts of the town. These include not only the villas built by the homecoming emigrants who have acquired fortunes through a lifetime's work as shepherds in the western United States, but also the newly opened (July, 1964) Hostal Baztán. This contemporary structure, in wood and concrete, though it provides a balcony for every room, and a swimming pool in its grounds, yet harmonizes well with the countryside which it has made more accessible to those tourists who like their creature comforts.

Three miles to the north of Elizondo lies the village of Arizcun. Nina Epton, in *Navarre*, describes her search in a part of Arizcun called Bozate for the strange race of 'untouchables' called *agotes*. Perhaps gipsy, perhaps gothic, perhaps the descendants of lepers, they were a depressed substratum of western Pyrenean society until the last century. But she uncovered only faint memories at Bozate, and I had even less success when hunting for the same elusive race at Ciboure, alongside St. Jean-de-Luz, where they are also supposed to have survived.

Neither peaceful Baztán nor friendly Ciboure seem likely places to conceal such dark mysteries as that of the *agotes*. But off the lovely road which joins them hide darker mysteries still. In search of them we must cross the Maya pass, which here forms the watershed of the Pyrenees. The frontier, however, lies six miles farther on, for we meet here the first of several exceptions to the general rule that the political frontier exactly follows the crest of the range. The two streams on either side of the road will unite just after they have crossed into France to form the Nivelle, the river which reaches the sea at St. Jean-de-Luz. And just on the Spanish side of the frontier a road to the left leads after four miles to the village of Zugarramurdi, dominated by the 2,500-foot hill of Aizchuri.

This summit was one of the favourite gathering places of the *sorgiñak* or witches, who seem to have been even more prominent in the Basque country than in England during the seventeenth century. Witchcraft had existed for long before the sudden flare-up during these years on both sides of the Atlantic, and Margaret Murray has convincingly argued that it probably represented a survival into Christian times of a pagan cult, with a secret organization and strong emphasis on fertility rites. The fact that the Basque vocabulary of witchcraft: *Jaun Goŕi*, the Red Lord, *akelaŕe*, the witches' Sabbath, and so on, seems entirely indigenous, tempts us to wonder whether the unusual strength of the cult amongst Europe's oldest race was due to an unusually firm and continuous survival there of the 'old religion'.

The great persecution of witches in the Basque country took place at the beginning of the seventeenth century, some fifty years earlier than the great period of witch hunting in England. In neither land was repression complete, and *brujos* and *brujas*, as the *sorgiñak* are called in Castilian, still appear in conversation amongst the Basques more frequently than in other parts of Spain. The persons referred to are occasionally regarded with genuine suspicion because of their odd behaviour or eccentric habits. But the more general use of the word is now metaphorical: today's *bruja* is not so much a witch, as a bitch.

Lying beyond the watershed, Zugarramurdi forms geographically no part of Baztán. But one group of villages, although some way from the Bidassoa, certainly lie within the same catchment area. We must in any case pass them if we are to proceed south along the only road which follows this part of the Spanish Pyrenees. Retracing our steps to Irurita, we need have no qualms about taking the road to the left signposted 'Berroeta', which Michelin marks as a *parcours difficile ou dangereux*. It is neither, and one must regret that all Pyrenean highways are not as wide or as well surfaced. It is true that it runs high up along a succession of hillsides, but the views are breathtaking rather than vertiginous. Halfway along, one particularly fine viewpoint has been provided with seats: this is the *mirador de Baztán*, commanding the whole valley.

After skirting a number of high-set hamlets, this road rejoins the main road from the coast, which had left the floor of the valley at Mugaire, and after a sharp climb enters the last village of

The Basque Pyrenees

Baztán, Almandoz. The average traveller no doubt speeds through it, hardly conscious that it has passed, a 'gloomy little village', to echo Hemingway, like so many others. I had passed through it many times myself without even being able to recall its name, when a chance German acquaintance invited me to join him up there for a few days.

'I'm staying at the Casa Jauregui, the big white house at the end of the village on the left. If that description isn't enough to help you find me, just ask for *Carlos el alemán*. That's how I'm known throughout Ulzama and Baztán.'

Karl was reading for his doctorate in geology at Münster University, and his thesis was to be a detailed survey of four hundred square kilometres of the Basque Pyrenees. I later heard of two other such surveys in preparation: one by another student of Münster, based at Leiza near Lecumberri; and the other between Jaca and Sabiñanigo, by a mysterious figure whom my informants described as Polish. Some might be led to entertain suspicions that a hidden, Ian Flemingesque authority was using post-graduate research for some sinister end. I had no such suspicions myself, and no wish, in any case, to play the part of James Bond. I considered myself lucky to be able to accompany Karl on his expeditions, penetrating to lost valleys and distant woods which I would never have reached by myself, and returning with weary feet each evening to enjoy, with him, the cooking and the company of the Casa Jauregui.

There was nothing outside to indicate that it received guests. '*Hacen fonda*' as they say of a particular house in so many villages of the Pyrenees where there is no visible sign of an inn. The phrase implies that the business of putting people up is altogether secondary to the main activity of being the home of the people who live there. And this was exactly the situation at the Casa Jauregui. Through the big door and up the steps to the first floor, one crossed the polished oak floor of the wide windowless hall, its gloom relieved by a gleam of brass which would not have shamed a coaching inn of old England. At the end lay the door of the vast kitchen, its huge open fireplace still in very necessary use throughout the winter. And although the cooking now took place on a bright new stove operating on bottled gas, the meals produced were no less tasty.

Karl and I were served with ours at a round table in the corner, covered with a yellow oilcloth, whilst the Jauregui family, drifting in and out at odd intervals, ate theirs at a long rectangular one stretching down the centre of the room. Even now, after so many subsequent visits, I still cannot work out the full details of their relationships. There was the old mother, who did the cooking, and who seemed to have a casting vote in any major decision – such as whether or not a newly arrived traveller should be allowed to stay. Her husband remained in the background, mainly because he was of French nationality, having been born in the French Basque country, and after forty years at Almandoz had half forgotten French without fully mastering Spanish. For the only language which he needed to use was Basque. Then there was a daughter who seemed to have almost equal authority with the mother, and a one-armed son who managed the electricity generating station fed by the stream which joined the Bidassoa at Mugaire. And there were other agreeable but indeterminate personages who might be sons-in-law or cousins or nieces or just friends. Indeed, the Jauregui family must be related to almost everyone else in the village; and it was certainly to their home that the village turned for the set pieces of village life, such as marriage breakfasts.

Almandoz has a fine new marble church, built of local stone from one of the parish's three marble quarries. The last time that I passed through there I was particularly lucky in my day, for when I entered the Casa Jauregui I found that one of the quarry owners was giving his annual *banquete* to his thirty-two workers. The long room reserved for such occasions was full, and the noise of merriment only subsided when the assembled company were fully occupied in consuming yet another course. Seated as of old at the yellow cloth I had an ample share of each course as it went in, and renewed my friendship with various village worthies who one by one joined me for a glass of wine and a chat.

The three small quarries have done nothing to disfigure the landscape, and a mile or two away from the main road one is far from the modern world. The shepherds on Mount Sayoa (4,700 feet) often stay up there for months on end. Karl and I, plunging down one day through a dense forest of beech and oak, emerged into a clearing. A woman of about fifty was working in a maize-field beside an isolated farmhouse. But she had to call her husband before we could make ourselves understood. For she only spoke Basque.

4. Ulzama

After the steep climb from Almandoz through the forest, the road runs for a level mile of open pasture before dropping again. This is the Col de Velate, and the traveller must be ready to halt for a courteous Civil Guard who will step from his checkpoint to examine passports and note vehicle registration numbers. This is no useless exercise or training programme. For although Velate is thirty miles by road from the frontier, the frontier has been running south parallel to the road, and is still a mere eight miles away as the crow flies, on the other side of Mount Sayoa.

We owe this phenomenon to the peninsula of French territory formed by the valley of Les Aldudes. This quiet enclave is connected with the rest of France and the outside world by a single road beside a branch of the Nive; but a whole series of three thousand feet summits, with Basque names such as Izterbeguy or Argaraicomendia, mark its division from Spain, and are the highest we have yet encountered on the frontier itself.

By comparison with the mountains which we shall find farther east, however, the heights surrounding Les Aldudes are merely hills. Although the valley is served by only one road, several paths and mule-tracks wind over these hills into Spain. The nearest Spanish villages are eight or ten miles away, and it would be illegal to reach them by these unofficial crossings. But on my own visit to Les Aldudes I felt that I must at least find out what the frontier looked like in this particular sector, so I drove up towards it from Urepel, on the *voie ordinaire* which Michelin marks as ending exactly at the frontier.

Where the road came to a full stop stood a house all by itself marked 'Bar'. Going inside, I found that it was one of those general stores which not only sell everything from hams to hairpins, but which serve drinks as well. It is a type of establishment found more frequently in Spain than in France.

'How much farther is it to the frontier?' I enquired of the woman behind the counter.

'Twenty metres,' she replied, pointing in the direction from which I had come.

'But that means that we're in Spain.'

'That's right. And I'm Spanish, although I go to Mass at Urepel, and although my children attend a French school.'

As she spoke, I glanced up at the shelves behind her, and noticed a profusion of such familiar but un-French names as Gonzalez Byass, Larios, and Domecq, together with larger stocks of olives and anchovies than would be found in a large French supermarket.

'Have all these come from Spain?' I asked.

'Yes, we bring them by horse or mule. It's a long, rough track through the woods, but it's worth it, because we're able to sell them so much more cheaply than the liqueurs or tinned goods at Urepel or Les Aldudes.'

Knowing that within a few days I would be crossing back into Spain by the more official route, through Irún, I did not take the opportunity to replenish my supplies. But I was so fascinated by this remote and unexpected manifestation of the Spanish economy that I there and then purchased some olives and *chorizo* and half a litre of *vino tinto*. Then, sitting at a table under the trees, I ate a Spanish meal, at Spanish prices, ten miles by mule-track from the nearest Spanish hamlet, but only as many yards from France.

The checkpoint at Velate may have been set up to combat activities even more serious than smuggling. In the years after the Civil War remnants of the Republican armies survived as outlaws in the sierras all over Spain, but particularly in the Pyrenees, where they could if necessary retreat into France, itself then suffering the ferment of Occupation and Resistance. By 1952 these groups had everywhere been destroyed, together with the last of the bandits who had never been absent from the Spanish scene since before the time of Borrow.

The long Pyrenean frontier, however, remained a standing temptation to the thousands of exiled Spaniards scattered throughout France. Their numbers are particularly high in the south-west, in departments such as the Basses-Pyrénées and the Pyrénées-Orientales, and in Bordeaux and Toulouse, cities at all times so familiar to the Spaniard that he has hispanised them as *Burdeos* and *Tolosa*. Throughout the 1950's there was hardly a year when rumour or report failed to tell of the activities in the Pyrenees of armed bands of Republicans who had crossed over from France.

The last such 'invasion', and the most serious, took place in 1961. Its importance lay not in its numbers, which were insignificant – perhaps a score or so of veterans – but in its leadership. For it was organized and led by the one Republican commander who still enjoys an international reputation.

Valentín González was nicknamed *el Campesino* because of his humble Estremaduran origins. Although backed by the Communists as a genuine proletarian commander, he became suspicious even before the Civil War had ended that Russian help was all too self-interested. After the fall of Barcelona he retired to Stalin's Moscow, where his Spanish independence of temper soon got him into trouble. It was only after many years in a Siberian concentration camp, and untold miles trudging on foot around the Soviet Union, that his second attempt at escape brought him in the late 1950's to a West which was no longer as critical of the Franco régime as during the heady anti-fascism of the 1940's. His autobiographical *Listen Comrades* enjoyed a minor success, but he was not invited – as ten years earlier he might just conceivably have been – to organize the 'liberation' of 'Fascist' Spain. Any such expedition would have to be a personal affair.

When Sir Roger Casement came ashore in Galway Bay in 1916, he had spent two years in Germany, and was sadly out of touch with the Ireland he had come to free. But *el Campesino*, as he picked his way with a few companions through the Irati forest on a dark night in the summer of 1961 was re-entering Spain after an absence of almost twenty-three years. He perhaps expected all the non-Communists opponents of the government to rise at the sound of his name. But an entire generation had grown up which had been born after the Civil War had ended. Even his own memories should have told him that Carlist Navarre, whose *requetés* had perhaps tipped the scales against the Republic, was the least suitable province to have chosen for his return.

I happened to be staying at the Casa Jauregui in Almandoz when the report came through of *el Campesino*'s ephemeral reappearance on Spanish soil. I should rather say reports, for there were three. There was a brief, bald announcement on the Spanish radio to the effect that after a clash had taken place between the police and this group of desperadoes, in which one Civil Guard had been killed, *el Campesino* had beat a hasty retreat across the frontier. On my transistor set I then picked up the French report, which was only an expanded and embroidered version of the Spanish.

The fullest report of all, however, had reached Almandoz some hours earlier, by the bush telegraph linking valley to valley by elusive forest guards and lonely shepherds. It spoke of a more serious clash, and of several lives lost. It, too, told us that *el Campesino* was back again on the other side of the Pyrenees, and what interested me most of all was everyone's reaction to his brief intrusion. They were annoyed, at once with him for disturbing the peace, and with the French government which had not prevented him from launching his attack. And they were bored, with that air of pained boredom of an old soldier who for the twentieth time in a day feels the throb of an old wound.

' "*El Campesino*", indeed! Why does he want to come over here upsetting things? Why can't he leave well alone?'

There was a general sigh of relief when it was learnt that the French government had decided to take measures to curb *el Campesino*'s more extrovert activities.

The col de Velate has also a purely geographical importance which it would still possess if the frontier was hundreds of miles away. Hemingway himself may not have realized what this importance was, but his description of the change in country on crossing Velate is so vivid that it almost enables us to guess the reason for the transformation.

'We climbed up and up and crossed another high col and turned along it, and the road ran down to the right, and we saw a whole new range of mountains off to the south, all brown and baked-looking and furrowed in strange shapes.

'After a while we came out of the mountains, and there were trees along both sides of the road, and a stream and ripe fields of grain, and the road went on, very white and straight ahead. . . .'

We have crossed from a pastoral land to an agricultural land, from valleys which run swiftly coastwards to valleys which open on to the bare meseta, from a wet climate to a dry climate. In short, we have left behind us the last stream bound for the Atlantic. The more meagre waters of the rivers which we shall encounter from now onwards are all flowing – with one notable exception – towards the Mediterranean.

Perhaps it is a faint latinity in the air which has seeped up from the Ebro valley which every year leaves the Basque ethos of the valley of Ulzama a little weaker. Constituted by fourteen villages, scattered over a wide saucer of land sloping towards Pamplona, Ulzama hardly seems a proper valley by comparison with Baztán, or with the long, narrow trenches which we shall be encountering farther east. In the villages nearer to Velate the middle-aged still speak Basque, and even in those nearest to Pamplona the old still understand it. But for the young everywhere it is a strange tongue.

Yet there is nothing melancholy about the clear skies and prosperous farms of Ulzama. In every village two or three fine new white silos have gone up, and the district has benefited from its proximity to Pamplona, which for its size is the most prosperous and rapidly expanding city in Spain. This prosperity has been due not only to tourism and to state-sponsored industrialization, but also to the spontaneous growth of the natural centre of a naturally rich province.

To a certain extent Ulzama has suffered from Pamplona's prosperity, which has attracted many of the valley's young people to the new factories. Indeed, the village of Lizaso became so worried by this flight from the land that in 1963 it decided to put itself up for sale. The offer excited world-wide interest, and received publicity in the international press. Perhaps this was the main intention of the inhabitants, for they soon took their village off the market when the provincial government, thus made aware of their troubles, promised to take an interest. Now a syndicate has already started to lay out a golf course in the parish.

This venture should prove a commercial success, for Ulzama forms a natural rural playground for Pamplona. On a Saturday or Sunday afternoon in summer the by-ways between Arraiz and Ciaurriz are noticeably less empty than most secondary roads in Spain. The Citroen Dos Caballos and the Seat 600's draw on to the verges, and, as in Warwickshire or Surrey, the laughing urban families emerge to sport in their weekend Arcadia.

The simile is well chosen. For if Andorra is the Boeotia of the Pyrenees, Ansó the Athens, and Baztán the Sparta, then Ulzama must be the Arcadia. For the Arcadians, when their cities were at

4. Carolingian capitals in crypt of monastery of Leire

5. Santa Cruz de la Serós, beneath the Sierra de la Peña

6. Two monuments of the old kingdom of Aragon: the cloister of San Juan de la Peña

7. —and the abbey church of Siresa in the valley of Hecho

last free to federate after the defeat of Sparta, deliberately decided to prevent any one city from dominating the others by building themselves a new capital altogether. And in the same way the people of Ulzama in 1953 built themselves a fine new Casa Consistorial at the geographical heart of the valley, on the lane joining Iraizoz to Larrainzar. The large, white, half-timbered building, standing all by itself amidst the fields, will remind them of their origins long after the last old man in the fourteen villages to speak *euskara* has passed to his rest. For the inspiration of its architecture is unmistakably Basque.

5. Pamplona and *Sanfermines*

In a book about the Pyrenees, there is no room to say very much about Pamplona, which other writers have in any case treated in greater detail. But to write about the Basque Pyrenees without even mentioning the capital of Navarre would be like drawing a wheel without a hub. For the valleys of Navarre are like so many spokes of a wheel, and the vital link of each is the bus to Pamplona: the *Baztanesa*, or the *Salacena*, proclaiming by its name the valley which it serves.*

Mention has already been made of Pamplona's present prosperity, and of its newly acquired university. Its charm depends not upon any specific buildings of architectural importance, of which, indeed, it has few. The visitor without a map could wander for some time before finding the late Gothic cathedral, hiding behind an eighteenth-century neo-classical façade at the top of a cobbled rise which leads off a quiet alley. It depends rather on the arrangement of the city and on its situation. The wide, straight avenues of the new districts, their junctions picked out by fountains, meet the winding, narrow streets of old Pamplona in the Plaza del Castillo. This vast square, its deep arcades sheltering half a dozen pavement cafés: the Perla, the Iruña (Iruña is the Basque for Pamplona), the Choko, each with its clientèle, is at all times the heart of Pamplona. But never more so than during the second week in July.

'Siete de julio, San Fermín.' The fiesta of San Fermín is like no other fiesta in Spain. Not even the *Feria* of Seville requires such endurance, or inspires such affection. And this affection is shown by a willingness, indeed, by a craving to return year after year. No other fiesta has been given a nickname, and no other fiesta has its own *aficionados*. For it is possible to have no great interest in bullfights, and yet to develop an abiding love for *sanfermines*.

* But not, surprisingly, the *Roncalesa*, which is instead the name of the 'bus service between Pamplona and San Sebastian.

Pamplona and Sanfermines

Nevertheless, the whole of each day between 7th July and 14th July in Pamplona leads up to the bullfight late in the afternoon. The entire fiesta is in a sense the apotheosis of tauromaquia. This is the more remarkable because it takes place so far north, away from the heartlands of the taurine art – just as the finest wines come from the northern limit of the vine, from Champagne. But there is an ingredient in the spirit of *sanfermines* beyond and greater than the ecstasy of the arena. We shall only isolate and recognize this ingredient by describing what it is like to live through one of those seven days.

First of all, however, we must sense the atmosphere in Pamplona just before *sanfermines* begin. There is an almost palpable tension in the air. Even although everyone is going about their business as usual, the pressure of excitement which has been building up for twelve months is like the electric charge hanging heavy in a storm cloud. Those with the time to spare would be well advised to spend a few hours in Pamplona a week or so before 7th July, on their way to somewhere else of interest – Ordesa, for example – and then to return later for the fiesta itself. Hemingway nowhere refers to this tension, but he evidently relished it, for he causes his narrator to spend a night at Pamplona before taking the bus up to Burguete for five days' fishing. And he gives us a clue to the pressures waiting for release when he opens a chapter with the bald words: 'At noon of Sunday, July 6th, the fiesta exploded.'

Let us drive into Pamplona one morning after this explosion has taken place, and the fiesta is well and truly under way. It is as well to reach the city not later than half-past six, for we shall not be the only arrivals. And from the outskirts onwards we shall have to drive slowly, for there will already be many people about, singly or in groups, all with a red kerchief round their neck, and some a little unsteady on their feet.

There is generally space to park a car in the side streets between the bullring and the Half Moon Gardens, and this is also conveniently near where we want to get. Walking towards the bullring, we shall find that a double palisade has been erected between its principal gate and the main street of the old town. Along the corridor thus formed will pass the runners of the famous *encierro*, on the last lap of their sprint before the pursuing bulls.

Wedging ourselves as near to the palisade as possible, we shall have almost as good a view as those privileged beings who are now lining the balconies of the houses along the streets where the bulls will pass. Promptly at seven o'clock we shall hear the pistol shot which announces their release, and then a gradually rising crescendo of shouts as they approach us. Very soon the first of the runners will pass, probably a middle-aged man at a leisurely lope. He will have jumped the starting-gun by several minutes. For whatever the critics of the *encierro* may say, its dangers are assumed voluntarily; and just as each victim may be regarded as his own executioner, so each runner is free to set his own handicap.

Then will come more runners, and more: a confused mass of white shirts and red kerchiefs whose very numbers prevent them from reaching the speed to which we suddenly hear our own voices urging them. The bulls themselves come as rather an anticlimax. They are smaller than we expect, and their dark brown colour seems dowdy beside the garish dress of the runners and the onlookers. Besides, they are past us in a moment. There will still be a few runners to come, who have stepped aside or under the palisades, while the bulls have swept by. And some of the most dangerous moments of an *encierro* can come when all danger seems past, on the sudden appearance of a lone bull, a *manso*, lagging behind his fellows, and therefore even more frightened and unpredictable than they.

Dowdy though they may appear, frightened though they certainly are, it is the bulls who are the heroes of the *encierro*. These six god-kings of the fiesta race through the streets in ritual triumph, chasing the worshippers who less than twelve hours later will applaud the slim young priests who carry out the sacrifice.

Once the runners have reached the bullring, they are able to play a more active role – although a comic one. The bulls are soon rounded up, and a series of steers with horns bound are released for these amateur *toreros* to try their hand. It is well worth playing the few pesetas' entry fee to enjoy this spectacle, especially if one has friends who are trying to demonstrate their skill down there in the arena.

But all the seats in the bullring are filled before the *encierro* has even started. We cannot be in two places at once, and the comedy with the steers must wait until tomorrow. We are in any case hungry after our early start. So we repair to one of the cafés round the Plaza del Castillo, for rolls and coffee.

Pamplona and Sanfermines

Sanfermines is always more enjoyable if enjoyed in company with a *cuadrilla* of friends with whom we can share the fun and later laugh over the memories. And if we have come as members of such a group, we shall probably already have decided on the particular café where we are going to meet after the confusion of the *encierro*, for only thus can we hope to find each other again. Indeed, *habitués* of *sanfermines* can only distinguish one year from another by two things: by the quality of the bullfights, and by the café which their *cuadrilla* used as their headquarters that particular July. Jake and Brett and Mike and Bill and Cohn used the Iruña, which is one of the biggest, and which is very central and comfortable. But whichever we choose, it will become a home from home for us during the next few days. Whenever we feel lost, or tired, or bored, or lonely, we shall return to the Plaza del Castillo. And whatever the hour of the day or night, we can be sure to find one or more of our *cuadrilla* in some corner of our chosen café, with a coffee or a beer in front of them, and with an increasingly wine-stained red kerchief round their neck.

As we sit over breakfast, we shall suddenly realize that we alone are still without this emblem of the fiesta, this other red flag whose happier message might be read as 'Drinkers of the world, imbibe'. We can soon repair the omission, however, for every shop and every street pedlar offer a wide variety of red kerchiefs. But we must make our choice with care. This is a purchase we intend to keep for many years. For it is said that so long as we retain the first red kerchief we wore at *sanfermines*, so long are we sure of returning some other July to Pamplona.

Time flies as one coffee follows another, and we watch the kaleidoscope around us. Pamplona is more accessible than Andalusia, and its fiesta falls in a more convenient season than the Fair of Seville. The crowds who converge there are not only uninhibited, but cosmopolitan. They soon find, however, that this is a Bacchanalia with rules. One is licensed to go mad, but not to play the fool. A French friend of mine decided late one night to take a swim in one of Pamplona's public fountains. But his bath cost him a fine of a hundred pesetas!

Ever since we arrived we have heard snatches of a jolly, piping tune, something between a bagpipe march and a sailor's hornpipe. But towards noon it becomes more insistent, and presently a long procession winds slowly into view. Although its progress is slow, it expends a prodigious amount of effort in its gradual move-ment forward. The saint's statue requires the strength of several bearers. The grinning giants are for ever turning as they gape this way and that, now towards the crowd, and now towards each other. And the dozens of groups who follow, each with a banner proclaiming their village of origin, never stop dancing. Now their steps follow some variant of the *jota*, now an old Basque air. But every few minutes, as if to renew their energy and their inspira-tion, there strikes up once again the theme song of *sanfermines*:

> '*Uno de enero, dos de febrero,*
> *tres de marzo, cuatro abril,*
> *Cinco de mayo, seis de junio,*
> *siete de julio, San Fermín.*
> *A Pamplona hemos de irnos,*
> *con una media, con una media,*
> *A Pamplona hemos de irnos,*
> *con una media y un calcetín.*'

This procession will be repeated later in the afternoon, im-mediately before the bullfight. Now, as the last group of dancers come round for the last time and are lost to view, the square seems suddenly empty, and we become aware that it is not only the dancers who have disappeared. Half the onlookers, too, have gone off, and we realize that it is time for lunch. There are many good restaurants in Pamplona, but we shall get nearer to the heart of the fiesta if we follow the example of the majority of partici-pants, and take a *bocadillo* of bread and cheese and garlic sausage (the famous *chorizo* for which Pamplona is famous) into one of the scores of back-street wineshops.

The atmosphere in each is at once welcoming yet intimate. The gnarled faces above the black suits, the younger and more-rounded features above the white shirts smile as we enter, and we are soon members of their community, swopping *chorizo* for olives, or unsuccessfully trying to pour into our mouths a stream of tarry wine from a supple leather *bota*.

It is a real community into which we have been so easily accepted, and we shall soon learn that our new friends are all from some particular village of the Ribera, or all from one of our Pyrenean valleys. I once found myself in a wine shop along with all the *valencianos* who happened to be at the fiesta. When they had finished eating, they gave an impromptu display of dances from the Levante, of which Valencia is the capital.

There may be other days when we shall drive out into the country for lunch, to eat our *bocadillos* after a swim in the river Arga, and then, overcome by the sun and the wine, and sleepy after a late night and an early rise, to doze away the golden afternoon.

But in any case, before half-past five we shall be in our seats in the bullring, to watch three of the greatest matadors of Spain – only the best are good enough for *sanfermines* – dispatch the six bulls whom we saw running in the *encierro* this morning.

The *corrida* over, we are bound to lose our friends in the crowds who stream out from the bullring. But we shall find them again in our café under the arcades of the Plaza del Castillo, where we shall sip our apéritifs as darkness falls. It was at this hour of the day that Ernest Hemingway used to be at his most genial and approachable. As he sat laughing with a few cronies on the terrace of the Perla, or as he strolled across the centre of the *plaza*, he would turn with a smile towards each trousered girl, or youth with beard so much less trim than his own, and obligingly autograph their tendered copy of *Fiesta*, or *For whom the bell tolls*. He always returned, year after year, to the scene of his first and perhaps his greatest novel. And gloom settled on Pamplona on 2nd July, 1961, when from mouth to mouth was passed on the unbelievable news of his death. He had not only created an image of *sanfermines* for the outside world, but had himself become part of that image. For the first few hours of the fiesta – of his Fiesta – that year, we all of us, tourists and *navarros* alike, went through the usual rituals with hushed voices and little enthusiasm. And then, mercifully, we realized that the tribute to a man's memory must bear some relationship to his character. And by nightfall the *botas* and the *porrones* were being raised higher and more frequently than ever, and through the streets of Pamplona rang the old song as it had never rung before:

> '*Uno de enero, dos de febrero,*
> *tres de marzo, cuatro abril,*
> *Cinco de mayo, seis de junio,*
> *siete de julio, San Fermín!*

The Basque Pyrenees

Late in the evening there are fireworks to watch. Later still, there will be a dinner to linger over. But at some point during the three hours after midnight we shall realize that we must snatch a little sleep if we are to be awake to see the *encierro*. Even if we have been lucky enough to book a room in Pamplona some months before, we shall be disturbed by the noise of revelry, which is never stilled at any hour of the twenty-four. The one sure way to find quiet is to drive out of town, into the summer night. And what better road than the three miles to Villalba, and to the right towards Roncesvalles?

We need not drive far in search of peace. We are soon in countryside more silent than any we have known. This must be due to the contrast with the noise we have left behind us. Looking back, a wide glow marks the unsleeping city. But often, especially if the moon is up, we find ourselves driving on, up the long white empty road which Charlemagne and Roland knew. There is not a soul astir, yet the very landscape seems to possess some personal quality which the fiesta has conditioned us to recognize for the first time. We feel that we want to drive on and on, to deliver some unknown message to the farthest valley of the Basque Pyrenees.

And then at last we understand that *sanfermines* is not the fiesta of Pamplona alone. It belongs to all Navarre.

6. Roncesvalles and the Forest of Irati

The road to Roncesvalles follows the Arga, the river of Pamplona, for its first twelve miles. It then climbs across an intervening ridge into another valley, which it only follows for a few miles before crossing to yet another. But it reaches each stream at a higher point of its course, so that the last has hardly had time to form a valley. In twenty-seven miles the road has climbed from an altitude of 1,350 feet at Pamplona to 3,150 feet at Burguete, a long street of solid white houses at the centre of a plain.

There is often a cool breeze across this plain, and the combination of altitude and good communications has made Burguete an old-established favourite of summer visitors seeking a relief from the heat of the big cities. For many years it has therefore had several good inns, and this was probably why Hemingway takes Jake and Bill up to Burguete for their fishing in the Irati river. It involved them, as readers will remember, in a long hike across country every day before they could even start to fish. But 'the nights were cold and the days were hot, and there was always a breeze even in the heat of the day. It was hot enough so that it felt good to wade in a cold stream, and the sun dried you when you came out and sat on the bank'. How accurately that describes so many happy days in the Spanish Pyrenees! I was pleased to see that the brief shot of this sequence which was included in the film of *The Sun also rises* showed the Irati as the fast, relatively shallow Pyrenean stream which it is.

If Jake and Bill had wanted their fishing nearer to hand, they would have taken rooms in Orbaiceta or Orbara, villages which stand just beside the river. They can be reached direct from Pamplona, taking the road to Aoiz over the flat cornlands, off which lead several private roads, serving large estates. Although the kings of Navarre once had a residence there, Aoiz is today only a large village, with a population under two thousand, and a dark church above the Irati.

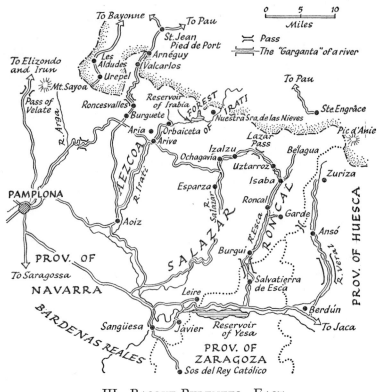

III Basque Pyrenees—East

Roncesvalles and the Forest of Irati

From Aoiz we can follow the river almost to its source. The valley of the Irati is known as Aezcoa, and the first ten miles are wild and almost empty. After Oroz-Betelu comes a steep climb to meet one of the few lateral roads joining the upper valleys of the Spanish Pyrenees. This runs high above the Irati for a mile or two, and then crosses the river at Arive, where we turn off towards Orbara and Orbaiceta, villages of solid houses in whitewashed stone. Soon after Orbaiceta the river splits, and the road does likewise. The track to the left leads to a disused wood processing plant, the *fabrica de Orbaiceta* after which was named the Rio de la Fabrica, mentioned by Hemingway.

The Irati itself, and our own road with it, bears away to the right. But it is now a road no longer, but simply a forest track, or *pista* – a word which we shall encounter to an increasing extent as we penetrate deeper into the range. Like most other *pistas*, it is practicable enough in dry weather, but a quagmire after rain, when it is torn to pieces by the timber carrying lorries for which it was developed.

The source of this timber presently comes into view. The trees appear at first sight in well-spaced groves, with open glades between, but they are soon packed more and more densely, so that we begin to understand why the Spanish word *selva* translates both 'forest' and 'jungle'. The forest of Irati is neither flat nor monotonous, however. When from a rise we can see some way ahead, the green carpet below us is formed not by grass, but by treetops. And the trees themselves are a pleasing mixture of oak, beech, and fir.

The deep valleys carved in the forest by the Irati and its tributary the Urio have given Spanish engineers the opportunity to build one of their dams, behind which waters can build up to provide power for their energy deprived land. The reservoir of Irabia, occupying part of both valleys, and of their joint valley after union, has filled out into the form of a 'Y', and therefore adds two or three miles to the route. But the views of steep tree-covered slopes down to the water make the diversion worthwhile. So does the knowledge, as we cross the log bridge over the Urio, that we are very nearly in France – with not a frontier guard in sight.

Then on the other side of the reservoir the track leaves the Irati and climbs for three miles, finally degenerating into a mere footpath. We are higher here, and the trees are beginning to give way to open pasture. Half-way up a hillside two stone houses stand side by side for warmth – it would be inappropriate in this setting to speak of them as being semi-detached. And higher still stands a small, white chapel, the aptly named sanctuary of Our Lady of the Snows.

These unpretentious houses are the 'capital' of the forest of Irati. The two families who spend seven months of the year there both receive guests, and to judge by the smell proceeding from the huge, brown-enamel dishes on the stoves of their wide clean kitchens, they offer the right fare for the healthy appetites engendered by the mountain air. To reach them from where the track ends we have to cross a narrow stream – the infant Irati, which has curved round to meet us. And in crossing the stream we cross also from the part of the forest which is *patrimonio del estado*, property of the State, to the part belonging to the valley of Salazar. The largest village of Salazar, Ochagavía, happens also to be the nearest to Irati, and it is to Ochagavía that the two families retire for the five winter months. For their task is to care for the valley's trees, and there is no point in their remaining up here in discomfort and isolation when the forest is covered by snow.

In summer their isolation is far from complete. Apart from visitors staying with them, there are various foresters and tourists around Irati who call in for a drink. Then there is Pablo, the one-eyed shepherd, grazing the cattle of all Salazar on the tender mountain turf. And above all there is Don Santos.

Don Santos Beguiristain, a tall and strikingly handsome Canon of Pamplona Cathedral, has for many years cherished a strong affection for the Basque Pyrenees. This is the more unexpected, because although he is regarded as an authority on ancient Castilian, he speaks not a word of Basque. But even if his keen, hawk-like face did not reveal his racial origin, his name alone would prove his Basque ancestry, for the suffix-*ain* is as typically Basque as the suffix-*ian* is typically Armenian. And his homing spirit brought him, summer after summer, to the woods and pastures which lie beyond where the last valleys end.

Such a devotion eventually had to find a physical – dare we say a sacramental? – expression. In 1954 Don Santos persuaded the villagers for miles around to help him in building the sanctuary of Nuestra Señora de las Nieves in the heart of the countryside which in spirit he had made his own. It is a simple square structure with a wide entrance porch, and the walls inside are covered by murals. Behind the alter these represent Basque worshippers in the old costumes of the valleys; and on the lateral walls are depicted the four sanctuaries of Our Lady in the valley of Salazar. The only one of these known outside the valley is that of Muskilda, near Ochagavía. But no chapel stood where Don Santos decided to raise his own tribute to Our Lady, and as the site belonged to all Salazar, and not to Ochagavía alone, it was fitting that in establishing this new sanctuary he should remember all four of the shrines where she had long been venerated.

Every Sunday in summer Don Santos travels up to Irati to say Mass in the new chapel. And on the first Sunday in August, the day of its patronal festival, he goes not for a single day, but for two weeks, staying with one of the forest guards just below. 'Don Santos is up there now,' say old and young alike from Orbaiceta to Izalzu, as they point towards the mountains with a smile. It is as if a familiar and well-loved star is once again showing over the horizon. And every morning little groups will trudge several miles over the forest paths to hear Mass at Our Lady of the Snows. It may be misty when they finally emerge on the bare hillside of the sanctuary, but Don Santos, a true shepherd, will be waiting outside to embrace them, his soutane overlaid by a full sheepskin cloak, a *manta de pastor*.

Below the sanctuary winds the Irati river, early on its journey from its source at the foot of the Pic des Escaliers. A French name? Yes; for the Irati, like a number of lesser Spanish streams in this sector, rises over in France, just as the Petite Nive begins its life in Spain.

To see the latter phenomenon, however, we must retrace our steps to Burguete, from which we have been led into the depths of the Irati forest on the track of Hemingway's heroes. A dead straight road runs the two miles which separate Burguete from the cluster of houses beside the great collegiate church of Roncesvalles.

Like the Elsinore of Hamlet, the Roncevaux of Roland is one of the most evocative names of western literature, the basis of childhood dreams and youthful fantasies. It must be some system of celestial justice which has invested both sites with a feature which brings the visitor down to hard reality with a bump. For the spectre of Elsinore has been frightened away by a shiny green copper roof. And the paladins of Charlemagne would feel equally out of place under the roof of corrugated zinc which Roncesvalles bears today.

Nor is there any authentic relic of the eighth century, either in the well-restored thirteenth-century church, with its fourteenth-century virgin of Roncesvalles, or in the museum attached to the community of canons. The treasures of this museum are of interest in their own right, without any dubious connexion with Roland or Oliver or Archbishop Turpin. There is hardly likely to be any authentic relic of the great engagement in which the Frankish rearguard was destroyed, for this would be to expect the egg before the chicken. The church did not exist when the battle was fought, and only exists now because a need was felt to raise a memorial in stone to parallel the memorial in verse, the *Chanson de Roland*. Nor need we be surprised that more than four centuries passed before King Sancho the Strong of Navarre decided to erect such a memorial. For if we go back behind the legends to the earliest, prosaic account of what happened, that of Charlemagne's biographer, Einhard, we learn that it was not the Moslems who attacked the rearguard, but the *Wascones*, the Basques themselves.

They had good reason to do so, for Charlemagne had just attacked Pamplona. In this he was pursuing a policy of alliance with one of the two Arab factions struggling for control of Saragossa, a policy which makes sense when viewed in terms of his global strategy at the time. But this particular expedition of 778, as it turned out, had no sequel. Its only historical significance – forgetting its literary repercussions – was that it was the only occasion that the Emperor himself crossed the Pyrenees. He did not avenge the loss of his rearguard, the Basques never came under his rule, and the Carolingian influence in early Navarre, although profound, was indirect. Twenty years later he was to initiate a new, and historically a far more important policy in other parts of the Spanish Pyrenees, but of this we shall speak as we come to the regions concerned.

If the church of Roncesvalles had been intended purely as a memorial to Roland, it would have been built high up in the defile where he died. But it was founded for a more practical purpose too, as a staging post for pilgrims travelling to Santiago de Compostela, to the shrine of St. James, the patron of Spain, in far Galicia. This was the second most popular pilgrimage after Jerusalem throughout the Middle Ages, just as Spain was the second most popular theatre for Crusades against the 'infidel' after Palestine.

Roncesvalles marks a particularly happy moment in that long struggle. For its founder, Sancho the Strong, was the king of Navarre who united his armies with those of Castile and Aragon for the campaign which smashed the power of the fanatical Almohades at Las Navas de Tolosa in 1212, opening the way for the conquest of the Guadalquivir valley and the Levante. The tent of the Moslem leader was protected by stout chains, which formed part of Sancho's trophies, and which feature still on the arms of Navarre. Parts of these chains have been preserved in a number of places in Navarre, amongst which Roncesvalles is one.

The pilgrims on their way to Santiago, whether they came from France, northern Europe, Germany, or Italy, were bound to cross the Pyrenees, and this is only the first of several passes where we shall find that provision was made for them. It is pleasant to know that the Basques, who had once attacked the Franks here, were later to offer hospitality to the pilgrims of 'Francia' as they came down from the pass of Ibañeta (as the actual pass of Roncesvalles is called). The twelve canons of the collegiate church are strongly Basque in their sympathies to this day, and some of their number, born and brought up in the Basque speaking parts of Navarre, can always welcome a Basque visitor in the language of Roland's assailants. But they are the last outposts of the tongue, for at this point the domination of Castilian has crept right up to the watershed.

It has not crept right up to the frontier, however. For beyond the Ibañeta pass, as beyond the Maya pass, there lies a little pocket of Spanish territory which geographically belongs to France. There Basque is spoken just as it is in the neighbouring French districts around St. Jean-Pied-de-Port and Les Aldudes. These two little pockets: Zugarramurdi and Valcarlos, both on the wrong side of the range, are linked by a melancholy historical association. For the younger Don Carlos, the pretender in the Second Carlist War of 1872–6, entered Spain at Zugarramurdi. Like the young Pretender in Britain, he was an attractive and romantic figure by comparison with the old Pretender, the Don Carlos of a generation earlier. And just as Bonnie Prince Charlie got as far as Derby, so Don Carlos's brother and sister-in-law penetrated all the way to Cuenca. But Carlists and Jacobites alike were fighting against the stream of history, and when Don Carlos recrossed to France from the Val Carlos where another and greater Charles had known defeat, he was ne'er to come back again.

It is only two miles from the village of Valcarlos to the bridge across the frontier river, the Petite Nive, and the French village of Arnéguy. And from there it is only another five miles to St. Jean-Pied-de-Port, the capital of Basse-Navarre, one of the seven Basque provinces, and the only part of the old kingdom of which Henry of Navarre was ruler when he united the crown of Navarre to that of France in 1589.

The tourist is brought up against the inconsistencies of the frontier line when the waitress who serves him a delicious pair of freshly caught trout at the open-air restaurant beside the Nive in St. Jean turns out to be a girl from Valcarlos. She is one of many who bicycle to and fro' across the frontier on their way to work. The political division has some justification, however, for a whole series of heights several hundred feet greater than the pass mark the boundaries of the *défilé de Valcarlos* on either side. The real anomaly is not that Valcarlos should be in Spain, but that the hamlet of Ondaroles should be in France.

Ondaroles forms part of the commune of Arnéguy, but is four miles away from the main village, up a narrow road between the Pic de Beillurte and the Petite Nive. Valcarlos, however, lies within hailing distance across the river – and the frontier. The people of Ondaroles have therefore always found it more convenient to use the church of Valcarlos, even after a church was first built at Arnéguy in 1656.

During the eighteenth century, when France and Spain were ruled by members of the same Bourbon family, they generally co-ordinated their foreign policies. This alliance had its moment of triumph when Britain, their arch-enemy, attacked whilst trying to put down the rebellion of her American colonists, was forced to sign a Peace of Versailles of the vanquished in 1783. It must have been the euphoria of that victory which brought about the signing of a treaty at Elizondo on 27th August, 1785, whereby Ondaroles was to be ceded to Spain.

Roncesvalles and the Forest of Irati

But in helping the American Revolution, France had invited a revolution of her own, and the defenders of the Rights of Man proved to be more chauvinistic than the absolute monarch whom they displaced. Ondaroles stayed French, and a more efficient and centralized system of government allowed no waiving of the rules for special cases. By 1842, a soldier was being stationed at the door of any house in Ondaroles where a death had taken place, to prevent the body being carried over to Valcarlos for burial. In retaliation for this theft of his spiritual children, the Bishop of Pamplona was at the same time declaring that all who married at the church of Arnéguy were merely concubines. And as recently as 1940 the Germans, perhaps with a view to reviving old conflicts, drew their line of Occupation between the village and its dependent hamlet, so that Arnéguy was in the occupied zone, whilst Ondaroles was administered by Vichy.

Today no one tries to stop the people of Ondaroles from worshipping in Valcarlos. And this has one unexpected result. For by law, every Frenchman who marries must not only go through a civil ceremony as well as a religious ceremony, but the civil must take place first. In Ondaroles alone can the bride and groom slip across the river for their wedding by the priest, and then return, already man and wife, for the official formalities before M. le Maire.

We must hope that the same easy-going attitude is extended towards those who live in the extreme north of the wedge of Spanish territory beyond Valcarlos, who find themselves in the reverse position. For by an error of frontier drawing three houses, although in Spain, remain in the parish of Lasse, and thus under the ecclesiastical jurisdiction of the Bishop of Bayonne.

7. Salazar and Roncal

These two valleys of eastern Navarre, *les hautes vallées des Pyrénées navarraises* as the *Guide Bleu* calls them, have so much in common that they can be treated as a unity. They have more roads joining them together than roads linking them to the outside world. Here, and nowhere else in the Spanish Pyrenees, a lateral road connects the head of one valley to the head of another, so that it is possible for the tourist to travel up Salazar to Izalzu, 'over the top' of the Alto de Lazar to Uztárroz, and down Roncal all the way to Burgui.

I have suggested a clockwise itinerary not merely because that is the general direction in which we are proceeding, but in order that the traveller may enjoy the exaltation of passing from west to east through the little Lazar pass. The road is good: the climb is not unduly steep. We hardly realize that we have reached the summit when we find ourselves between the two faces of a short cutting in the rock. We have left Salazar, and a minute later all Roncal lies below us. And beyond so much else.

Ever since we left the sea we have been climbing up and down hills. Big hills. Awkward hills. Wooded hills. Grassy hills. But in essence, nothing more than hills. And now, at last, we face the true mountains. Fifteen miles away rises the Pic d'Anie to 8,216 feet. Beside and beyond rise others to a height little less. There is an unwonted sharpness in their angles, and an unaccustomed bareness about their rock. And there is snow.

But these first peaks of the high Pyrenees, which mark the end of the Basque country, lie between France and Aragon. In Salazar and Roncal we are still in Navarre, where the frontier heights are some two thousand feet lower, and the cols between them correspondingly easier to negotiate. It is this which distinguishes them from the two parallel valleys of Ansó and Hecho, over in Aragon.

Roncal in particular has much in common with the valleys farther east. We find here, as we have already found in Aezcoa and

Baztán, and as we shall find many times later on, that the name of
the valley is not the same as that of its river. Roncal may be
defined as the valley of the Esca, together with the valleys of its
tributaries, from their sources to where it leaves Navarre. 'Where
it leaves Navarre' is no artificial line. It is a long narrow gorge, in
which there is not really room for both the river and the road.
This is a phenomenon typical of the central Spanish Pyrenees, for
which we shall be offering an explanation later on: it is here that
the phenomenon first appears.

This narrow gorge is a natural frontier between two types of
country and two ways of life. The valley above the gorge is
pastoral, well watered, and with solid villages not unlike those of
the Pennines. The parched plain into which it opens out, on the
other hand, has an almost Mediterranean vegetation, and is
dotted with clustered villages of that primitive yet exotic
character which conform to the popular concept of a Spanish
pueblo.

Just at the point where Roncal and Salazar meet the plain these
pueblos are in fact even more primitive than usual. For here, on the
frontier with Aragon, lie *las Bardenas reales*, the arid badlands
where only the game hunted by the kings of Navarre grew fat.
The irrigation made possible by the huge new reservoir of Yesa is
gradually enriching this countryside, but until a few years ago it
suffered from an Andalusian poverty. Small, dark, walnut brown,
and earthy, its people mouth a crude Castilian which the newcomer
finds difficulty in following. Before 1960 there was only one petrol
pump in all the one hundred and eight kilometres between
Pamplona and Jaca: at the very junction of this road with the
road up to Roncal. Nor was petrol the only liquid in short supply.
For at that very petrol pump – itself a quaint relic from the very
earliest days of motoring – I once asked for a glass of water. But
they *had* no water. Would not a glass of wine, they asked, quench
my thirst equally well?

In earlier centuries Salazar and Roncal found these plains inaccessible, inhospitable, and alien. So, perhaps, did Hecho and
Ansó, which responded by developing into isolated communities,
conserving ancient dialects and costumes. They could do little
else, for a high mountain wall cut them off to the north. But their
Basque neighbours in Salazar and Roncal suffered less impedi-
ment: beyond the hills at the head of their valleys lay other

Basque villages similar to their own, speaking not merely the
same language, but the same *souletin* dialect. For the really big
purchases of life: a silk dress, a gold watch, or a sporting gun, they
went not to Pamplona, but to Mauléon or Oloron. And when,
with winter, the life of the farms was stilled, and the pastures lay
under snow, there were few young people to be seen in the streets
of Isaba or of Ochagavía. For they were working in factories or in
domestic service across the frontier.

Today this trans-Pyrenean traffic is no more. Nor is it only
passports and work permits which are responsible. For in the
motor age, man travels only where the roads lead, and the roads
from these valleys lead not to Pau, but to Pamplona. The de-
ficiency is being mended, however. Both from Salazar and from
Roncal roads are being driven north to meet French roads which
are being extended to the south. Once linked up, these will trans-
form the life of the valleys through which they pass. Those who
would prefer to see them before they become busy through
routes, however, still have an opportunity. Work was in noisy
progress on the road from Salazar when I passed that way in 1959,
and I was assured that it would be open in 1960. But in 1964 the
sound of the pickaxe was hushed, and shrugs of the shoulders
greeted my enquiries as to when I would be able to drive through
to Tardets. And although from Roncal a road now runs up to the
wide, high plain of Belagua, it has been built independently by
the village of Isaba, when the valley as a whole refused to act. To
push it farther, beyond the so-called Venta de Arraco to meet the
road from Sainte Engrâce or Arette will require the efforts not
only of the whole valley, but of the province of Navarre.

This road, when it is at last completed, will pass very close to
the frontier stone of Saint Martin. Here, on the morning of 13th
June, there takes place every year a curious ceremony which in a
paradoxical way illustrates the links in this sector between the
two sides of the Pyrenees. Ever since 1375 the valley of Barétous
(which includes the villages of Arette, Aramits, and Lanne) has on
that date paid a tribute of three cows to the valley of Roncal. The
origins of this are uncertain, but it is the best of all the examples of
private treaties between Pyrenean valleys, made regardless of
national frontiers, which we have mentioned when writing about
Baztán.

On the Spanish side, the principal role in this ceremony is

taken by the mayor of Isaba, and this village retains two of the tribute cows. The other goes to the neighbouring village of Uztárroz, and I am told that Garde also has some share of the tribute.

Talking of the different villages of the valleys brings us to the way in which they are organized. We have already compared the differing systems adopted by Baztán and Ulzama to those of Sparta and Arcadia, and we could, if we wished, find Hellenic parallels for those of Salazar and Roncal. Both have shown at once statesmanship and sense in not making their biggest village their capital; for Ochagavía in Salazar, and Isaba in Roncal, fine places though they are, stand almost at the head of their valleys, and would be inconvenient capitals for the majority of the inhabitants. Instead, Salazar has chosen to have no fixed capital: the council of the valley meets every year in a different *pueblo*. In 1964, for example, this was Esparza.

Roncal, on the other hand, although it has a fixed capital, has placed this in its geographical centre, Roncal itself, which is one of the smaller of the valley's seven constituent villages. There, on their common business, gather the seven mayors, from distant Uztárroz, from lordly Isaba, from Urzainqui just off the main road and across the Esca, from Roncal, from Vidangoz and from Garde to east and to west in subsidiary valleys, and from Burgui in the far south.

Little Roncal is not only the valley's capital, but the birthplace of its most famous son, Gayarre, the operatic tenor who in the generation before Melba had a reputation in the musical world equal to hers. His bust stands in the gardens between the Esca and the splendid schools which he presented to Roncal, and in the cemetery half a mile up the road to Vidangoz stands his tomb. This is surrounded by a huge bronze group executed by Benlliure, the sculptor from Valencia who was at his prime when Gayarre died in 1877.

Although neither Ochagavía nor Isaba rank as capitals, both have a certain pre-eminence in their valleys, which they well deserve. Ochagavía, although its church stands on a rise, is built mainly on the level, on both sides of the river Salazar. If it was not for the gleaming whitewash which covers several of its fine, four-square houses, the traveller might imagine himself in a Cotswold village, where a river is often just as much at the centre of things.

The Basque Pyrenees

There is the same peace and stability in the bare hillsides and the thick stone walls, and the same intimation, too, even on an August afternoon, of the bitter winds which make such walls necessary.

Isaba, on the other hand, is Pennine rather than Cotswold; or perhaps it is simply more typically Pyrenean. It was there that I first saw a Pyrenean herd of sheep and goats arrive home in the evening. They entered the village as a confused indistinguishable mass, and when I saw stray beasts turning to left and right down side streets, I thought that they must be quite out of control. Then in the centre of the village the entire herd disintegrated, as part went in one direction, and part in another. But these were neither cloven-hooved goats nor lost sheep, as I was soon to learn. Each knew where she was going, and made straight for the door of the house where she belonged. Within a few minutes the last of the hundreds of bells which had drowned every other noise had tinkled away down a distant alley.

These and other animals do not actually live with the families who own them, but their stables form an integral part of the houses which line the streets of Pyrenean villages. From the valley of Roncal onwards, the goat is the most numerous domestic animal, and the goat herd is a figure of importance in village life. (The great flocks of sheep are so often and so far away from home, on the high pastures in summer, or in the plains in winter, that it would be a misnomer to call them domestic). Any inhabitant of the Spanish Pyrenees if he were not from the valley of Arán would subscribe to the old English definition of the goat as 'the poor man's cow'.

Yet however excellent the quality of its milk, and however high the ratio of milk produced to food consumed, the goat remains an inefficient cow substitute. Three or four cows, tethered near the village, would provide all the milk which its population required with a quarter of the trouble. But mere milk production is not the goat's only role. The Pyreneans cling to her for other less tangible reasons. An agriculturalist, urging the enormous superiority of the cow, found all his arguments accepted with the fatalistic resignation of those who intend to do nothing whatsoever about them. When he had at last finished, an old woman turned to him with a slight shrug of the shoulders. 'Yes, sir, you are quite right. But the truth of the matter is that we each have a great affection for our goat.'

In Roncal, however, it is not goat's milk, but sheep's milk which is used to make the cheeses by which the valley is best known throughout the rest of the country. Spain has few cheeses, for the simple reason that she has few cows and little milk, and the only native variety found everywhere is the white *manchego*. Roncal is a deep yellow cheese, with a brown rind, made in huge round wheels. But it is not always easy to locate on its native heath, and a little enquiry will be necessary before a bony hand tenders a newly axed segment through some dark doorway of Uztárroz or of Urzainqui.

The four chapels in Salazar dedicated to Our Lady have already been mentioned. Roncal has no shrine as popular as Ochagavía's Virgin of Muskilda. Indeed, the best-known chapel of the valley, that of the Virgin de la Peña, lies just outside Navarre, in the province of Saragossa, and is now peacefully shared – after many past disputes – by the villages of Burgui and Salvatierra (the birthplace of the wife of my friend the Civil Guard sergeant).

But two miles to the north of Burgui, in the midst of the sunny corn bowl which forms the southern third of Roncal, an uneven clump of vegetation stands separated by a small field from the left bank of the Esca. The road runs on the opposite side of the river, which in summer, though pleasantly fresh, will not have that icy coldness which melted snow gives to the streams of Aragon and Pallars. With trousers rolled up, a man can wade across and barely get his knees wet. And he will find the clump of vegetation to be a true 'ivy-mantled ruin', still awaiting rescue and clinical cleaning by Beaux-Arts or Ministry of Works.

This was once the monastery of Burdaspal, founded in the ninth century. It flourished during the two or three hundred years when the Pyrenean valleys knew an intense religious and political life, a life which ebbed away as the Christian lords rediscovered wider horizons in the re-conquered lands to the south, leaving Burdaspal as one of the many casualties.

The greatest glory of Roncal today, however, was not made by man. Or rather, it was only made by man in the negative sense that he has cut timber and grazed herds to bring about the bare beauty of Belagua. Two streams meet at Isaba, and a road follows each. That to the left, from the pass of Lazar and Uztárroz, we already know. To the right, the road runs in a narrow gorge, crossing and recrossing the river as it climbs – the first of many similar roads we shall travel in the upper reaches of the central Pyrenean valleys. After about five miles it opens out, and we find ourselves seemingly on top of the world. Or at least we would feel on the roof of the world, in the open lonely landscape, beneath a sky truly empyrean, were it not for the hills beyond, which rise higher still. All the maps mark an isolated inn at the head of Belagua, with the name of Venta de Arraco. But it must be many years since any of the cartographers came to see for themselves, for there is no inn now.

'Yes, I think that someone used to keep a *fonda* of some sort up there. My father occasionally used to speak about it,' said a man of my own age as we stood drinking in Isaba. It is not the only part of the valley's past which has slipped away almost beyond memory. Once everyone wore the costume of Roncal. The men's was in its essential features – the breeches and the wide black hat with tassel – closely similar to that still worn in Ansó, which we shall be describing in due course.

The women's, however, was more distinctive, including a blue skirt, a red sash, and a large red square worn over the head and reaching below the shoulders. For widows the costume was the same, except that every garment was black, giving the wearer the appearance of a nun of one of the humbler and less-secluded orders. At the time of writing only one old lady in Isaba, aged ninety, still wears this. When I passed that way in 1959 she had two or three friends still alive, with whom I heard her chatting in Basque.

The last report I have heard of the men's costume was given me by Don Francisco Bejarano of Ansó. He saw a man in *roncalés* dress working in a back garden of Uztárroz in either 1953 or 1954. Uztárroz, the last village at the head of the valley, is the place where one would expect old customs to linger longest. I was more surprised to hear that as recently as 1950 there lived in Garde an old man who not only still wore the traditional dress, but who could still speak Basque. For Garde, although two miles away from the main road, and the new fashions which the main road may be expected to bring, has always stood at the very limit of Basque-speaking territory, where Navarre meets Huesca and Saragossa provinces. Its proximity to conservative Ansó made it understandable that the old dress should have survived there until the mid-twentieth century. But that Basque was still spoken so recently at Garde seemed almost incredible.

For it is the death of the language which has wrought the fundamental change in the life of Salazar and Roncal. With Basque have gone the costumes and the traditions, and the trans-Pyrenean freemasonry with the French Basques of Soule, whose dialect is almost identical to 'that sonorous ancient tongue', as Rodney Gallop called *roncalés*. Nina Epton visited Isaba in 1955, and describes the same old ladies in traditional widows' weeds whom I was fortunate enough to see still alive four years later.

'They were the spiritual keepers of the valley lore, of the old Basque words peculiar to it and of songs that only they can remember.'

The reader has perhaps already guessed that I had become fascinated by the last flickering of Basque in this, its farthest outpost. I set out to discover for myself how much still survived, in 1964, of the dying tongue.

8. The Dying Tongue

The withering of Basque in the eastern valleys of Navarre was perhaps inevitable once there was no longer a continuous belt of Basque-speaking territory along the Spanish side of the Pyrenees. So I decided to begin my little investigation by confirming that such a break had in fact occurred.

I knew that it was spoken in Soule, in Valcarlos, and in Les Aldudes, all on the north side of the range. I knew, too, that it still survived between the Arga and Ulzama, as my friend Don José Maria had been appointed as parish priest of Arano specific-ally because his home was in Egozcue, and he could therefore speak Basque to his parishioners. The likeliest place to test for its survival seemed to be Burguete.

I was a little taken aback, therefore, when the first person in Burguete to whom I spoke, an elderly man who came out of his home to operate the single petrol pump, alongside which I had drawn up, told me that he could not only speak Basque, but that he had been able to speak it before he knew a word of Castilian. He added, however:

'But there's no one else in Burguete who speaks a word of it. You see, although I've been living here for forty-three years, I wasn't born here. I was born and brought up at Azcoitia, in Guipuzcoa.'

Seven miles farther east, at Arive, I asked a boy where I could get a drink.

'At the restaurant across the river.'

But I had already seen half a dozen cars parked there, some with the number plates of other provinces. It would be no place to hear any Basque.

'No, not there. Somewhere smaller. Where do the men who live here go for a drink?'

He took a look at me, as if to assure himself that my style of dress was sufficiently informal, and then led the way down the road, stopping at a plain house marked *Carnicero* (Butcher).

'Here.'

I pushed my way through the chain curtains into a lit but empty room. It was scrupulously clean, with only a white tiled counter and the gleaming wood of a 'frigorific wardrobe' to indicate its daytime use. Shops in the Spanish Pyrenees do have a tendency to double as bars, but they generally perform their two functions at one and the same time, and I had never known of a butcher's which served drinks. But one must never be surprised, and I leaned against the counter hopefully waiting for company. None came, and presently I became aware of the low sound of talking behind a door at my back. I knocked and entered.

Eight men aged from about thirty to fifty-five were seated on benches round a deal table covered with a blue check oilcloth. Some, but not all, had a drink in front of them. They were there, obviously, to talk as much as to drink, but as soon as I appeared every mouth was silent. They were not unwelcoming, but simply struck dumb. Asking the old woman in the corner for a glass of red wine, I sat down at the table, and looked in turn at each of the faces around me. Most were long faces, and only one was fat. Three wore bérets. Five at least had long hooked noses. All shared certain characteristics of physiognomy possessed by only one race on earth.

'It's easy to see,' I remarked, 'that you are all Basques.'

'But of course we are all Basques.'

'. . . all Basques.'

'. . . all Basques.'

They chimed assent, like a school assembly singing the chorus of a hymn in canon. The ice was broken. In one who recognized their origin, they saw a friend.

'Do any of you speak Basque, then?'

'Just a few words. But I can't understand it if anyone starts talking it to me.'

'Our fathers and mothers used to speak it amongst themselves. But they never tried to teach it to us.'

'If you want to hear Basque, you should go to Aria. It's only twenty minutes' walk away, but it's right off any main road, and hasn't had the influences from outside.'

'Yes, in Aria the children still play together in Basque. Why, it must be fifty years since the children here did that.' The speaker, a man of about forty, turned to the oldest of the party, who looked some fifteen years his senior. 'Did you play in Basque when you were small?'

'No, we always played in Castilian. It was before me that that finished.'

The younger man turned back to me, and pronounced, a little nostalgically:

'Then there have passed more than fifty years since the children of Arive played in Basque.'

I was later to hear, from a priest who had once had charge of Orbara and Orbaiceta, that these more isolated villages, as might be expected, preserve more memories of Basque than Arive. I wish that I had gone to Aria, to see for myself if its children still learn the language from their mother's knee, and one day I shall. But I was anxious to reach Salazar, where two middle-aged man in 1959 had assured me that quite a lot of Basque was still spoken. So I pulled up in the centre of Ochagavía, and approached a group standing outside the most frequented bar.

'Is Basque still spoken at all here?' I enquired.

'Oh, no. It's years and years since that died out.'

'Aren't there any old people who still know a few words?'

'The odd word, perhaps. I know that it used to be spoken here, long ago. But it's lost now, that is.'

They were a pretty representative group, several of them at least fifty. Perhaps those men I had spoken to five years earlier had been from outside the valley, and had not known what they were talking about. Pablo, the one-eyed shepherd who looked after the valley's cattle up in the forest of Irati, knew a fair amount of Basque. But he must have picked it up, I surmised, from his opposite numbers, the French shepherds of the wild country between Tardets and St. Jean-Pied-de-Port, where it was still spoken by young and old. The judgement of these eminently sensible men of Ochagavía seemed final. The Basque of Salazar was dead. Reluctantly, but with resignation, I turned back to my motor-caravan.

I had re-crossed the road, and already opened the door of the driving cab, when I heard footsteps coming after me.

'There is one old man in the village who knows a bit of Basque, and he's just gone into the café. If you like, I'll introduce you to him.'

The Dying Tongue

The café was L-shaped, and most of its clients were sitting or standing in the longer arm of the L. In the shorter arm stood only one table, and round this table sat six old men playing *mus* (the most popular indoor game amongst the Basques, played with the Spanish pack of forty cards). Not one of their shrewd, well-worn old faces had seen a day less than seventy years.

'This señor has been asking if anyone here speaks Basque, so I've brought him to you.'

The old man thus addressed looked up at me. 'Yes, I speak Basque. Why do you ask? Do you speak Basque, too?'

'Only a few words.' I recited the catalogue of my tiny vocabulary. All six of the old men looked up at me with interest.

'You learnt those words in Guipuzcoa,' said a second old man. 'I can tell from your accent.'

'So you can speak Basque, too?' I asked him.

It was a third old man who replied: 'He could speak Basque before he could speak Castilian, like all of us round this table. But we never taught our children, although we went on talking it amongst ourselves. And then, as everyone around us was talking Catilian, we dropped it altogether. When would that be?'

'It must be fifteen years since we stopped talking it amongst ourselves. Yes: it must be fifteen years.'

'But could you still talk it if you wanted to?' I was getting excited.

'I suppose that we could still talk it. But we never do.'

He spoke a few words of Basque, and they all laughed.

'Please go on, and say some more,' I asked him.

He shrugged his shoulders, and leaned across the table. Slowly, almost visibly searching for each word, he constructed a few sentences to the grey stubble and black béret in front of him, whose reply was just as halting. Then the conversation became general. But it was never really fluent; and every now and again one of those taking part would ask for a word which he had not understood properly to be repeated. They were like mechanics trying to start up a rusty machine which had lain too long forgotten and unused.

The sight of those six old men struggling to recapture the language of their earliest memories, and of the long history of their ancient race, was the most touching I have ever seen.

The Basque Pyrenees

For the first time I learnt that a man can forget his mother-tongue.

As I cruised down from the Alto de Lazar a sudden bump made me aware that my spare wheel had again been dislodged. It was neither the first nor the last time that the vibrations caused by Pyrenean roads had brought this about. But it happened now at an unfortunate moment. For although the pass had been clear and bright, down in the valley was that drenching drizzle to which the Basques of the coast give the almost onomatopoeous name of *siri-miri*. As I bent down to put things right, the last thing that I wished for was polite conversation.

'You are English?'

In the drizzle, I had not noticed a short round figure, large black umbrella in hand, who had stolen up behind, and was now addressing me in the best accents of Berlitz. I would have guessed him to be the *cura* of Uztárroz, taking his constitutional, had it not been for his unaccustomed command of my own language. For my purposes, he turned out to be someone more interesting still: the chaplain of the Hospital of San Fermín in Pamplona, who returned for a month every summer to Uztárroz, the village of his birth, to take charge of the church whilst the parish priest had a holiday.

'And last summer, there were two English people staying in Uztárroz,' he went on. 'They were Mr. David Butler of the University of Oxford and his wife. He is the nephew of Mr. R. A. Butler, the famous English Minister. After they had visited the San Fermín fiesta they were so tired that they asked the Office of Tourism to tell them which was the quietest and farthest village of all Navarra. So they sent them here.'

I enquired whether the quietness and isolation of Uztárroz, which had so commended it to Mr. David Butler, had also enabled any Basque to survive there.

'Well, not much. But some of the old people remember a little: more, anyway, that is remembered in any other village of Roncal. When I was a child' (he looked about sixty) 'people of thirty or forty could speak Basque, but my generation never learnt any. My mother and father knew Basque, for example. But the only time they used to speak it to each other was when they didn't want us children to understand what they were saying.'

94

The Dying Tongue

I have already said that in 1964 there only survived one of the Basque-speaking old ladies whom Nina Epton saw in Isaba in 1955. There are still two or three other old people in the village who have some knowledge of Basque, but this old lady, now aged ninety, and completely deaf, is the only inhabitant of the valley who can speak the old dialect perfectly. Indeed, until she was eighteen, she could speak no other language, and perhaps this is why she has not merely retained it, but – so I am assured – has passed it on to her daughter, a woman in her 'fifties, who lives in Madrid.

Another last ember of *roncalés* has been scattered even farther afield.

Having slept in Isaba, I had driven two villages farther down the valley to Roncal, the capital, and parked my motor caravan on the hill beside the cemetery, where Gayarre lies buried. Sitting outside in the early morning sunshine I ate bread from Isaba with honey from Espot, and drank coffee made from milk bought in Roncal, listening to my transistor tuned to Radio Andorra. Was it possible, I wondered, to have a more Pyrenean breakfast?

My reverie was disturbed, when I suddenly found myself and my vehicle engulfed in a moving sea of animals: the goats of the village of Roncal on their way to pasture. And behind them came their master, the goat herd, a fine figure in his sixties. For a long minute he stood surveying me with a broad smile, and then came the first of a whole series of questions about myself and my motor caravan, England, and the world in general. At last his curiosity seemed satisfied, and it was my turn to put questions to him

'No, I don't know a word of Basque. None of my generation learnt any. Even our parents only used it when they didn't want us to understand something. There is not a soul in Roncal today who speaks any.'

'When did the last Basque-speaking man or woman die?' I asked.

'It must be ten or twelve years ago. No!' he suddenly remembered some other venerable figure. 'Five or six years ago.' He again puckered his brows. 'I'm wrong. There is still one old woman of Roncal who knows something of Basque. She must be 97 or 98. Close on a hundred. But she's still alive, and she still remembers a little Basque. But she lives now in America.'

The Basque Pyrenees

The houses of Burgui, Roncal's southernmost village, have a Basque solidity, and there is a savoury Pyrenean quality in the cooking at the Casa de Huespedes, rendering it appetising to the northern palate. But the countryside around is browner than at Roncal: the road into the village is dustier: we have moved from pasture to cornlands. Here the pull of Castilian must always have been strongest. I hardly expected success when I stopped to ask an old man of seventy-five if he could speak any Basque.

'No, no.' He spoke as though I had asked him if he had ever been on the moon.

'Did your father speak any Basque?' He did not hear me properly, and his son, who looked a few years older than myself, replied for him.

'I don't think so. His father-in-law, my mother's father, is still alive, aged 90, and I know that he never knew any Basque. Papa', he shouted. 'The señor wants to know if your father spoke Basque.'

The old man turned to me. 'No. He didn't speak any. He understood it a little, when he heard the old ones speak it. If he were alive, he would now be 99, or 100. But although he understood it a little, he never spoke any.'

My search was over. Here, in Burgui, the dying tongue was dead.

9. Where Navarre marches with Aragon

The contrast between Roncal and Salazar, and the dry dusty country into which their rivers open out, has already been made. But this country offers the visitor several monuments of an important historic past, and one recent monument which should guarantee it a more prosperous future.

Nor is it without present fascination for even the most casual visitor. For in taking the road from Pamplona to Jaca he finds himself for the first time in a 'typically Spanish' landscape, as northern Europe understands that description. A brown plain bounded by strangely shaped mountains is traversed by a straight narrow road. This is Spain at her most monotonous yet at her most exotic, if exotic be taken in its strict meaning of 'strange, bizarre, of abroad'. Nowhere else in the Pyrenees except in the Conca de Tremp is there a region like this. But to discuss its geographic explanation we must wait until we reach Aragon, into which this region extends along the great depression called the Canal de Berdún.

The road east from Pamplona is not always flat, and the Irati river, which it follows for part of the way, has to cut a narrow passage through some grimly eroded hills which give the country a bare lunar appearance. Near this defile, the Foz de Lumbier, the foundations of a fourth-century Roman villa have been uncovered just beside the road. The country gentleman who lived there sixteen hundred years ago probably enjoyed an even better view than the tourist of today. For then, before the goat and the woodcutter had completed their work, the forests still spread down from the high Pyrenees to within sight of the Ebro valley, and these grey and brown rocks were hidden by green leaves.

A few miles farther on these hills become higher, and although covered here by an aromatic green undergrowth – what the French would call *maquis* – they end in giant red teeth against the skyline,

G

a little after the style of Montserrat in Catalonia. High on these slopes stands the earliest monument of the kingdom of Navarre, and the most splendidly situated: the Monastery of San Salvador de Leire.

From 1835 until 1950 it was left to fall into ruin, and I would never have guessed its existence when I passed this way in 1951 unless some newly-made friends in nearby Sangüesa had insisted on accompanying me up there. We had to follow a rough track, but the work of restoration – which here, as everywhere, distinguishes and dignifies Navarre – had already begun.

Now a metalled road makes the steep climb – a thousand feet in only two and a half miles – as easy as it will ever be. But the greatest moment of the restoration came in 1955, when the first of a small community of Benedictines moved into residence. It was not one century, but nine, since members of their Order had occupied Leire, for Cluniacs were introduced into a royal monastery which was already old, at about the time of the consecration of the present church in 1057. This church is a lovely example of eleventh-century Romanesque: the carvings above the main door should be especially studied.

But the capitals of the columns in the crypt below are two centuries older. They have seen monks of the simpler rule of St. Benedict saying mass before a whole line of kings of Navarre of the ninth and tenth centuries, of whom we know little except their names, and that they were buried here at Leire. They seem shadowy figures from a dim past. The modern side-chapel where their names are recorded brings an even more poignant reminder of the passage of human greatness than that other pantheon of the royal line of Navarre, at Lescar near Pau. For at Lescar the bones, though disturbed and desecrated during the French Revolution, have been identified with some degree of probability – and the fifteenth century is twice as near to us as the tenth.

Historically, however, these shadowy kings played an important role, and Leire is an epitome of Pyrenean history as we shall see it reflected at Siresa, at San Juan de la Peña, at Roda, at Bohí, and in Andorra. Only in answer to pressure from the rich plains to the south could communities of such importance have grown up clinging to the edge of the Pyrenees. There, they served at once as nuclei for resistance to Moslem advance, as refuges for Christian culture, and as bases from which to launch the reconquest when this became practicable. Their role was at once political and religious, for in face of the Moslem threat Church and State became two facets of the same authority. Leire was above all a monastery, but not only a monastery. For here, as later at the monastery of San Lorenzo del Escorial, kings lived, ruled, and were laid to rest.

It is not only in its relationship to the south that Leire illustrates the most dramatic period of Pyrenean history. For the ninth century saw not only the rise of a series of Christian states along the southern slopes of the entire mountain chain, but also a uniquely intimate association between those southern slopes and the rulers of the lands to the north.

When the Spaniard of today talks about *Francia* he is referring to the leading modern Latin state, with its capital at Paris, and its boundaries 'the Pyrenees, the Alps, the Rhine, and the Ocean'. The Visigothic nobles who retired to the Cantabrian Mountains and the Pyrenees during the years after the defeat and death of King Rodrigo at Guadalete in 711 were also familiar with *Francia*. But although it was the direct ancestor of modern France among other things, the *Francia* which they knew was a very different state. The Rhine was not its frontier, but the very axis on which it moved, and during the eighth century it came to straddle the Alps far into central Italy. Its aristocracy, though German like the Visigoths, had never severed their connection with their land of origin. Nor had they made the Visigoths' fatal mistake of accepting a heretical form of Christianity, alienating them from the inhabitants of the Roman lands which they conquered.

For the Visigoths, when they arrived in Spain, were Arian heretics, and the resulting persecutions and resentments set a pattern in Spanish society which the Arab dominion and the long reconquest only intensified. The Franks, on the other hand, though they remained pagans almost until the year 500, chose the Catholic form of Christianity. When their leader, Clovis, defeated the Visigoths near Poitiers in 507, and seized from them the wide lands of Aquitaine, from the Loire to the Pyrenees, he actually described himself as freeing them from the Arian oppressors, and was so regarded by their populations.

In 732 an even more important battle took place near Poitiers. The armies which were now advancing from the south were Moslem armies – not merely heretical, but infidel. The leader of the Frankish forces which barred their way was Charles Martel, the head of a vigorous family which had come to the fore as the descendants of Clovis had degenerated. In defeating the host of Abderrahman he saved *Francia* for Catholicism, and was at the same time playing the same part which Clovis had played more than two hundred years earlier.

During the rest of the eighth century his family became more and more closely associated with the Church, and closer, likewise, to the fulness of power. Charles Martel's son, who first took Frankish armies to Rome, became King of *Francia* in name as well as in fact. And the marriage of Church and State culminated in the coronation of his grandson, Charlemagne, as Emperor of the renewed 'Roman' empire by the Pope himself, in St. Peter's cathedral on Christmas morning of the year 800.

This great ruler, from his Rhineland base, successfully incorporated in his empire many of the lands which Rome had once ruled, and some which she had not. Spain had once been a Roman province, and the Pyrenees then had none of those subjective associations which Louis XIV was later to seek to destroy with his famous quip 'Il n'y a plus de Pyrénées'. For Charlemagne the Pyrenees, as a sancrosanct frontier, did not exist.

It is in this light that we must view the decisive Carolingian intervention in the Spanish Pyrenees. The tiny mountain kingdoms of northern Spain came into being in conscious reaction to the Moslem conquest, and it can be further argued – it has been argued, by one of the most distinguished historians of this century – that the whole Carolingian Empire was an involuntary reaction to the rise of the Arab world state. 'Without Mohammed, Charlemagne would have been inconceivable' was the way that Henri Pirenne put it. The proposition is so immense, the surmise so wild, as to have caused endless debate. But the central facts on which he based his thesis are less open to argument. The Arab conquests did polarize the early medieval world into two camps in a way in which the barbarian invasions of the Roman Empire had never done. And the Christian Empire which grew up, partly in reaction to those conquests, was essentially a land empire, for which land routes were the important routes. The Mediterranean coast of *Francia* did not even include Septimania, the land from the Pyrenees to the Rhone, until 759.

For the first and only time in history the Spanish Pyrenees

looked hopefully for support to the power to the north. And that power, imbued with a philosophy which might be described as 'Maginot line in depth', was deliberately surrounding itself with a wide series of buffer territories, called Marches, into which the Spanish Pyrenees conveniently fitted. There was a Saxon March, just as later there was to be a Danish March (hence Denmark), and an East, or Ostmark (hence Austria). And to mention the Breton March is to think at once of Count Roland who was in charge of it, and of the expedition in which he took part, one of the earliest in the series of events which led to the creation of a Spanish March.

The fate which befell Roland at Roncesvalles shows that the success enjoyed by the Carolingian intervention was uneven. Indeed, that particular expedition – the only one in which Charlemagne himself passed beyond the Pyrenees – was directed not specifically against the Moslems, but in alliance with one rival Arab family in Saragossa against another. In the process, it involved an attack upon the Christian city of Pamplona. But these seeming inconsistencies only show how infinitely more complex was the tactical position at any given moment than seems apparent to us at twelve hundred years' distance. From his palaces at Aix-la-Chapelle and Paderborn the ruler of *Francia* was able to follow in detail the internal politics of Saragossa and of Cordova, of Oviedo and of Barcelona, and to adjust his day to day decisions accordingly, never losing sight of the aims of his grand strategy.

That strategy was the creation of a deep sphere of influence along the Spanish Pyrenees, to protect the southern flanks of *Francia*. Where the Moslems were in occupation, and had to be forcibly ejected by Carolingian representatives, the sphere of influence was a direct one, and in this way there came into being the Spanish March proper, the *Marca Hispanica* between Pallars and the Mediterranean.

Where Christian states already existed, however, the sphere of influence was indirect. It was none the less noticeable for that. The capitals of the crypt of Leire are the architectural evidence that the ripples of the brief 'Carolingian Renaissance' spread to this outpost of the tiny Christian world of the ninth century. But the books of the monastic library, which once provided the literary evidence, have disappeared.

Now the Benedictines are back at Leire. Their number could be

counted on the fingers of two hands when last I visited them in
1962. But they are friendly and communicative, and will invite
the visitor on a hot day to refresh himself with a swim in the
reservoir from which they irrigate their vegetable garden. Anyone
wanting more of their good company can enjoy it by staying for a
few days at the privately run and inexpensive guest house attached
to the monastery.

The monks' invitation to a swim is worth accepting, if only
because nowhere else can it be possible to swim with a view of
another, far greater sheet of water a thousand feet below, which
is itself already a thousand feet above sea-level. This is the huge
pantano, or reservoir of Yesa, which lies beyond the scope of this
section, over in Aragon. For Leire lies very near the boundary
between the two ancient kingdoms.

Then why was it the palace-capital of the early kings of
Navarre? Because in those early centuries the frontiers between
the Christian states were still fluid: indeed, their very identity one
from another was still uncertain. Sometimes Navarre was united
with Aragon, sometimes with Castile. From Leire Sancho the
Great (1004–35) ruled a territory stretching from Leon in the
west along the Cantabrians and the Pyrenees as far as Ribagorza
in the east. Though the Christians often quarrelled amongst themselves, the really serious business of making war was with the
Moslems to the south, and Leire was excellently placed as
Christian fortress and headquarters.

But after the last native king of Navarre, Sancho the Strong,
had taken a leading part in the victory of Las Navas de Tolosa in
1212, the danger from the south no longer existed. For two and a
half centuries Castile, Aragon, and Navarre neglected to extin-
guish the one remaining Moslem kingdom of Granada, whilst
they fought each other. It was during this period that two other
places in eastern Navarre became important, for they stood at
strategically vital points on the frontier with Aragon.

Samgüesa stands near where the Irati river empties itself into the
Aragon, and near where the road coming up from the romantic-
sounding (but in fact rather depressing) Cinco Villas de Aragon
joins the east-west highway from Pamplona to Jaca. The market
towns of Navarre are amongst the pleasantest small towns of
Spain. Expatriate engineers prospecting for the big oil companies have settled happily into the social life of Estella and Tudela,

dividing their leisure between the terrace cafés of the main squares and the more private world of the local casinos (the social clubs).

Sangüesa, although much smaller, is equally friendly, with its eleventh and twelfth century church of Santa Maria la Real, two other Romanesque churches, and two Gothic cloisters. A number of mansions with carved façades give the main street the air of a country capital. These are not 'town houses'. They were the headquarters of the country estates of families who lived mainly in Pamplona or Madrid – or even, in one case, in Peru. One of these houses, now the town hall, belonged to the Prince of Viana – the title, like that of the Dauphin in France, or the Prince of Asturias in Spain, given to the eldest son of the King of Navarre.

This title was a late development, being granted for the first time by Charles III in 1423. Only eighty years later, in 1503, the last rightful sovereign of Navarre to be born on Navarrese soil first saw the light of day here in Sangüesa. And little Henri d'Albret was only nine years old when his parents were driven from their kingdom by Ferdinand of Aragon. Our feelings as we think of him in quiet, rural Sangüesa are not, however, of regret for his lost kingdom, but of wonder that so great a line should have had such a provincial background. For that little boy was the grandfather of Henry IV of France. And he was the grandfather of *le roi soleil*.

The first time that I stopped at Sangüesa, I was puzzled to find the walls of the excellent *fonda* covered with recently executed murals, depicting hooked-nosed thin-faced men in bérets. Who were they? '*Vascos.* Basques.' For years I wondered why they should be depicted there; for it was only long after that I realized how near Sangüesa lay to the Basque valleys of Salazar and Roncal, for which, indeed, it was the nearest market town on the Spanish side of the Pyrenees.

Sangüesa is the main centre of these eastern marches of Navarre, but their buckler against the Aragonese lay even nearer the frontier, at Javier. This was not a town, and hardly even a village, but simply the fortress-home of the family entrusted with the defence of the eastern approach to Pamplona. Many perfectly sober historians have explained the Spanish conquest and settlement of the New World as the expenditure overseas of the continuing pressures built up by the long *Reconquista* inside the peninsula. And it may not be fanciful to suggest that the immense energy of St. Francis Xavier may have owed a little to the absorption of Navarre into the rest of Spain in 1512, when the defensive role of Javier lost its meaning, and the pressure of centuries was released.

Even today, however, there is no road from Javier into Aragon. It can only be reached from Navarre, either from Sangüesa, or from the Pamplona to Jaca road, just below the great dam of Yesa. Although the original fourteenth-century castle has not actually been destroyed, it has endured, like the home of St. Ignatius at Loyola, a restoration which would render it unrecognizable to the man whose birth there made it famous. Francis, if he returned, might feel himself more at home in the parish church, for although it was built two hundred years after his time, it still shelters the eight-sided font where he was baptised.

Javier, after Loyola, and perhaps Manresa, is the most beloved sanctuary of the Society of Jesus. One of their members at Javier is generally able to show visitors round in whatever language they happen to speak, and in doing so honours the memory of St. Francis himself, perhaps the greatest cosmopolitan of all time.

Born in the last decade of Navarre's independence, he grew up in a family which divided its allegiance between the legitimate French kings of Navarre at Pau, and the new Hapsburg rulers of 'all the Spains'. When the French tried to reconquer the forfeited kingdom in 1521, a brother of Francis fought beside them at the battle of Pamplona. So when the nineteen-year-old Francis set off for Paris in 1525 he was no more going to a foreign country than if he had left for Castile or Aragon.

Four years later a Castilian visitor of thirty-eight came to stay for some months at the College of Sainte-Barbe in Paris where Francis was studying. As a Castilian, this visitor had taken part in and been wounded at the battle of Pamplona, but on the opposite side to that of Francis's brother. But the two men had a bond in common which transcended any such 'local differences'. They were both Basques.

They soon found that they had even more in common. On 15th August, 1534, seven men made the Vow of Montmartre, which marks the effective foundation of the Society of Jesus. One was this Castilian visitor, Ignatius of Loyola. Another was Francis of Javier.

The Roman church owes its greatness to its more than imperial government, and the new Society had no more official status than the groups of heretics who were gathering beyond the Rhine and the Channel until it had received written Papal recognition. Francis was in Rome with Ignatius during the negotiations which led up to this, but before it had actually been granted he had left for Lisbon, in answer to a personal appeal by the King of Portugal. On 7th April, 1541, he sailed with the Portuguese fleet of the Indies to evangelize the East.

The scene, as the great ships lay at anchor in the Tagus, whilst Francis prayed for the last time within sight and sound of Europe, is a favourite theme with artists depicting Jesuit history. The invitation to sail east from the highest quarter is indeed typical enough of the Society's later development. But the intensely personal nature of Francis's missionary journeys – one is tempted to call them his adventures – in India and the Far East, is far from characteristic of the impersonal discipline with which the later Jesuits carried out their work in Poland or Austria. This may be partly because in leaving Europe when the Society had barely gained recognition, he had hardly had time fully to be moulded to the Jesuit pattern as we now know it.

It may also be partly due to the fact that Francis was born at Javier. The child is father of the man. The saint who on 2nd December, 1552, died alone within sight of the strange land of China had wandered alone as a boy amidst the arid badlands of Las Bardenas, under the strange cliffs of the Sierra de Leire.

Interlude at Arano, a village of the Basque Pyrenees

From the coast of Guipuzcoa three roads run inland towards Pamplona. There is the road already described, which follows the Bidassoa before striking away to the right, to assault the pass of Velate. Then there is the main road from San Sebastian, through Tolosa and Lecumberri.

Narrow, little known, and not easy to locate, there is also the so-called interior route to Navarre. To find this it is first necessary to find Hernani, a small town with numerous ancient private houses, and with a church which shelters the tomb of the Spaniard who captured Francis I of France at Pavia in 1525. Today many of its inhabitants commute daily to San Sebastian; and, like so many 'commuter suburbs' of north London and Surrey, Hernani is somewhere one often hears about but never passes through. And, as every way there is equally hard to find, I shall recommend the one which at least has the advantage of interest. This is the road passing by Ayete, the summer residence presented to the Chief of State by the city of San Sebastian. The wily Basques thus ensured that General Franco would continue to lead the *gente de categoría* of Madrid each summer to the resort made fashionable by King Alfonso XIII and by his mother the Queen-Regent Maria Cristina.

The interior route to Navarre starts only a couple of hundred yards from the centre of Hernani, immediately on the other side of a bridge, and opposite a small factory. And it follows the river which flows under that bridge, and which provides the power for that factory: the Urumea. This is the same river which, polluted in its lower reaches by the waste of paper factories, flows out to sea at San Sebastian.

At first the valley, though rapidly narrowing, is flat. Then, after passing a small, quiet reservoir feeding a hydro-electric station, the road begins to climb. Presently the traveller passes a stone building marked *Arbitrios-Guipuzcoa*, and shortly afterwards another marked *Arbitrios-Navarra*. These are the miniature customs houses which collect dues on commercial freight passing from one province to another. The amounts of these dues are small: a halfpenny on a bottle of cider entering Navarre, or three farthings on a bottle of wine entering Guipuzcoa. But they are sufficient to justify the elaboration of ingenious schemes for their circumvention.

Beside the second of these customs houses – the one belonging to Navarre – there stand a couple of cottages, and one of those shops-cum-bars which fulfil all the functions – and more – of our own 'village general'. This cluster of houses, which takes the name of the bar, Venta Berri, is not only just inside the province of Navarre, but also just inside the first parish, or *municipio* of Navarre: Arano. The road climbs on, steadily gaining height above the Urumea. Two miles on, at the point where it begins to drop towards another cluster of houses beside the river called Arramendi, stands a low white cottage labelled *Camineros*, and here a much steeper road runs off to the right.

In Navarre, as in the other provinces of Spain, there is a policy of replacing the *camineros*, or road menders, as they die or retire, by *brigadas* or teams of workers based on the towns, who travel out by lorry. With the machinery which accompanies them, these can repair in one day a stretch of road which the individual *caminero* would have needed a month to cover. In Navarre at least, where the workers of the *brigadas* all wear the red Carlist beret, they add a touch of colour to the landscape. Socially, however, they represent the substitution of the footloose constructors of the motorways for the protagonist of Michael Fairless's great work.

For although his philosophy may be less exquisitely expressed than that of *The Roadmender*, the *caminero* of Spain is a philosopher just the same. And no one more so than the *caminero* of Navarre, which is so proud of being the only province to have preserved its *fueros* or self-government, and of the good roads which those *fueros* have made possible.

The swarthy dark-eyed figure in blue shirt and trousers who may wave from the door of the white cottage is no exception.

Despite his meridional appearance he is himself *navarro*, from no farther south than Mañeru near Estella. His children have grown up to speak Basque, and although he speaks none himself this has in no way cut him off from the Basque-speaking community amongst whom he has made his life. He is an outsider who has completely integrated into the village of which he is such an essential member. This is obvious whether you enjoy a drink with him at one of the bars after Mass on a feast day, or whether you stand beside him where he is working at a turn on the long road up to the village, and discuss the trout in the Urumea far below, or the wild boars in the woods of the farther hills.

This road, which we must now follow from where it leaves the interior route to Navarre at his white cottage, forms about half the five miles of roadway which are his responsibility – the other half being Arano's section of the interior route itself. His task is easier since it was tarred seven or eight years ago, but the traveller to Arano will find it just as steep as in the old days, even if better surfaced.

At Hernani we were already 150 feet above the level of the sea which we left at San Sebastian, and we have climbed twice as far again to reach the roadmender's white cottage. But we now climb a further thousand feet, all in a distance of a little over two miles. This may sound an impossible gradient, but a series of well-engineered zigzags up the mountainside make it perfectly feasible in a low gear, and lines of trees provide ample shade. The pedestrians for whom they are designed, however, often prefer to take short cuts to avoid the long detour of the zigzags. In doing so they make use of various footpaths, well-worn and well-known tracks like countless others which we shall tread as we explore the parish.

The road at last takes a right-angled turn, a change from the twists of a hundred and seventy-nine degrees to which we have become accustomed. Presently a building comes into view, and it is only when we reach and turn left in front of it that we realize we have started to climb the village street of Arano.

Climb is still the operative word, as we drive up a single street of houses, in a few cases whitewashed, but mostly of unadorned stone. The church appears on our left, standing above a primitive public fountain, and then the gradient suddenly becomes steeper than ever before, and the surface degenerates to hard cobbles. We change back to bottom gear and grit our teeth, but almost at once we find ourselves on the level for the first time since leaving Hernani. Very much on the level, for the broad square of concrete on which we stand is limited on two sides by high concrete walls – it is the village *frontón*, or pelota court. Here, between the *frontón* and the church – the true heart of any Basque village – the road ends, or 'dies' as Spanish more vividly expresses it. We have arrived.

The walls of the *frontón* form two sides of this miniature *plaza*. The church, low, unassuming, yet complete with clock tower and deep Basque porch, forms a third. Half of the fourth side is formed by a low stone wall, no higher than one's knee. At first sight, it seems little enough protection against the chasm which we imagine yawns beyond. It is only when we have looked over, to assure ourselves that the drop on the other side is of a mere five or six feet, that we can stand back and enjoy the view given by the sharply falling ground, which created the illusion of a sudden fall.

Beneath us opens a deep green valley, formed by a tributary of the Urumea. We cannot follow it as far as its junction with the parent stream, nor can we see the road which we have ourselves followed. But we can make out the double line of hills between which the Urumea flows, and following them to the horizon we seem to descry a diminutive but familiar silhouette against the skyline. Can it be the tower of Mount Igueldo, the folly which dominates the almost landlocked bay of San Sebastian? By night we would have no doubts: the distant glow between the dark hills can only be the collective illumination of an entire city. And that city can only be San Sebastian, seventeen miles away by road.

It was this proximity to San Sebastian which led to my own discovery of Arano, in the days before I had acquired a motor caravan. Desperately tired of the crowded coast one August, and unwilling to drive forty or fifty miles into the interior in search of peace and quiet, I studied my map in search of somewhere nearer, yet inaccessible, where I could relax during my five days of freedom. Just inside Navarre, and at the dead end of a twisting road, Arano seemed a possible answer.

It was an answer indeed! Driving up the zigzags for the first time, I wondered if the village would ever come into sight. At last I stood in the *frontón*, beside the low wall, and looked down the valley towards Mount Igueldo. Not even amongst the monks of the Ile St. Honorat opposite Cannes have I felt a sharper contrast between the ephemeral bustle of one world and the timeless peace, only a few miles away, of another. Down there, seventeen miles away, the high society of Madrid would be filtering on to the Ondarreta beach. The crowds would already be surging to and fro along the promenade of the Concha. They were happy, kindhearted crowds. Many of my friends would be amongst them. But I wanted peace, and as I gazed around me I knew that I had found it.

Across the deep green valley rose hills as high or higher than the one to whose side Arano precariously clings. Their upper slopes were as bare and green as any down, but below these pastures stood woods, increasingly dense as they approached the river. Clearings had been made in these woods, however; and, each at the centre of a neat but asymmetrical pattern of tiny fields, stood four Basque farmsteads, which at that distance seemed as though they had been specially made for Basque dolls to live in.

These four farms: Arola, Ipiñabar, Descarga, and Enazti form part of Arano, and their distance from the *casco urbano* (as the nucleus of the smallest *pueblo* is grandiloquently called) is even greater on foot than it appears looking straight across at them from the *frontón*. When children from these farms first come to school, it is sometimes the first time that they can remember coming to the village.

As I got used to the view, I realized that one of these farms, even at that distance, appeared uncared for. Saplings had sprung up in its fields, and the woods were reclaiming their own. On enquiry I learnt that this was deliberate.

'In 1956 the owner of Descarga moved to Hernani, and sold his farm to the *ayuntamiento*. They have planted it with pines, which bring such a good return. The house? It is just being allowed to fall to pieces. The damp and the frost will soon break it up. There is nothing else to be done. No man today could persuade a woman to go and share such an isolated life. The owner of one of the other three farms over there also wishes to leave, to come to live here in the *casco urbano*.'

Later I was to poke my way through the undergrowth around Descarga, past the doors askew on their hinges, amongst the broken remains of furniture and the damp ashes of the last fire in a hearth around which generations had been reared. Like so many of the more isolated houses in the Spanish Pyrenees, it had been a living home only a few years before, but was now doomed more certainly than ever the ruins of Angkor Wat.

Gazing now towards the head of the valley, I saw that there were no more houses, but only woods and pastures, leading on to a high lonely country, where green hills made a clean line against a blue sky. And then I turned to my right, to the other half of the fourth side of the *plaza*, formed by a large house over the doorway of which ran the legend *Bar Frontón*.

It proved in fact to be not only a bar but a *fonda* and a farm as well. Each of these functions gained from the others. Visitors to the bar enjoyed the society of the occasional resident in the *fonda*, who in turn enjoyed hearing the village gossip. The farm found in the *fonda* a market for its produce. And what the *fonda* gained from the farm can only be appreciated by one who has enjoyed the meals which that produce went to make.

Looking back across a seeming infinity of gargantuan repasts one remembers best the thick vegetable soups, the hams, the earthenware dishes full of fried mushrooms, each the size of a saucer, and the roast chickens. There was never any attempt to 'hang' these chickens: only a few hours would separate their execution from their appearance on the table, a delicate but appetising study in sepia, set in a frame of succulent red peppers. But they never tasted any the worse for this; and when, to my announcement that I had invited friends from San Sebastian up to lunch the next day, I was told '*Matarémos pollos,* we *shall* kill chickens', I could relax in confidence that both Gambrinus and Bacchus would smile upon my party.

Bacchus inevitably, for this was Navarre, the country of strong wine. Arano itself, in the extreme north of the province, produces only an excellent cider. But whenever a few *vecinos* (neighbours) found their supplies getting low, the village lorry would be chartered for a trip to the Ribera, the far south where Navarre's frontier rests on the Ebro. In the west, the Ribera runs to within four miles of Logroño, the capital of La Rioja; and there is, indeed, a Rioja of Navarre, a good, full-bodied wine, comparable to the heavier French table wines.

It was not towards La Rioja, however, that the Arano village carrier would direct his lorry, but farther east, where at Tudela Navarre throws out a salient across the Ebro. There grow wines not of ten or eleven degrees – the strength of the average French table wine, nor of twelve or thirteen degrees – the average of Spanish table wines; but instead wines of fourteen degrees, wines of sixteen degrees, wines even, it is said, of eighteen degrees. At this point they are very little weaker than the fortified wines like sherry, port, or madeira. Many would say that they are too strong, and that if drunk as table wines at all, they should be well diluted with water. But at the *Bar Frontón*, although a bottle of wine from the Ribera was put in front of me at every meal, a jug of water was not. In Navarre I did as the *navarros*. I enjoyed my siestas at Arano, lost to the world on the bracken under the beech trees. And I slept well at nights.

This was the more unavoidable since the village carrier, on his way back from the Ribera, would pull into a wine warehouse in Pamplona to take on a cask or two of brandy. In a magic line of that magic book *The Enchanted Mountains* Robin Fedden refers to the brandy to which he was invited to help himself in the shadow of the Encantados. 'It smelt of violets, a phenomenon unfamiliar to connoisseurs of *fine* but not unusual in upper Aragon.' This phenomenon is no more unusual in Navarre, and no less accept-able. '*Una copita?*' How could I say no, with the glass already on the tray beside my coffee, and the bottle, 'full of the warm south', already leaning appealingly in my direction.

The hand which held it was generally that of Milagros, the daughter of the house, a well-made tranquil woman of about thirty, who generally seemed to be expecting a baby. Her tran-quillity did not mean that she was lazy. On the rare occasions when she was not pregnant, and her husband, Santos, was not actually working at the factory in Hernani to which he went to and fro on his motor-cycle, they made a fine picture, both with an implement in their hand and a sun hat on their head as they set off to some corner of the family fields.

Work, and good work at that, was indeed the Egurrechea family's main characteristic. Milagros's father had worked all over the Basque provinces in the building and quarry trades before 're-tiring' to his farm-cum-*fonda*. And her mother was the cook responsible for the wonderful meals. The English phrase 'she is a good cook' fails to convey the nature of her gift as fully as the more active Spanish '*sabe guisar*' (literally 'she knows how to dress victuals').

8. Hecho: the Selva de Oza

9. Hecho: farther up the valley, where the woods end

10. Hecho: *chesos* in traditional costume in front of house with
characteristic covered chimney

Interlude at Arano, a village of the Basque Pyrenees

Besides Milagros they had two sons. The elder had married and left home, but the younger was still a bachelor and worked, like his brother-in-law Santos, in Hernani. His excellence extended to sport, in which he had brought glory not only to his family, but to Arano as a whole. This sport, of course, could only be pelota, which he had played since a child in the *fronton* just outside his front door.

Players of pelota are often known by another name than their own. It may be compared not so much to a nickname as to the new name adopted by a layman who enters a religious order, and perhaps indicates the single-minded thoroughness with which pelota is regarded. And on the first floor of the *fonda*, in the dark dining-room which is never used – family and guests alike eating at trestle tables in the wide bar below – there stands like a Roman *lar* a silver cup bearing the name of Bengoechea. It proclaims that in the year 1958 Bengoechea won the world championship of *pelota a mano* (the original form of the game, often known as *trinquete*). In doing so, he had to defeat not only his Spanish Basque rivals and his French Basque rivals, but also opponents from all over the world, notably from Latin America, and from certain states of the U.S. where the game has become popular since it has been commercialized by bookmakers.

It was a great moment for Arano when he returned from his final match in triumph, and he was given a hero's welcome. Although he was playing less when I used to stay there, he would still occasionally make up a friendly team, to represent Spain against the French at Hasparren, for example. And of an evening he would sometimes stroll out of his home to watch and encourage the youngsters of Arano as they played amongst themselves, until he was inevitably drawn into the game, and the youths watched intently, anxious to learn every possible gambit from the maestro.

Such easy camaraderie, such unsophisticated freedom of social intercourse are characteristic of all the smaller villages of the Spanish Pyrenees. By smaller villages I mean those of less than about three hundred inhabitants; and although the total population of Arano in 1964 was 376, barely 200 of these lived within the actual *casco urbano*. These 200 were like one big family. Their children ran in and out of each other's houses. Besides the *Bar Frontón* there was another *fonda*-cum-bar in part of the ground floor of the municipal offices, and also two shops-cum-bars farther down the street. After Mass on a feast day one could wander from one to another of these four places of refreshment, buying drinks and having drinks bought for one, not as if pub-crawling, but rather with the easy familiarity of a guest moving from room to room at a cocktail party in a house which he already knows well.

Happiest of all, perhaps, were the informal gatherings in the *plaza* at sunset. Sitting on the low wall, gazing across the valley, and trying to communicate with a little girl of four who, like all the children of the village under school age, spoke only Basque, I would be joined by Milagros with her youngest child and her mother. And then a bluff figure in clean white shirt and dark trousers would come round the corner, accompanied by his young wife, like Milagros well on the way to a happy event.

Together, the *secretario* of the *ayuntamiento* and the girl he has married from his native village of Lodosa in the Ribera would serve as excellent models for a portrait entitled 'The Navarrese man and wife'. It is not only their appearance – they are both pleasant to look at in a rugged way without actually being handsome – but also their attitude which is characteristic. They are completely happy in total acceptance of the way of life into which they were born. Lodosa, their home village, is a metropolis by comparison with Arano – it numbers some five thousand souls.

'I must say that I find it rather boring here,' said the *secretario*'s young sister-in-law, a girl of twenty who was spending a few days with them.

'Then doesn't your sister find it even more boring, for she is here all the time?' I enquired.

Her response was immediate and revealing. 'Oh, no! She is *colocada* (placed, settled) for life. She has her husband, her home. Soon she will have her children. She is happy, for here she has all that a woman seeks. For her, therefore, it is quite different.'

For the husband, too, appointment to such a remote village might by many be regarded as an exile. For he is both an educated man himself, and comes from a family which has other members in the professions. His own brother, before his early death, was already in the priesthood, having been a contemporary at the seminary with Don José Maria – of whom more later. To become a *secretario* a man has to pass a stiff examination, and even when qualified he will not automatically secure an appointment. He can best be described as the Town or Parish Clerk, appointed by the provincial government to advise the *alcalde* and councillors, and to carry out all the work of administration. In other parts of Spain I have found *secretarios* who combined their post with other work: one was an estate agent, another a butcher. But then in the rest of Spain there are two grades of *secretario*: first-class *secretarios*, who have passed two examinations, for the larger localities, and the second-class *secretarios*, who have passed only one for the villages. Navarre, here as elsewhere, is unique: with only one grade of *secretarios*, who are all full-time.

Being unique has its price, for the Navarre-qualified *secretario* can practice nowhere else. But he would not wish to. One reads how in Andalusia or Galicia young men of promise rot away with boredom and brandy. But for the *navarro* the world centres not on Madrid, but on Pamplona. It is true that the *secretario* of Arano welcomed a visitor like myself from the outside world. He enjoyed a good talk. And once he insisted on lending me a book. It was a history of Sancho el Fuerte, Navarre's greatest king.

As we all sat talking, watching the sunset, and exchanging greetings with the occasional farmer returning down the path from field or pasture, we would look up to see that we had been joined by a young man in black, with heavy glasses and a broad smile.

'Good evening, *padre*, how nice to see you. Do sit down for a few minutes' talk.'

Don José Maria never would sit down, however. But he would stand for a little while, insensibly giving a more general, and – without priggishness – a more elevated tone to our conversation. During the day he had often visited a parishioner in one of the more distant *caserios* or farmsteads, and would tell us how the widow in Suro was getting on, or how the maize crop was ripening on the way to Goizueta.

He was a shepherd who well understood his flock. For he was in every way their parson, their *persona* or representative as the word means. He had grown up in just such another Pyrenean village as Arano, forty miles to the south-east. Like them, he had spoken Basque as a child before he spoke Castilian, so that he was able to read the vernacular offices in Basque, and to preach in a language which both the old people and the young children could follow without difficulty. And like them he had grown up with an intimate understanding of country things, of the crops and cattle upon which the economy of a Pyrenean *pueblo* depends. Nor was this knowledge merely theoretical. It was never easy to make him sit down, but he once confessed himself more than glad to join me for a pot of English tea.

'I really am quite tired this afternoon,' he said. 'I've been helping the farmer with whom I lodge to gather his harvest. He was short of hands, and the least I could do was to lend him mine.'

And just as the people of Navarre, who furnished the fierce *requetés* to Don Carlos and to Franco, identify their cause with that of their church, so their parsons are priests first, but they are *navarros* too. 'I was born a *navarro*,' he said to me one day, the skirts of his soutane swirling almost rakishly in the breeze, 'And I must admit that, despite my cloth, when I hear the music of *sanfermines* my heart rises within me, in pride and in exultation. No *navarro* can ever hear that sound and feel otherwise.'

Like the parson of the Middle Ages, he was both nearer to his people than the average Church of England clergyman of today, yet intellectually had travelled to continents of which they had never dreamed. We would talk together of Newman and Manning, of whom he knew as much as I, who had lived and studied where they had worked and undergone conversion. Twelve years in a seminary had left a rich deposit in his mind.

They had left their discipline too. Between half-past seven and eight every morning he could be seen pacing up and down the *frontón*, reading his breviary before saying Mass. And he would never stop for more than a few minutes' chat on those arcadian summer evenings. Excusing himself with a last smile, he would turn away towards the church. Presently the bell would begin to toll for vespers.

The church to which he was thus summoning us is dedicated to Saint Martin, whose day falls on 11th November. One would therefore expect this to be the day of Arano's fiesta. Even in the mild Basque Pyrenees, however, winters can be cold at fifteen hundred feet, and November days are everywhere too short for the prolonged celebrations which go to make a fiesta. So the date for the village fiesta has been fixed as 25th July, St. James's day, to which the people of Arano have as much right as any other Spaniards. For is not Santiago the patron saint of all Spain?

Had they wished, however, they could even more appropriately have chosen the day of San Sebastian or the day of San Roque. For to these patrons are dedicated the two *ermitas* or chapels outside the *casco urbano*. At least half the *pueblos* of Spain have a chapel, at greater or less distance from the parish church, to which a *romería* or pilgrimage will be made once a year; and which will sometimes be visited, too, by solitary worshippers, young girls or old men, who for private reasons have acquired a devotion to the saint, and unconsciously, perhaps, to the *genius loci*.

Why Arano should have two such chapels we shall never be sure. There may once have been records which would have given the explanation of this and of much else. But although individual documents earlier than the nineteenth century have survived, and although there are references to Arano from as early as about 1140, there is no continuity in parish records until 1841. Why a clean break at 1841? The Carlists were active all over this country, and the first Carlist war ended in 1840.

'Did the Carlists burn the records?' I asked the Secretario outright. He smiled shrewdly from behind his desk, every inch a *navarro*.

'We can be certain that in those wars, as in other wars, some documents were burned by somebody. But we do not know by whom.'

It was a cautious answer which not even the most meticulous historian could have faulted. But it was also the answer which he wanted to give.

Legend often steps in, however, where the written word fails. The smaller of the two chapels, San Sebastian, is a plain square building atop a small steep hill overlooking the village. Although lower than the surrounding mountains, it is the only place which commands a view both of the main Urumea valley, and of the tributary valley below the *frontón*.

Here, according to the legend, came a pair of lovers, fleeing from their families in San Sebastian who had forbidden them to marry. It all happened 'about a thousand years ago', which is no doubt another way of saying 'once upon a time'. Finding themselves safe at last, the couple decided to build a house and to call it San Sebastian after the town they had left.

They must have had faith in their own fertility, and in the long-term workings of the population explosion, for they also

117

decided, then and there, to determine the territorial limits of the village which would grow around them. So the young man took his bow, and pulling three arrows from his quiver sent each flying off in a different direction. He was evidently as powerful as an archer as he was passionate as a lover, for the three arrows came to rest at the three extreme points which mark the rough triangle formed by the *municipio* of Arano on the map. Nor was his feat forgotten, for the three arrows are still to be found in Arano's crest, which is reproduced in the woodcut forming the letterhead of this chapter.

It was perhaps because of this legend that Milagros used to say that the village had once stood on the hill around the chapel of San Sebastian, and had only later moved down to its present position. I could find no other reason for this unlikely theory. But some time may well have passed before the *casco urbano* developed where it did. For, quite apart from the isolated farm-steads, and the two clusters of houses down on the interior route to Navarre, Arano has two *barrios*, or suburbs. Many, indeed, would say that it has three, referring to the *casco urbano* itself as the *barrio de arriba*, the upper suburb.

The corresponding *barrio de abajo*, or lower suburb, lies a couple of hundred feet below, but at least half a mile away by the series of narrow tracks which connect the two. The actual number of its households is about half that of the *casco urbano*, but the strength of its inner life is far less than half. Less attempt is made to keep the houses in good repair, and no one ever comes there except on brief business. There is no shop and no bar. This is the provinces as opposed to the metropolis. One house seems to be no more than an uninhabited ruin. But this is in some ways the most interesting house in the *barrio*. For it is the official 'home' of a titled aristocrat, who by thus establishing his domicile in Navarre benefits from some of the fiscal advantages deriving from Navarre's *fueros*.

I had made several stays at Arano before I visited the third *barrio*, Suro. Perhaps simply because it was a full mile and a half away from the *casco urbano*, it had none of the absence of vitality which had depressed me in the *barrio de abajo*. It contained only seven households, stretched at long intervals on either side of a wide grassy lane. To walk from the first house to the last one had to cover about half a mile. But it was a happy half mile. Suro was an Arcady within Arcadia. One would pass a group of *vecinos* combining to give the outer wall of one of the farmsteads a new coat of plaster. The seven households had even joined forces, independently of the *ayuntamiento* of Arano, to make the track from Suro to the main road suitable for motor traffic.

It was in Suro, surprisingly enough, that I met the only other foreigner that I ever saw at Arano. The daughter of one of the farms had trained as a secretary and married her boss. Returning to *veranear* (spend the summer) with her parents, she had brought along an *au pair* girl from Lausanne to help with the babies. I found this girl surrounded by her charges as she sat on a tree trunk beside the wide grassy lane. She was at once surprised and delighted that in the process of learning Spanish to qualify for work with Swissair she had been carried up to this remote hamlet.

'The people are so welcoming, and so kind. They have so little, but what little they have they want to share with you. They will insist on giving you an apple, or some nuts. Of course, you cannot really say that they are poor', she added with a Swiss calculation. 'They have their solid stone houses, with oak floors and oak furniture. And they have their land, which provides them not only with an income, but with everything they need to live.'

This was true. Apart from wine – the importation of which from the Ribera we have already followed – the average family needs few outside purchases beyond coffee, sugar, and cotton cloth. Cloth, not clothes, for the attractive red check dress of the girl in the shop, and the workmanlike blue trousers of the man in the field are alike cut and sewn at home. Fifteen years ago ready-made clothes were almost unknown in Spain, and although the industry of *confección*, as it is called, has recently made tremendous strides, its products are still never seen in the *pueblos*.

Such self-sufficiency depends upon owning land, as the Swiss girl had shrewdly observed. I was offered a pleasant well-built house in the *casco urbano* at a cheap price 'because no land goes with it'. Almost the only inhabitants without land, apart from the priest and the *secretario*, were the baker and the schoolmistress, who alike had 'external' means of support.

The teaching profession is no better paid in Spain than anywhere else, but the mistress at Arano when first I went there, tiny though her salary, found this much enhanced by gifts in kind. One pupil would bring a rabbit, another a dozen eggs. After several happy years she only left because her husband, who had occupied himself at Arano with a little shoe mending, secured a good job as sacristan to one of the larger churches in San Sebastian. Navarre's schools are no 'closed shop'. Each *ayuntamiento* can appoint a mistress from anywhere in Spain. And on my last visit I was pleased to find that as many as twelve women, only half of whom were from Navarre, had applied for the vacant post.

But although the possession of land is normally essential for living, only 240 out of Arano's 1,370 hectares are privately owned. These 500 odd acres produce the standard crops of Cantabrian Spain, from the Atlantic slope of the Pyrenees to Galicia: maize, potatoes, greenstuffs (both for human consumption and for cattle), and apples. They also have a rather more specialized line in cherries and in nuts.

The other 1,130 hectares are common land, but common land as it was known by the medieval peasant, rather than by the contemporary inhabitant of Clapham. For it is just as productive as the privately farmed sector, and in terms of hard cash more profitable.

In the first place it provides pasture, and thereby produces meat, milk, and wool. By tradition, each house has the right to graze a certain number of sheep and cows, and a man will often purchase a house not because he wishes to live there, but to increase his head of cattle (the house which I was offered was cheap because it had not only no land, but no grazing rights either).

In the second place the common land produces timber. The area planted with trees is on the increase: we saw how the farm of Descarga was bought by the *ayuntamiento* – thus becoming common land – and planted with pines. This is not the only variety of tree to be found; but whereas the beech requires 80 years to reach maturity, the native oak 90, and even the imported American oak 60, the *insignis* pine can be cut after only 22 years' growth, and is naturally given preference in new plantations.

The majority of this common land lies farther up the tributary valley, and can be reached by the unmade track which winds up from the *frontón* where the main road comes to a halt and 'dies'. For three-quarters of a mile it runs between cultivated fields, and then passes through a small grove of beech trees, offering a dappled but welcome shade on a hot day. Here, where one could

Interlude at Arano, a village of the Basque Pyrenees

– I did – happily spend whole afternoons sleeping, reading, or just gazing out across the valley, stands a whitewashed, rectangular building about twelve feet high. It is the chapel of San Roque. From there onwards one is amongst pastureland, and after another half-mile comes a spring, never dry and of excellent taste. Here the road divides.

To the left the track cuts a short passage through to another valley, and bears right along a series of hillsides. About two miles farther on is a much larger beech grove, and a lawn like expanse of well-cropped grass dotted with a number of stone huts of various sizes. It was after these that it was called Las Bordas, a name used everywhere in the Spanish Pyrenees to describe the isolated buildings where animals can shelter, and where shepherds – and sometimes, notably in Andorra, whole families – camp out for the summer. In and around Las Bordas grow the best of those giant mushrooms, the *setas* which tasted so delicious at the *Bar Frontón*. From there a path runs down into the main Urumea valley, and provides a short cut to Goizueta.

Goizueta is three times the size of Arano, and has several amenities which the smaller village lacks, with the result that a strange procession can be seen winding its way past Las Bordas once every fortnight. In front walks a woman, and behind her – often fifty or a hundred yards behind her – comes a man, carrying over his shoulder an extraordinary object which at first sight appears to be a portable pillory. By this time tomorrow a metamorphosis will have taken place amongst the women of Arano. For this is nothing less than the twice-monthly visit of the hairdresser, whose husband accompanies her bearing the apparatus on which her clients rest their heads during their transformation.

The right-hand track at the spring, however, runs on high above the same tributary of the Urumea above which stands Arano itself. With each hour as we proceed the church clock is fainter. Fortunately it always strikes the hour twice, giving us a second chance to listen carefully. The track plunges into woods for a couple of miles, and emerges at last much higher up. At the head of the tributary valley it branches again, and it is possible to follow one path right round to Descarga and the other three, still occupied farms of the farther slope. Don José Maria and I once planned how we would spend a whole day walking this route, beating the parish bounds as it were. Now he has gone off to the mission field in Venezuela, and I suppose that we never shall.

The path which leaves the valley runs straight ahead towards the grassy summits. Although no higher than 2,500 feet, one feels on top of the world. I never got beyond the point where one is arrested at the sight of a circle of great stones, projecting only a few inches above the grass. That evening I asked Milagros what they were.

'You've been a long way. They say that the Carlists put those stones there, but I really don't know.'

She didn't refer to them again until one day the following summer, when she greeted me with a searching glance as I re-entered the *fonda* after a day's picnic.

'Have you been up beyond the head of the valley, Enrique, near those stones which you once asked me about?'

'No. I've been in quite another direction. Why do you ask?'

'Because this morning we caught sight of a figure moving about up there, on the skyline. We wondered if it might be you.' She looked at me again and pursed her lips. '*Sería un pastor*. It must have been a shepherd.'

Timber does not dominate Arano's economy as it does that of some of the Aragonese *pueblos* which we shall be visiting in the next part of this book. But it is a useful prop, and it has had one unexpected side effect. For the last time that I was there I felt that something was missing, even during the Corpus Christi celebrations, as we males all walked in procession down the herb-strewn village street after Mass, to the altar which had been erected outside the last house.

It was only at the open-air dance in the *fronton* that evening that I realized what was the matter. There was not a man between twenty and thirty years of age to be seen, and the girls were sadly dancing with each other for want of partners. It transpired that the young men – twenty-five of them, all told – had gone as a team to work in a forest of the French Alps. There was a need there for men with their skill and woodcraft. They were not only able to earn a much higher wage than they could in Spain, but were also given their board and keep, so that they could bank almost every franc. Perhaps the girls were not really so sad after all. For, as Milagros's mother said:

Interlude at Arano, a village of the Basque Pyrenees

'Next year they will all be back, with enough money each to buy his house and to get married.'

But where would these houses be? For Arano itself, the story might not have quite such a happy ending. I thought of Descarga as she added:

'Then, with their homes already paid for, they will each be able to settle down to a nice job in a factory.'

Part Two

The Aragonese Pyrenees

PROV. OF
NAVARRA

To Pau

Pic d'Anie

Zuriza

Isaba

Roncal

Garde

Pass of Matamachos

Ansó

Fago

Salvatierra de Esca

Leire

Tiermas

Biniés

Berdun

Reservoir of Yesa

Ruesta

Sos del Rey Católico

Petilla de Aragón (TO NAVARRA)

PROV. OF ZARAGOZA

Pass of Santa Barba

R. Aragón

Selva de Oza

Aguas Tuertas

Pic du Midi d'Ossau

Somport Pass

Portalet Pass

Infierno

Sallent

Spa of Panticosa

Ibón of Estanes

Candanchú

Siresa

Hecho

Urdués

Aragües

Jasa

Embún

Javierregay

Canfranc International Station

JACA

Sta. Cruz de la Serós

San Juan de la Peña

Peña de Oroel

Sabiñánigo

Biescas

Pass of Cotefablo

R. Gallego

PROV. OF HUESCA

Castle of Loarre

Bolea

To Huesca

To Huesca

+—+—+ Railway

The "Garganta" of a river

0   5   10
Miles

R. Esca

RONCAL

VALLEY OF ANSÓ

R. Aragón Subordán

VALLEY OF HECHO

CANFRANC

TENA

CANAL DE BERDUN

IV UPPER ARAGON

The term 'upper Aragon' is sometimes used for the entire
Aragonese Pyrenees, and sometimes in a still wider sense to
include all the province of Huesca. In this map, however, and
throughout this book, it is given the narrower but more natural
limits of the old Kingdom and county of Aragon, based on the
valley of the river Aragon and its tributaries.

1. The Canal de Berdún

We have already traversed the highway from Pamplona to Jaca as far as the point where it leaves Navarre, with Leire high on the left, and Javier away to the right. The dry, monotonous yet exotic countryside becomes perhaps even more dry and monotonous as we enter Aragon. A river has joined the road: it is not the Irati which we crossed a few miles back, but the Aragon, into which the Irati flows at Sangüesa. It is not named after the old kingdom of Aragon. On the contrary, that kingdom was named after this river. For shallow and unnavigable though it may be, its flow more fluctuating than many mountain torrents, the Aragon is the most important of the many rivers of the Spanish Pyrenees.

It is important in the first place because it fails to cut a passage through the sub-Pyrenean sierras, a wide belt of tangled formations to the south of the principal chain which we here encounter for the first time. Leaving the Pyrenees proper – as a geologist would define them – at Jaca, it is deflected by the Sierra de la Peña, and for fifty miles runs from east to west, before turning south again at Sangüesa. The only other river which does this is the Segre, from its source to as far as Seo de Urgel, and the high 'latitudinal' valley of the Segre, though shorter, is so exceptional that it has been given the special name of the Cerdaña (or in French, the Cerdagne). The high 'latitudinal' valley of the Aragon has also been given a special name: it is called the Canal de Berdún.

This may not at first sight seem a very appropriate name. For Berdún is today an unimportant village of some six hundred souls. Perhaps it was never much bigger, for its appearance is deceptive. From its commanding knoll it dominates the road for miles before one actually reaches it, and by night its lights – like all lights in the Spanish Pyrenees, so low in watts yet so rich in promise – seem to hang suspended like a mirage from some earlier century. Its unbroken circle of houses, with only a single gateway, seem as if they might shelter several thousand. But it is a hollow circle, and one finds little life on actually climbing up.

Before the road to Jaca was built through Puente la Reina, however, the valleys of Hecho and Ansó found their chief market in Berdún, where they would purchase everything they needed except wine. This last was brought on mules from the Cinco Villas de Aragon, passing through Garde in Roncal over the steep little pass of Matamachos – though why this uncomfortable detour into Navarre was required, I have never discovered.

Even before the road was built the Canal de Berdún was a natural highway, providing a ready-made route from Navarre into Aragon. In their early years ndeed, these two kingdoms were as often as not united, as we have noticed when visiting Leire. In a sense, the Canal de Berdún *was* the old kingdom of Aragon. It was only a small kingdom: four valleys, and their surrounding sierras. But three of those valleys – Canfranc, Hecho, and Ansó – ran into the valley of the Aragon, to which the fourth valley, Tena (the name given to the valley of the river Gallego) was linked up by the continuing depression of the Canal de Berdún from Jaca to Sabiñanigo.

Huesca, the province of which these lands now form part, is one of the five least densely populated provinces of Spain. Over fifteen years I have spent a total of four months in upper Aragon, yet even on this casual acquaintance I find it possible to enter any bar between Biescas and Berdún, and to establish a relationship with someone present on the basis of 'If your brother-in-law is the forest guard at San Juan de la Peña, and your uncle is the *alcalde* of Guasa, then why haven't we met before?' In the eleventh century the population of the Pyrenees was probably higher than it is today; but it was still relatively tiny: and as the kings of Aragon moved up and down the Canal de Berdún, from Siresa to Santa Cruz de la Serós, and from San Juan de la Peña to Jaca, they must have become familiar figures to almost every one of their subjects.

Small though the kingdom was, therefore, it was well knit together. Nowhere else in the Spanish Pyrenees are four valleys able to communicate so easily. The Canal de Berdún provided the only possible nucleus for a major state between Navarre and the coastlands of Catalonia.

11. Castle of Loarre

12. Plaza of Alquézar

13. The Hospital de Viella, at southern end of tunnel to Arán

The Canal de Berdún

It performed too – and still performs – a useful economic function in bringing an almost Mediterranean cultivation right up to the threshold of the high Pyrenean valleys. Coming down from the Somport, after passing between the narrow green fields and the high pastures of the valley of Canfranc, the traveller is hit by a sudden contrast with the dry brown plain stretching away towards the Peña de Oroel, the great sub-Pyrenean landmark which dominate Jaca. It is like coming straight from wettest Wales into dryest Norfolk. This climatic contrast may be the explanation for the variety and excellence of the fruit and vegetables for sale each morning in the market opposite Jaca cathedral.

But it is not a truly Mediterranean cultivation. Those figs and onions would never taste so good had they been grown anywhere near sea-level. The Canal de Berdún, dry though it may be, stands at 2,500 feet. There is a freshness in the evening air even in July and August. The trees which provide shade for the new luxury camping site near Puente la Reina may look like olives, but they are in fact a variety of holm oak.

Berdún itself is today the only village directly on the road between Navarre and Jaca. There was once another, which would have claimed greater importance than Berdún, for its very name, Tiermas, proclaimed it as a spa. Its healing waters were recognized as such by the Romans. Part of the village, with the church, still stands, but the road no longer passes through it. And the spa now lies beneath the waters of the reservoir of Yesa, upon which we looked down from the heights of Leire.

For although named after the village of Yesa in Navarre, the reservoir lies wholly within Aragon. Now that it has at last filled up, and the new road along the north shore has been properly surfaced, we can admire its ten sinuous miles, sometimes green, sometimes bright blue, as a pleasing addition to the scenery. A farmer has recouped himself for the loss of some of his fields by establishing a camping site and boating marina on those which remain. And when the water level is low, the hot spring of Tiermas can still be seen bubbling away below the surface.

It was not to enhance the scenery, however, that the Aragon was dammed above Yesa, but to irrigate the badlands of Las Bardenas. This is the latest service of the Canal de Berdún to Navarre and to Aragon, across the frontiers of which lie these dry but potentially fertile marches. Forty miles to the south of the reservoir, between Sádaba and Ejea de los Caballeros, the new roads are under construction, and villages with names like Bardena del Caudillo are receiving the families to whom the newly irrigated lands have been allotted.

Sádaba and Ejea are two of the Cinco Villas de Aragon. These five towns of the cornlands stretch in a long line, like an incomplete and far from celestial Plough, from Tauste almost on the Ebro, through Ejea and Sádaba to Uncastillo and Sos. Sos, though by far the smallest and the poorest, is also the most interesting, and it is the only one sufficiently far north to justify a description here.

For Sos was the Aragonese stronghold set against Sangüesa and Javier, from each of which it is distant a mere eight or nine miles. Indeed it faced the enemy on two sides, for to the east lies Petilla de Aragon, which although entirely surrounded by Aragonese territory belongs to Navarre. It was acquired, so the legend runs, at a game of *mus* between the neighbouring sovereigns when the stakes were pitched particularly high.

If fortune on that occasion favoured the king of Navarre, its ultimate decision was for the king of Aragon. Just as the one often resided at Sangüesa to watch the frontier, so the other just as frequently, and for the same reason, resided at Sos. We have seen how Henri d'Albret was thus born at Sangüesa in 1503. But at the Sada palace in Sos half a century earlier, in 1452, was born a greater prince: that Ferdinand who amongst other things was to drive little Henri d'Albret and his parents across the Pyrenees in 1512.

The 'other things' included, of course, marrying Isabel of Castile in 1469 after a secret, adventurous and romantic ride to where she was practically imprisoned at Valladolid. The crowns of the two catholic sovereigns thus united, Ferdinand saw his arms triumph in Granada and in Italy, whilst Columbus laid a New World at his wife's feet. Even England was affected by this marriage, for one of its children was our ill-fated Queen, Catherine of Aragon. And it all began here in Sos, which with justification is now styled Sos del Rey Católico.

It is a little town of some fifteen hundred inhabitants, standing at about two thousand feet. The palace where Ferdinand was born has been well restored, but the ramparts have needed no restoration, and still present a bold front towards a Navarre which no longer threatens. Sos is high enough to be reasonably cool in summer by comparison with the Ebro valley, and here, year after year, come families from Saragossa who prefer somewhere a little cooler and a little cheaper than Jaca. So that there are doctors in Teruel, and lawyers in Calatayud whose earliest summer memories are of the steep cobbled streets of Sos, and of picnics in the valley of the Onsella.

All along the Basque and Aragonese Pyrenees there is a friendly rivalry amongst antiquarians as to which was the most ancient and popular pilgrims' road to Compostela. With a view to gathering evidence to support the claims of the route across the Somport and down the Canal de Berdún, the *cura* of Navardún, five miles from Sos, set off one day a couple of years ago in the direction of Ruesta. This *pueblo* lies in the Canal de Berdún, beside the reservoir, and its church is dedicated to St. James, the saint of Compostela. On the way, he turned aside and 'casually entered' (to use his own words) a chapel attached to Ruesta dedicated to St. John the Evangelist. It was many years since worship had taken place there, and the building had served as a *borda* for shepherds and their flocks. Casually, still, he began 'to scrape on the surface of chalk', and was astonished when evidence of painting appeared underneath.

The mural thus uncovered in the apse of San Juan Evangelista de Ruesta is of the twelfth century, and some authorities are already speaking of it as the third finest Romanesque mural in Spain. Its upper part represents the *Pantócrator*, Christ in glory surrounded by the angel of the Apocalypse and the four evangelists; whilst the lower consists of portraits of people who figured in Our Lord's life on earth. Although the subject is thus similar to those chosen by the Master of Tahull for his paintings of the same period in the valley of Bohí and at Roda, it is thought that the artist at Ruesta was neither the same nor of the same school. For reasons of safety the mural has been transferred to the newly-opened Diocesan Museum in the cathedral of Jaca, after having first been on exhibition in Barcelona. The fame which the discovery has brought to his diocese has led the bishop of Jaca to issue instructions to all his clergy to keep their eyes open; and the young priest of Santa Cruz de la Serós told me that he had high hopes of discovery in a remote chapel of his parish called San Salvador, at two hours' walk and 6,000 feet!

2. Ansó

At Berdún a road leads away to the left up the first of the purely Aragonese valleys. Ten miles earlier, at an unlikely point in the middle of a near desert, a signpost has pointed to the fresh green 'Valle de Roncal'. The directions at Berdún run simply 'Ansó 25', for Ansó is the name both of the valley and of its only *pueblo*. Fago, in an adjoining valley, is in fact closely dependent upon Ansó, but to all intents and purposes Ansó and Hecho are unitary states. Reverting to our Greek constitutions, we are amongst the Athenians of the Spanish Pyrenees!

Travelling up alongside the Veral, as the river of Ansó is called, a traveller might dispute this statement when he saw the village of Biniés with its ruined castle high up on his right. But Biniés forms no part of the valley of Ansó, from which it is cut off by a long narrow gorge, called the Foz de Biniés, which the road presently enters. For two miles there is room for only the river and the road, and only just room for them. Often a way has had to be cut for the road beneath overhanging rocks, and sometimes tunnels have had to be driven through them.

We have already encountered this phenomenon at the southern end of Roncal, between Burgui and Salvatierra de Esca, when we described it as a typical formation of the central Spanish Pyrenees, for which we would be offering an explanation later on. The explanation is as follows.

During the series of Ice Ages which descended over Europe between the geological eras known as the Tertiary and the Quaternary (in which we are still living) there was inevitably a profusion of those rivers of ice which we call glaciers. There are still glaciers in Europe today: in Scandinavia, for example, in the Alps, and in the Pyrenees. But only one of these is in the Spanish Pyrenees: it is a relatively small glacier curling round the north face of the Maladeta massif. And the Maladeta not only includes the Aneto, the highest peak of the entire range, but it also lies entirely within Spanish territory. This means that although this glacier lies inside Spain, it faces north away from Spain, and has therefore not been produced by typically Spanish Pyrenean conditions. For glaciers have survived in the French Pyrenees precisely because they face north, and are less exposed to the sun.

Even when the last Ice Age was at its height, and the climate of the Pyrenees was much like that of Scandinavia today, there was a difference between the glaciers on the two slopes. Northward the glaciers were not only more powerful, but with greater rainfall they also had more 'raw material' on which to put that power to work. So that they were both bigger and stronger than the glaciers on the southern slope, and they were forcing their way down valleys which were much shorter.

For one of the greatest contrasts between the French and the Spanish Pyrenees is in their extent. The traveller from Biarritz to Collioure who does not wish to brave the almost fairground ups-and-downs of the scenic *Route des Pyrénées*, can follow a busy but almost level highway through Pau and Tarbes, St. Gaudens, St. Girons, and Foix. At no time will he be more than about forty miles from the crest of the range, and at times he will be as few as twenty.

No comparable road exists on the Spanish side. The best is the one which makes use of the Canal de Berdún and the Cerdaña, the two faults between the main range and the sub-Pyrenean sierras, and it faces some awkward passes when it leaves these faults, between Jaca and Huesca, and again between Puigcerdá and Ripoll over the pass of Tosas. But a road following the plains all the way would sometimes be as far as a hundred miles from the crest. At Barbastro a signpost to Benasque reads 98. From Lerida to Andorra la Vella there are 153 narrow kilometres to be negotiated along the floor of the Segre valley. And Benasque and Andorra lie only at the start of the ascents towards the passes.

The result of this contrast was that during the Ice Ages the more powerful glaciers on the northern slopes were able to force their way right down the shorter French valleys and into the open plains beyond. There, at the points where the glaciers finally melted, they deposited groups of heavy boulders which still remain. This process, far from being unusual, was typical of glacial action everywhere; and the presence of these moraines, as the masses of debris are called, is normally regarded as essential evidence that such action has in fact taken place.

In the Spanish Pyrenees, however, although there are many apparently glacial valleys, with their suave rounded contours, and their level floors, there are only two points where such moraines are to be found. And it is significant that one of these points is near Jaca, and the other near Puigcerdá. In other words, they are situated exactly where the Aragon and the Segre decide to break the rules. For all other Spanish Pyrenean rivers from Velate onwards flow – albeit with many a twist and turn – from north to south. It is precisely at Jaca that the Aragon, and at Puigcerda that the Segre choose instead to flow for many miles from east to west along those high 'latitudinal' valleys which we have already described as so exceptional: the Canal de Berdún and the Cerdaña.

For the Aragon and the Segre were not the only rivers to have glaciers. As evidence of this we have not only the formation of the valleys, but also one river, the Esera, which although it has no moraine still possesses its glacier, even if in an attenuated form – the glacier of the north face of the Maladeta. But because these other glaciers had less power than the French glaciers they were unable to force their way right down to the plains, which were three times more distant.

At the point where the glaciers ended, the broad smooth glacial valleys ended too, and the melted waters cut themselves deep trench-like passages to the south. The force of the torrents was sufficient to carry away the debris which would otherwise have gone to make moraines.

These deep trenches still exist, and are the most characteristic feature of the central Spanish Pyrenees. They go under various names. The most generally used is *garganta*, but in Pallars and Sobrarbe the more common term is *desfiladero*, whilst in Ribagorza we encounter *congosto*. And in western Aragon and Navarre this type of narrow gorge, where once a river sprang fully grown to life – a naiad emulating Aphrodite – is named a *foz*.

This geological phenomenon has created some unusual human environments, of which Ansó is one. For had the glacier of the river Veral been only a little more powerful, it would have forced its way past the four miles which separate the Foz de Biniés from the Canal de Berdún. The *ansotanos*, open to the world, would then have been as extrovert as the people of neighbouring Hecho, whose *foz*, left evidently by a much weaker glacier, lies high above the village, below the forest of Oza.

The road up to Ansó requires careful driving even today, and untarred was a real disincentive when first I went there in 1951. And a few years earlier still only a narrow mule track along the Foz de Biniés had linked the *ansotanos* with the outside world. Thus isolated from the south, they were cut off from the north by mountains 2,000 feet higher than those over which the inhabitants of neighbouring Roncal used to travel to France. They lived, therefore, not so much in a valley as in a long, mountain-girt island; and, as islanders often do, they developed their own ways of speaking, of dressing, and of running their affairs.

It would have been easy to have made Ansó the centre of this book, treating it as the most typical, the least evolved, the ultimate in all that a Pyrenean village ought to be. I have deliberately adopted what I would like to regard as a more sophisticated approach – and some readers may think that I have been too clever by half. For I have pointed out that in neighbouring Roncal Basque was spoken and a local costume worn within living memory. And for my more detailed account of a village in the Aragonese Pyrenees I have chosen not Ansó, but its neighbour Hecho, partly through having *cheso* friends, and partly too because it is so much less widely known.

For although Ansó is an extraordinary place, it is not unique. Hecho in most respects, and many other villages in certain respects, have the same interesting features. Both Ansó and Hecho have conserved, for example, slightly different dialects of the ancient Aragonese, but Hecho's dialect, known as *cheso*, is both purer and in more general use than *ansotano*.

Having said all this, if I were asked to advise someone who had time to visit only one village in the Spanish Pyrenees, I would tell him to go to Ansó. For only in Ansó will he see local costumes being worn every day by ordinary men and women as they go about their daily business.

And I would tell him to go soon. A generation age he could have seen in daily use in Roncal and in Hecho local costumes which now lie in the *ayuntamiento* to be used only when the young people dress up at fiestas. And a generation ago more than half the population of Ansó had never worn 'normal' modern clothes. As I write, there are only eight old men and between fifteen and twenty old ladies in Ansó, and two old men in Fago who have never worn any dress other than the customary dress of their valley, and who therefore wear it still.

There lies the rub. Once a man had slipped into the convenient jacket and trousers of the twentieth century, he could never again bring himself to don the heavy black breeches, the white stockings, the purple *faja* (a sort of wide and noble cummerbund), the piratical black cotton headscarf with dangling tassel and the broad felt hat. Here as in so many aspects of Spanish life, the Civil War marked a watershed. Many *ansotanos* went off to fight in their *faja*. If they returned, it was in the drabber garments of 1939.

John Langdon-Davies was fortunate enough to visit Ansó four years before that war began, in 1932, when the old dress was the rule rather than the exception. He was fascinated by this 'unexpected fairyland' where 'at the butcher's shop you buy from a lady who might be Queen Elizabeth'. He was equally fascinated by the miniature welfare state of the valley: a free village health service, with a municipally paid doctor and a municipally paid chemist, and even a municipally paid barber providing every adult male with a free weekly shave. Writing under great pressure late in 1936, in the agony of soul of an English intellectual who knew and loved Spain well, he saw in Ansó a co-operative commonwealth, typical of what philosophical anarchism, left to itself, might produce all over the peninsula*.

It is certainly true that given similar conditions, other Pyrenean villages often provide similar services. Almost the only free service which Ansó provides for its inhabitants, and Hecho does not, is the advice of the municipal veterinary surgeon. And little Santa Cruz de la Serós, under a capable *alcalde*, will now lay a piped water supply to any house within 200 yards of the church free of charge, and will provide a free sink withal! And although it has not the population for a resident doctor or vet.', it will pay the fee for one to come out from Jaca to visit any *vecino* or *vecino*'s animal who may be ill.

How many services are provided depends far more upon the

* John Langdon-Davies *Behind the Spanish Barricades*, Secker & Warburg, 1936, pp. 68–73.

personality of the individual *alcalde*, and the wealth of the individual *ayuntamiento* than on any leanings towards 'practical communism' or 'philosophical anarchism' amongst the inhabitants. Pyrenean villages might with greater reason be likened to competing joint stock companies, with greater or less assets at their disposal, and with chairmen of varying competence. In such a simile the inhabitants are the shareholders, and the *ansotanos* owe their welfare state to their fortune in being the shareholders of a very wealthy and well-run company.

Mr. Langdon-Davies in his otherwise charming account of Ansó makes one extraordinary statement, when speaking of the parish priest. 'He is a good man, and no one minds joining him in a smoke, but that is about his only function. For here, too, religion, even so long ago as 1932, had lost its hold.'

Whatever the position in 1936, or 'even so long ago as 1932', the *ansotanos* are today regular worshippers at their church, with its gallery at the back filled with huge leather-bound volumes of chants, copied out by hand on parchment. Before or after the 10 o'clock Mass on a Sunday is a good opportunity for seeing the traditional female costume, as the old ladies enter and leave the church. Its essential feature is a long green skirt, differing from that of Hecho in that it falls straight, with no suggestion of a bust. Their headdress also differs from that of the *chesa*: they wear a coloured wimple, with a dangling square ornament inherited from mother or grandmother, which Sacheverell Sitwell has likened to a phylactery.

The reason why Ansó provides free veterinary treatment where Hecho does not may be the greater importance of animals in Ansó's economy. This is due to the much greater extent of its pasture land. For the entire belt along the international frontier from Navarre to the ski slopes of Candanchú is the property of Ansó, which has long-standing *facerías* or private treaties over pasture rights with the valley of Aspe in France, and more especially with the village of Borce.

Nine miles separate Ansó from Zuriza, the great glade where these high pastures begin, and where the road used to end. But the road has now been extended a few miles to a spot known as Linzas. There, at over 4,000 feet, a spring which comes to the surface in the shade of some great trees has been induced to flow neatly from a pipe, to provide that essential concomitant of a

Spanish picnic: a *fuente*. The water is 'rich', as they say; and in the further wood you can pick wild strawberries.

The road has been built and the spring has been tapped in order to attract tourists, of whom there are still surprisingly few. The *ayuntamiento*, I was told, are prepared to give a free site and a substantial monetary grant to any company which is prepared to erect a hotel in the valley without delay. For although the *ansotanos* are the Scots as well as the Athenians of the Spanish Pyrenees, grave and silent behind the closed doors of their clean but unadorned stone houses, they also have a canny flair for placing their wealth where it will bring their valley most lasting benefit.

The fine new cinema, large enough to hold almost all the population at once, may seem an exception to this rule. But the elders of Ansó realize that only by such means can the young people be retained, happy and contented in their native place. And they have been careful to ensure that its steep pitched roofs and its stone walls are in keeping with the austere but functional lines of their own homes.

Recently they made a shrewder and wiser investment still. Dr. Balcells, the Director of the Pyrenean Centre for Experimental Biology, is a man patently in love with his work. Clad in the corduroy jacket and trousers of the Pyrenean shepherds whom he so well understands, his powerful binoculars ready for vulture or izard, he may be encountered striding in his *chirucas** almost anywhere between Roncal and Ripoll. From his laboratories at Barcelona and Jaca, and from his experimental farm in the Canal de Berdún, he is working for improvements in the agriculture of the Pyrenean valleys, for greater returns from the flocks of the Pyrenean pastures, and for more and finer fish from the Pyrenean rivers.

Although a Catalan, Dr. Balcells regards Ansó as the most attractive village of all his vast territory, and in 1964 he purchased a house there, where he could spend his own holidays. It was in a very bad state of repair, and the *ayuntamiento* of Ansó at once made him a free gift of as many cubic metres of wood and stone as he would require for its restoration.

He very kindly allowed me to accompany the members of the

* Light canvas boots with rubber soles favoured by Catalans when walking or mountaineering.

first postgraduate course held by his centre on their visit to Ansó. Whilst there, he showed us over his house, where repairs had not yet started. As we emerged from the dark interior into the sunlight, I was interested to listen to the reactions of the three girls with whom I spent most of that day. For each was from a different part of Spain, and each reacted characteristically.

'*Es un gallinero!*' said the girl from Andalusia. 'It's nothing more than a hen-house!'

'But it will be very typical when he has made some reforms,' said the girl from Madrid.

Last spoke the girl from Aragon. 'It will be a home.'

3. Santa Cruz de la Serós and San Juan de la Peña

South of the Canal de Berdún – to the right of the main road from Pamplona to Jaca – rise the sub-Pyrenean sierras. They culminate in the Sierra del Cadí, to the south of that other great east-west fault, the Cerdaña, and in between they offer a wide variety of very 'Spanish' mountain country, such as we might expect to find in the hills on the edge of the meseta, or even over in Mexico. This Iberian quality is due to a single characteristic: this whole chain of sub-Pyrenean sierras is exceedingly dry.

We have already remarked on the difference in climate between the northern and southern slopes of the Pyrenees, but the main chain of the Spanish Pyrenees, and the valleys which lead off from it, at least enjoy some of the winter rains which fall on the summits, and in summer a share of the melting snows. More land in the main chain receives upwards of 2,000 millimetres a year of rainfall than receives merely 1,000 millimetres in the sub-Pyrenees. And even this restricted moisture is deposited mainly in seasonal storms, and quickly drains away from these steep eroded hills.

Yet as if to prove this general rule, the first village of the sub-Pyrenean sierras which we shall visit is as full of the sound of water as the Generalife summer palace at Granada. I have already described how the capable *alcalde* of Santa Cruz de la Serós will lay on a free water supply to any house within the *casco urbano*. But the springs of cool, 'rich' water which enable him to do so are exceptional: they stem from the fact that the village faces north, and lies below a sierra which towers fifteen hundred feet above it. On top of that sierra, at San Juan de la Peña, water is far from being so plentiful.

One day within the next few years it will be possible to drive straight up to San Juan from Santa Cruz. Until now, the journey by road from one to the other has involved a long detour of twenty-six miles through Jaca. But the last six of those miles, already bone shaking in 1951, and apparently untouched by *caminero* in the interval, are so bad that I recommend everyone in reasonable physical condition to travel to San Juan de la Peña on foot from Santa Cruz.

Although this is only a walk of three miles, it involves a climb of fifteen hundred feet, and takes a long hour. The midday sun is hot, and can be avoided by setting out early in the morning – not in the evening, for the traveller may easily lose his way if darkness falls before he gets back. The path requires a little finding even by daylight, but the parish priest, Don Jesús, is always prepared to point it out. So one should arrive at Santa Cruz soon after half-past seven, when he will be found reading his breviary in the little square outside the main church, preparatory to saying Mass at eight.

Following his instructions, the traveller will breast a steep bare spur, and after following a path up the side of a cleft will emerge on a plateau amidst great pine trees. He is at 4,000 feet, and may rightly guess that if he could see through the trees, he could command a good view across the Canal de Berdún to the main range. Fortunately, a well-situated *mirador* has been constructed to enable him to enjoy that view, where with the help of a *table d'orientation* he can pick out many of the great peaks of the central Pyrenees.

When he at last drops his eyes from the white wonders on the skyline, he will become aware of another wonder, owing almost as much to nature, in the chasm at his feet. As he gazes down to where Romanesque columns form an uncanny frieze along the base of the overhanging mass of rose coagulant on which the *mirador* is set, he will at last understand why El Greco found himself so at home in Spain. For there must be some fundamental sympathy between the Greece which has produced the monasteries of Meteora and of Athos, and the Spain which has produced Leire and the *monasterio viejo* of San Juan de la Peña.

It is often described as 'the cradle of Aragon' or as 'the Aragonese Covadonga'. In its appearance, surrounded by forest, and half excavated in the living rock, it indeed resembles the site of Covadonga in the mountains of Asturias, where the fleeing Visigoths first turned and snatched a victory from the pursuing Moslem columns.

The earliest resistance to the Moslems in this region, however, probably came from the valleys of Canfranc and Hecho alone, and was stimulated by Carolingian support. Count Aureolo, who was active thereabouts at the turn of the eight and ninth centuries, was a Frank. The Canal de Berdún was traversed by Moslem armies after the disaster of Roncesvalles in 778, and again early in the ninth century. It is improbable, therefore, that the fortress on Mount Pano, where the new monastery now stands, was a very early centre of resistance. But it is quite likely that individual hermits – legend speaks of a Juan of Atarés – established themselves in the cave nearby.

In the mid-ninth century, with the expansion of Aragon to the south of the Canal de Berdún, that cave came to occupy a central position in the enlarged county, whose rulers were now local men. And here were buried not only the early kings of Aragon, but their nobles also. The pantheon of the kings was restored in a pleasing Rococo in 1770 by the Count of Aranda, acting on the orders of King Charles III. But the pantheon of the nobles of Aragon looks much as it ever did, with its tombs bearing primitive devices of the type described by Sir Walter Scott in *Ivanhoe*, which a century or two later would blossom until full coats-of-arms.

The eleventh and twelfth centuries church runs right back to the bare rock, and makes a contrast with the feathery stonework of the fifteenth-century chapel of San Victorian. But the jewel of San Juan is the twelfth-century cloister, entered through a 'Mozarabic' arch which has remained from the original monastery of the ninth century. Although roofless except for the great rose rock towering above, the cloister has a more intimate air than the church, and is open to the forest lying beneath. One side has been lost, but the three which remain preserve a whole series of exquisite Romanesque capitals.

San Juan de la Peña was the first monastery in Spain where Cluniac monks chanted the Roman rite in place of the Mozarabic. The Mozarabic was the older ritual of the Mass, as it had been said all over Spain in the seventh century, before the Arab conquest. It continued in use while the Spanish Christians were out of contact with Rome, and the rest of the western church was adopting a new liturgy. Gradually, beginning here at San Juan, the Spanish church came into line; and now, to hear what the old rite was like, you must go to Toledo Cathedral before ten o'clock on a Sunday morning, and whisper to a sacristan '*misa mozarabe*'. He will guide you past gilded altars and past sumptuously dressed statues to a dim and distant chapel. Entering, you step back a millenium and a half to hear Mass as Bishop Hosius of Cordova used to say it, Mass as it was intoned by Bishop Isidore of Seville, Mass as it was heard by King Rodrigo on the morning of Guadalete.

On this occasion, therefore, San Juan was the avenue whereby ultramontane fashions reached the rest of the peninsula. Seven centuries later, however, when the heroic 'Augustina of Aragon' rallied Saragossa to face a two months' siege by Napoleon's Marshal Lannes, the 'cradle' of the old kingdom also played its part against the new infidels from the north. The monks no longer lived in the romantic but rather damp *monasterio viejo*, but had built themselves between 1668 and 1714 a spacious new Baroque palace half a mile away on the plateau above. Suchet's troops arrived there to find the birds flown, and all their treasures with them, taken to safety in Jaca. They proceeded to burn the 'new' monastery, and it is only recently that the province of Huesca has repaired part of it to form a hostelry, furnished after that simple but seemly style which so charms us in the State *paradores*.

The walk downhill to Santa Cruz de la Serós will be less tiring than the early-morning ascent, and should leave the traveller with plenty of energy to visit the village's two perfect churches. One alone would have been worth a journey of fifty miles. The smaller is known as the parish church, although services are only held there occasionally. But the description is correct, for it is the elder by more than two centuries, being built – wait for it! – in 848.

This means that it belongs to the very earliest years after the Moslems had been driven from the Sierra de la Peña, when the Canal de Berdún had only just become, once again, a Christian highway. And even if its simple squat arches and its plain semi-circular abside – the hallmark of primitive Romanesque from Congas de Onis in Asturias to Brixworth in Northamptonshire – had not alerted us to its antiquity, the dedication to San Caprasio might have led us to entertain suspicions. For he is a saint whom one encounters little in Spain. Like Santa Orosia the patron saint of Jaca, and Santa Barbara whose chapel stands beside the pass between Huesca and Puente la Reina, he was probably introduced here from beyond the Pyrenees. In other words the parish church, like the capitals of Leire's crypt, represents that moment of decisive Carolingian intervention in the Spanish Pyrenees, when the counts of Aragon were supported by Frankish allies or auxiliaries.

Some of these northerners may have settled here permanently. For the Reconquest was also a re-peopling. Again and again, as the Christian frontiers were pushed south, half-empty lands had to be filled by the kings of Leon, of Navarre, and of Aragon, until even the Alpujarras almost within sight of Africa had to be re-colonized after the last Moslem rebellion at the end of the sixteenth century. I have already remarked that the tiny nucleus of Aragon may well have been more densely populated in the eleventh century than it is today. For in accomplishing their part of the *Reconquista*, the Spanish Pyrenees drained themselves. England has her lost villages, given over to sheep in the fifteenth and sixteenth centuries, or deserted when the fall in population after the Black Death caused the abandonment of marginal farming land. But no English county can compete with the valley of the Aragon, where of twenty-eight villages mentioned in a document of 1208, thirteen have disappeared.

Another document recently discovered refers to a village, today unknown, named Santa María de Orcal. It describes it as situated about an hour's walk from Santa Cruz de la Serós. Don Jesús was asked if he had any idea where it might have stood. He had indeed. For although he knew of no ruins, he did know that one of his parishioners owned three adjacent fields with the significant names of Villar (from Villa?), Santa Marina (from Santa María?), and Orcal.

Santa Cruz de la Serós derives its own name from the nuns, *las Sorores*, who used to live there, and whose church alone remains of the convent founded in 984 by King Sancho Garcés. This massive building, as tall as broad, has an octagonal cupola sitting above a square Romanesque tower of an altogether heavier breed than those which soon after rose in Pallars. Within is the unusual and successful design of a single central pillar rising from out of the font. This church was built almost a century after the convent's foundation, in 1076. We can understand why so many of the slender resources of little Aragon were concentrated here when we learn that three of the sisters of King Sancho Ramirez: Doña Urraca, Doña Teresa, and Doña Sancha came to live at Santa Cruz when they decided that they had a vocation for the religious life.

Two of them decided rather late, for Doña Urraca alone renounced the world without first tasting it. Doña Teresa only became a nun here after the death of her husband, Count William Beltrán of Provence. And as for Doña Sancha, whatever her intentions may have been, she only got around to taking vows at the very end of her life. When her husband the Count of Toulouse died, she returned to her homeland and travelled around Aragon with the royal court, making herself useful.

Making herself useful did not merely consist in embroidering tapestries, like her contemporary Queen Matilda in England. At the battle of Alcoraz in 1096, when the Moslems, with Castilian help, attempted to relieve their besieged stronghold of Huesca, the main Aragonese force was under the command of King Pedro, the friend of the Cid and Doña Sancha's nephew. The vanguard was led by his son, Doña Sancha's great-nephew Prince Alfonso, the future conqueror of Saragossa. And the rearguard was urged on by that redoubtable figure Doña Sancha herself.

The original eleventh-century stone coffin, wherein lie her bones, is now in Jaca where the '*sorores*' of Santa Cruz moved in the sixteenth century. As we look at it, we remember this brave and energetic woman who helped to open up the road which led from her family's tiny kingdom in the Pyrenees beyond the Ebro to Valencia, to Majorca, to Sicily, and to Greece.

4. Jaca: a plain paradise in the Pyrenees

If Jaca did not exist, it would have to be postulated. Since leaving
Pamplona, we have travelled over sixty miles. For the first twenty
the villages have clearly looked to Pamplona as their centre, and
in the middle stretches Sangüesa has probably always been able to
supply the desert marches with their primitive needs. But since we
passed Berdún there has been evidence of a thriving, if primitive
cultivation in the Aragon valley, and every now and again a signpost, to Ansó, to Hecho, to Santa Cruz, telling of larger communities which presumably require some market place. Even a
physical map alone, showing neither roads nor localities, would
draw our attention to the 5,000-foot Somport pass, which joining
as it does the straight south-north valley of Aspe in France to the
straight north-south valley of Canfranc in Spain provides the
most direct natural route across the Pyrenees between Roncesvalles and Perthus.

Somewhere near here there ought, we feel, to be a town. It is
significant that the only three towns of any size deep in the
Spanish Pyrenees all lie on the two latitudinal faults, and in
similar positions. In the Cerdaña lies Puigcerdá near the frontier
at Bourg-Madame, and Seo de Urgel near the frontier with
Andorra. And in the Canal de Berdún, near the frontier at Canfranc, lies Jaca.

Not that Jaca is large by any absolute standards. But ten thousand souls are a host to conjure with in the Spanish Pyrenees.
Here are concentrated sufficient skills to supply everything which
the *pueblos* for forty miles around are unable to supply for themselves: a bishop with cathedral and seminary to supply them with
priests, surgeons with a small but adequate hospital to perform
their operations, a market to absorb the eggs, honey, and fruit
surplus to their needs, shops to supply everything from a type-
writer to a bar of *turrón* sweetmeat which is beyond the range of

the 'village generals', and finally a whole gamut of establishments, from the humblest bar to the new *Gran Hotel*, where over a drink or a meal they can mingle with people from outside the restricted circle of their own valley.

Not that all the ten thousand inhabitants of Jaca are specialists. For the traveller who arrives there directly from Pau over the Somport, rather than for those like ourselves who approach it by the lonely road along the Canal de Berdún, it seems semi-rural, and little larger than a big village. Not all the produce for sale opposite the Cathedral is brought by the leathery peasants who descend from the creaking buses, for the *hoya de Jaca*, the little plain beneath the Peña de Oroel, is itself under intensive cultivation. And as we walk along a side-street a semi-circular oak door in the line of white-washed houses will swing open to reveal the milking of a dozen tethered cows.

Jaca is an important garrison town, and the six thousand troops stationed in nearby camps do nothing to destroy the rural atmosphere. Spain's 'flight from the land' is accelerating, but a majority of the young conscripts doing their *mili* are still country boys, often from regions far poorer and more backward than the Pyrenees. It is eminently suitable that Spain's crack mountain regiment should be based here; and the clip-clop of hooves on the cobbles of the next street is as likely as not, when we turn the corner, to be seen to proceed from a fine animal urged on by the black top boots of a cavalry officer.

Iacca, commanding the road down from the *Summus Portus* (the Somport), was already a *municipium* in the second century. It could not then have had a garrison as numerous as six thousand, for a single legion sufficed to police and protect the whole of Spain and Portugal, the most peaceful of all the provinces of Rome, and the farthest away from the dangers on the imperial frontiers. Jaca today bears a closer resemblance to some town nearer to those frontiers: to *Eboracum*, for example, the Roman York. It has the same semi-rural atmosphere, the same 'small, and white, and clean' quality, the same good provision for secondary education and even (in its Summer University and its Centre for Pyrenean Studies) for higher learning, and the same straight narrow roads leading away over the hills to a wider world which yet seems a long, long way away.

Such oases in time and space are necessary to every age. If Jaca did not exist, it is not only in a geographical sense that it would have to be postulated. For to walk up the Calle Mayor of Jaca at ten o'clock on a summer morning is for certain temperaments to get as near to Paradise as mortal may. The full heat of early afternoon is already hinted at in the dry, still air. There is a smile from the grocer, who behind his chain curtains hides an Aragonese Fortnum and Masons – but with Pyrenean honey such as Piccadilly never knew. And there is a greeting from the leather merchant, who is just hanging out the shaggy sheepskin rugs, the wine *botas*, the hides and the harness from the skins of Pyrenean cattle. The plums and the runner beans are already spread out in the arcades opposite the cathedral, and we cross the bright *plaza* for a chat with two very frail and ancient canons who stand sunning themselves in attitudes reminiscent of Chelsea pensioners.

The cathedral is the first major Romanesque monument in Spain. It was probably begun in 1033, the date when King Ramiro I definitely selected Jaca to be not merely the most important place in the kingdom* (which it was already), but the permanent seat of the royal court. And it was consecrated just thirty years later, at the Council of Jaca, the decisive assembly which that monarch summoned just before his death. Its columns – unusually graceful for the eleventh century – its capitals and its vaults, its abside, and its porch – Don Ramiro's *magna porta* – are the direct inspiration of Santa Cruz de la Serós and of San Juan de la Peña: they are the witness in stone to that supreme moment when little Aragon stood poised for the great drive from the Pyrenees to the Ebro.

Another historical watershed is represented by the chapel of San Miguel, whose alabaster sculptures were finished in 1523 by the Florentine Giovanni Moreto. During the first quarter of the sixteenth century it seemed that Aragon, directly connected with Italy through the conquests of the *Gran Capitán*, might come to share in every aspect of the Italian Renaissance, then still in its earlier, springlike, pagan period. But the canker which was to split Christendom and to raise a deadly *cordon samitaire* along the

---

* The father of Ramiro I, Sancho the Great of Navarre, did not die until two years later, in 1035. But Ramiro had already been ruling Aragon for some years, as he was technically illegitimate, and his father had therefore specifically assigned him a territory in his own lifetime.

Jaca: a plain paradise in the Pyrenees

Pyrenees was already at work: six years previously Luther had nailed up his theses at Wittenberg.

Even in the straitjacket of Trentine theology and Hapsburg absolutism, however, the Spanish spirit could find subjects congenial to artistic creation, and we have one such masterpiece in Jaca's *retablo* of the Trinity, which can be dated as later than 1575, and which has been ascribed to Juan de Ancheta. *Retablos,* or altar pieces, are generally paintings, but as in this instance they can also be three dimensional, and Juan de Ancheta's God the Father is said to show the influence of Michelangelo's Moses.

The cloister, still showing traces of its twelfth-century construction, is covered in. This reminds us that Jaca has the winters appropriate to its height of 2,500 feet. Here, and at one or two other places in the cathedral, are windows still glazed with very thin alabaster instead of with glass. Only a cold, pellucid mountain light filters through the mottled stone: the very essence of upper Aragon.

The two dear old canons standing outside in the bright sunlight will almost certainly be Aragonese, although not necessarily from this province. For the diocese of Jaca includes not only those parts of Huesca which are not in the sees of Huesca or of Barbastro, but also all the Cinco Villas of Aragon in the north of the province of Saragossa. The bishop of Jaca, however, is unlikely to be a local man. And although the canons are old, the bishops are generally young. This is because the see is in most cases a first appointment for men who are being groomed for preferment to key positions. After five or ten years in Jaca they will move on, still vigorous, to Bilbao, perhaps, or to Malaga. And they may end their careers as Archbishops of Seville or even of Toledo, and as members of the College of Cardinals itself. Jaca loses nothing by this arrangement. It means that upper Aragon enjoys the administration of men who are already marked out as the Church's leaders, but in their prime of life, when they still have their careers to make, and are in possession of full physical and intellectual vigour.

Our purchases are completed, and it is a quarter to eleven. Hurrying back past the office of Jaca's weekly newspaper, *El Pirineo Aragonés,* the typographical wonder of the western world, and past the town hall, with its convoluted 'plateresque' façade of 1544, we cross the main road to France. We glance to the right up towards the *Hotel Mur,* that 'house of Constancia Mur' so well-beloved of Hilaire Belloc and of his friend and biographer J. B.

Morton. Then we follow the *Paseo*, the long shady garden where beside the well-watered flower beds the young mothers and nurse-maids up from Saragossa are already walking their exquisitely dressed children.

As we approach the long, low building set in ample gardens, the *Universidad de Verano* where the University of Saragossa holds its summer courses, we see others hurrying along, books in hand, or chatting with friends while waiting to enter the lecture hall. There are young people from most countries of western Europe and North America. Nor is everyone very young. We recognize a professor from Gothenburg, and the University Librarian from Besançon. The door of the lecture hall opens, and we file in. Promptly at five past eleven Professor Blecua enters with a mischievous smile, wearing one of those light summer suits which the Spaniards tailor so well.

The Venetian blinds are down to lessen the full force of the heat. But the windows are wide open, and sitting in our comfortable rush-seated armchairs we can hear the bees in the garden, and an occasional splash from the swimming pool. But these cannot distract our minds from the intellectual feast spread before them: a limpid exposition in chiselled Castilian of the poetry of Miguel Unamuno. And indeed we seem to have fulfilled the vision of Unamuno, and of the founders of the *Instituto de Libre Enseñanza* with whom he was associated, and to have returned to some idealized gymnasium in a remote province of a Hellenistic world which never was, to some garden of Epicurus set in the foothills of Pergamon or the valleys of Bactria. There are people who believe that all the lights in Spain went out in 1936. To realize how much of the 'spirit of 1898' survives, they should visit one of the *cursos de verano* in Jaca.

Lectures end with an ovation far more frequently in Spanish universities than in English, and Professor Blecua receives a well-deserved clap as he brings his theme to a triumphant close. Two hours remain before lunch, and we have the choice of three swimming pools: one at the University, one in the grounds of the *Gran Hotel*, and one belonging to the town. Whichever we choose, we have the assurance of pleasant company, and of the pure strong sunlight of upper Aragon to brown our bodies faster than on any beach of Costa Brava or Costa Blanca. And by two o'clock we shall have sufficient appetite to tackle a Spanish lunch.

Jaca: a plain paradise in the Pyrenees

After lunch we have a rendezvous for coffee with a friend on the stoa-like terrace of the Somport Bar, though we would probably drift there in any case, like almost everyone else at the University. There around a table in the corner sit three of the philosopher kings of Jaca: Dr. Blecua himself of the University of Barcelona, Dr. Monge of the Spanish Institute in Zurich, and Dr. Floristán of the Catholic University of Navarre. They are all men whose successful academic careers began at Saragossa, and who still return each summer to the upper Aragon which they then learnt to love.

There follows a siesta, and then at five we have arranged to meet another group of friends for a *paseo*, a walk in the cooler air of late afternoon. Save for the modern dress, we feel ourselves players in a scene lifted straight from the pages of Kilvert's *Diary*, as the young men and women innocently debate whether to go to Asieso, or past the fortified citadel begun by Philip II, and down to the medieval bridge across the Aragon. But the ideal goal of any Spanish walk is a *fuente*, where one can not merely quench one's thirst, but enjoy watching the water flowing so unsparingly in the parched landscape. And when someone says that he knows of a nice, 'rich' *fuente* on the road to San Juan de la Peña, the debate is over.

Arrived there, we sit talking and laughing under the shadow of the Peña de Oroel, and munching our *meriendas* – thick sandwiches containing slices of ham or fried meat or even an omelette. And we wander off into the bushes – for the entirely innocent purpose of stuffing our mouths with blackberries, which there dangle in Eden-like profusion.

As we walk back towards the town, the sun is going down behind the far hills to the west, where the Canal de Berdún at last closes in. With the cooler air our talk may also grow more serious, and we shall find Pili or Paloma, as they walk beside us, speaking with an unforced friendliness which in England one rarely encounters outside the relationship between brother and sister. And it is indeed as sisters that one comes to regard these delightful Spanish girls, whose simple cotton dresses give them a false 'little girl' quality which takes our mind back to a pre-Freudian world of children's parties on summer lawns.

In the evening there may be an orchestral concert at the comfortable new Oroel cinema. Or perhaps the retired Rector of Saragossa University will be playing on records his well-loved *Verbena de la Paloma.* And then after dinner, just twelve hours since we first walked into town, we shall again find ourselves walking up the Calle Mayor. The shops are shuttered now, and the banks are closed. In *The Enchanted Mountains* Robin Fedden makes one slightly unfavourable reference to the bank managers of Jaca, and I feel that I must speak up for them. They and their staffs will do everything possible to help the visitor. But like all bank managers everywhere, they understand best the population around them. I once asked the manager of the Banco Zaragozano where the Pyreneans put their money. He gave me a shrewd look which would not have been out of place on the face of the manager of the Midland at Market Harborough, or of the National Provincial at Melton Mowbray.

'They like to put their money,' he said, 'into something they know, and whose success they can visibly see for themselves. So the investments they prefer above all others are the shares of the hydro-electric companies.'

We have now almost walked the length of the Calle Mayor, which takes us in a very few minutes from one end of the little town to the other. Turning down a narrow street to the left, we enter a cul-de-sac which ends in a door bearing the legend *Casa Paco.*

Stepping through the crowded bar, we find ourselves on a vine-roofed terrace, with one side completely open. It gives out on to the circular road which surrounds the town. We are in fact in part of the old city wall, with a fine view by day of the country below. At half of the dozen or so tables we see friends, with hands raised inviting us to join them, and a moment later we are seated with a glass of wine and a saucer of olives in front of us.

Half an hour later we look up to see the mass of the Peña de Oroel sharply defined, lit by a great red globe like some celestial chinese lantern. Another pair of eyes at our table have noticed it at the same time, and a voice murmurs '*Mira esa luna que tu llamas la cosechera*'*. For although they have such lovely harvest moons, they never name them so.

Then, when the simple party is over, we take one last walk up the dimly lit *Paseo* before turning in. And we pause briefly at the *mirador* at the end, to contemplate the heartland of upper Aragon in an unfamiliar light. For there now presides over the Canal de Berdún that moon *que tu llamas la cosechera.*

* Look at that moon which you call the harvester.

5. Canfranc and Tena

The 5,000-foot Somport pass alone would have ensured the strategic importance of this section of the Pyrenees. But this gift of nature has been duplicated, for a mere eight miles to the east runs another pass, the Portalet, only 500 feet higher, and the last below 6,000 feet for 140 miles. The importance of this 'twin' formation was that it enabled an army to cross the range in two columns, and to concentrate with far less delay on the other side than if it had been spread out in a long cavalcade such as Charlemagne led back over Roncesvalles. The two rivers which run up towards these passes are the Aragon towards the Somport, and the Gallego towards the Portalet, but their valleys are known instead as Canfranc and Tena.

Their chief importance lies in their function as through routes, and it is just as well that Canfranc has had this second string to its bow. For its highest and best pastures were taken from it and granted to the citizens of Jaca by Ferdinand the Catholic in 1492, that *annus mirabilis* when so many other things seem to have happened in Spain.

Long before that, however, Canfranc was a route for traffic that was commercial and – in the broadest sense of the term – 'tourist', rather than merely military. There are historians who argue that as early as the eleventh century it was the customs dues on goods passing through Canfranc which enabled Ramiro I and his son Sancho Ramirez to build Jaca cathedral and San Juan de la Peña, and to set about the conquest of the plains to the south. And at the very beginning of the next century, in 1108, Gaston, Viscount of Béarn, built just below the pass, on the Spanish side, the hospital of Santa Cristina, some remains of which can still be seen. We shall be encountering a number of such 'hospitals' in the central Pyrenees: the term here means an inn – the French *hospice*.

The travellers for whom Gaston of Béarn was providing shelter were the pilgrims to the shrine of St James at Compostela. All pilgrims travelling by road to Santiago from the rest of Europe had naturally to pass the Pyrenees, and if this book only devotes an occasional reference to them, it is because the subject deserves – and is receiving from Spanish scholars – volumes of research by specialists. When first these pilgrims began to visit Santiago the Mediterranean was still a Moslem sea, and the Basques, even two or three centuries after Roncesvalles, were still something of an unknown quantity. So that the passes of the central Pyrenees, and Canfranc in particular, enjoyed a traffic such as they had never known before. Nor have they ever known it since. Once the easier routes at the ends of the range were safer, they became the inevitable choice of most travellers.

The optimistic 1920's, however, when all the world was booming, and neutral Spain under Primo de Rivera was booming most of all, saw an attempt to revive this route. A wonderfully engineered railway, culminating in a tunnel of five miles under the Somport was opened in 1928. But economic depression was followed by civil war, and when the Pyrenean frontier was at last reopened in 1950, railways were everywhere losing ground to 'personal transport'. At the monumental International Station of Canfranc both French and Spanish passport and customs formalities take place entirely on Spanish soil (whereas at Hendaye/Irún and at Cerbère/Port-Bou the two sides of the frontier split the pickings). But although international in function, Canfranc remains local in character. With all its echoing halls, it is but the Marylebone of the Pyrenees, where the local train from Pau connects with the local train to Jaca.

Yet the idea behind the railway was not entirely misplaced. Saragossa is the fastest-growing industrial centre in Spain. Pau, on the threshold of the Lacq natural gas field, is in France second only to Grenoble in the race for development since 1945. The importance of the route between the two can only increase; but it is the road, not the railway, which will mainly benefit.

Nor is the road across the Somport important only as a through route. For when the youth of Pau and of Saragossa think about winter sports, their minds turn at once to Candanchú. This is the name both of a mountain just inside Spain, and of an elliptical valley to which it gives rise, whose slopes are ideally suited for skiers. Although it is possible to stay in Jaca and travel to and from Candanchú each day, there are several hotels beside the main road built after the style of wooden Alpine chalets. From these, which are already well above the permanent winter snowline, a mile-long ski lift carries skiers up a further fifteen hundred feet.

The slopes of Candanchú, when free of snow, make excellent summer pasture. But the valley which owns them is not Canfranc, but the inaccessible valley of Aisa, one of the many areas of the central Pyrenees which is still without a properly made road. Aisa, however, and its associated villages Esposa and Sinués, can be reached by paths; and there are paths, too, along the long strip of frontier land which belongs to Ansó. A good reason for following them would be to visit some of the natural lakes, here known as *ibones* (possibly from *iba*, a French medieval word for water). The largest hereabouts, only just on the Spanish side of the frontier, is the Ibón of Estanes.

A path on the other side of the main road called the Canal de Roya would enable a traveller on foot to reach the 'twin' valley of Tena. By road the journey is five times as long: through Jaca, almost into the little industrial town of Sabiñanigo conjured into prosperity by French capital, and then up the sandy flats of the Gallego through the market town of Biescas. The most important village of the upper Gallego is Sallent, right at the head of the valley. Here is the Spanish customs post for travellers over the Portalet pass. But the greatest single attraction of the valley of Tena lies at the head of a subsidiary valley which runs off five miles below Sallent.

Attraction may not be the right word, if the visitor has come to the Spanish Pyrenees specifically to avoid his fellow men. For the Baths of Panticosa are one of their few long-established resorts, being situated, like Benasque and Bohí, on one of those frontiers between two different types of stone, where rain water, heated in deep faults where it has absorbed salts and other substances, can reach the surface again as mineral water. But even those who are mercifully in no need of a cure should take the steep road from Escarilla, beyond the village of Panticosa, to the *balneario*.

The hotels stand beside one of the lakes which are such a feature of the higher reaches of the central Pyrenees (there are over a thousand, all told, on both sides of the range). The circle of mountains around is utterly bare, and it is strange to see little pleasure boats in this grandiose setting at over 5,000 feet. Three thousand metres is the height at which Pyrenean peaks are re-garded as really 'making the grade', and two of those looking down upon the Baths of Panticosa come into this class: the Argualas at 3,061 metres and the Infierno at 3,076 metres. And out of view beyond the lakes of Brazato, right on the frontier, rises the lordly Vignemale, to 3,298 metres, all of 10,820 feet.

6. The Valley of Broto: Ordesa

At Biescas a good road leaves the valley of Tena and climbs painfully up to the pass of Cotefablo, through a short tunnel at the top, and down past Linás de Broto where a couple of hotels cater for summer visitors into the valley of Broto. Turning right, the village of Broto itself, with some half-dozen hotels, is only a couple of miles downhill.

The river on which it stands is the Ara, but as usual this has not given its name to the valley. And if we follow it fifteen miles downstream we shall see why, for we reach a narrow gorge which marks where the Ara glacier once melted. This defile, the Garganta de Janovas, effectively cuts off the upper valley of Broto from the lower valley centred round Boltaña. It probably also marked the limit of Moslem rule: Boltaña was probably for a time under the Moslems of Barbastro and Huesca, whilst Broto almost certainly was not. And from the tenth century, we know that the valley of Broto came under the ecclesiastical jurisdiction of the Bishops of Aragon, so that although geographically it belongs to Sobrarbe, it has always looked at least as much towards Jaca.

If instead of turning right for Broto we turn left, a steep climb will soon bring us to the village of Torla. Many previous writers about the Spanish Pyrenees have heaped every possible abuse on Torla, describing it as miserable, filthy and consisting of hovels. Perhaps they were merely trying to emphasize the 'classy' character of the inn where they eventually all found lodgings: the Viú. For mine host there was none other than the Marquis of Viú, and these writers have given pathetic accounts of how the noble family of Viú had been reduced to taking lodgers into their palace.

It all made a good story, but one must speak of Torla as one finds it, and I find it very much like many other places in these long central valleys. The road today runs round the edge of the village, and although one sees a Fonda Viú advertised, this has no connection with the Marquis, any more than another guest house run by a branch of the Viú family during the summer, deep inside the valley of Ordesa. One begins to realize that the Marquis may only be the most eminent amongst a widespread family in the

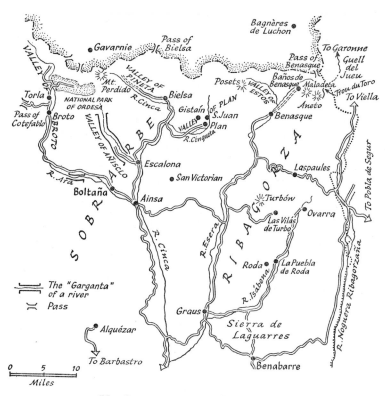

V SOBRARBE AND RIBAGORZA

district. And then one recollects passing a hamlet called Viú, on the road between Linás de Broto and Torla, and one wonders whether the word, so strange when first seen written, does not simply mean 'old', in this frontier land between French and Catalan and Castilian.

But when one starts to enquire for the Marquis-hotelier, one learns that there is no longer either a Marquis or a hotel.

'It was the grandfather who used to receive guests,' said the woman whom I had stopped to ask the way there. 'And he was the last to have the title. The house is still there' – it is indeed, with a fine coat-of-arms at the gateway, and a covered gallery looking down on the entrance courtyard – 'and it is the widow of the old Marquis's son who lives there now. But if you want to see what a *casa señorial* looks like, come and have a look at mine. The Casa Castillo is just as noble as the Casa Viú, our furniture is as old, and our stone floors are better!'

Unwittingly I had stumbled on the other leading family of Torla, who were evidently just a little peeved that for a hundred years every visitor had told the world of their Viú rivals, and none had referred to them. So I gladly followed Señora Castillo under her stone coat-of-arms, through a pleasant patio and upstairs.

She took me first into her dining-room, where a beautifully carved wardrobe formed one of the walls. Built-in furniture is no prerogative of the twentieth century, for this wardrobe is six hundred years old. Then, our steps ringing out on the stone floors of which she was so rightly proud, she took me to the kitchen. Its great central fireplace still stands intact, although the ubiquitous butane gas is now used for cooking. And beside the fire stood a black oak settle, in which the ingenious carpenter of an earlier age had devised a foldaway table which could be drawn out to allow two people to sit and dine from the one piece of furniture.

An older woman was in the kitchen, helping Señora Castillo with the household chores. In the course of conversation she told me that in her childhood, some sixty years previously, the older peasants of Torla spoke a dialect of their own. As Torla is equidistant between Hecho and Benasque we can surmise that it must have been a patois in which mingled elements both of *cheso* and of *ribagorzano*. We can be sure that its precise place, and its significant vocabulary, will be noted by Dr. Buesa, now a don at Seville, but born at Jaca, who spends all his summer vacations touring the central Pyrenees with notebook and tape recorder, talking to the oldest inhabitants.

The church of Torla is new, and even newer is a luxury camping site beside the main road just outside the village. It has every conceivable amenity including a swimming pool, but its greatest attraction is its proximity to the National Park of Ordesa.

To reach this we must turn right over a bridge known as the

Puente de los Navarros, leaving the road which runs on to the hamlet of Bujaruelo, from which it is possible on foot to reach Gavarnie in France by a pass rising 7,481 feet. High though this is, it is the only pass between the Portalet and the Bonaigua below 7,500 feet. The characteristic of these central Pyrenees is their unbroken cliff-like face, in which insignificant dents like the Brèche de Roland (reputedly cut by Roland with his sword Durendal) at 9,200 feet, or the Port d'Oo at 9,846 feet are proudly crossed by mountaineers who rightly derive almost as much satisfaction in doing so as if they had reached the summits which rise a mere 500 or 1,000 feet above these 'passes'.

From the Puente de los Navarros the road climbs steeply up the valley of a tributary of the Ara called the Arazas. Until Ordesa was declared a National Park in 1918 it was generally known as the valley of Arazas, and it must then have been even more remote than, for example, the upper valley of Plan today. Even five years ago it was often spoken of but little visited. But it has now been well and truly discovered, and on a fine day in August – and most days in August are fine in this part of the world – there are always several cars climbing up to the Casa Oliván, and a steady stream of hikers and picnickers on the footpaths beyond.

The Casa Oliván, once simply the forest guards' headquarters, but now also serving light refreshments, marks the end of the metalled road. The *Refugio Nacional,* a hotel owned and run by the Tourist Ministry as part of their excellent chain of *paradores,* is reached much earlier, at the very entrance to the valley. But it stands at the end of a drive, a couple of hundred yards from the road, so that visitors wishing to enjoy both comfort and solitude, with glorious views up and down the valley of Broto and of the circumscribing peaks, need have no fears that the noise of traffic will disturb them. And in any case the last of the cars and the motor coaches will have dropped down to Torla or Broto soon after sunset, leaving Ordesa in its secular stillness. For no camping is permitted in the Park, and the only visitors allowed to stay there are those who have taken rooms at the *Refugio Nacional* or the *Hospedería Viú* farther in, or who have in fact climbed right beyond the limits of the park, to spend a Spartan night at the mountain refuge of Goriz, on the slopes of Mount Perdido (known to the French as Mont Perdu).

To reach Goriz, their route is in its earlier stages the same that

14. View towards peak of Biciberri

15. Looking down the valley of Arán: to the left Salardú, to the right Uña, in centre Gessa, and in background part of massif of the Maladeta

16. Viella, capital of Arán

17. The twelfth century
'*Ecce homo* of Mig Aran'

less energetic visitors will follow. For the first couple of miles the river's course is fairly level, and the accompanying path runs through virgin woods. It becomes much steeper as it passes three waterfalls, each with special characteristics indicated by their names: the Cascada del Estrecho with a narrow channel; the Cascada de la Cueva or del Abanico which conceals a cave and is shaped rather like a fan; and the Grados de Soaso in which the water falls in a series of broad natural steps so regular as to appear artificial. These 'steps' being passed the visitor has reached Soaso, a wide bare cup of land with a level floor, a little reminiscent of Belagua at the head of Roncal, but as might be expected with more abrupt sides. And two miles farther still, where these sides eventually close, the river Arazas descends from Mount Perdido in the last and loveliest waterfall of all: la Cola del Caballo, the horse's tail.

And here I shall leave our visitor, munching his well-earned *merienda* and gazing up at the white water as it splays down into Soaso. He will not be quite alone, but he will not be troubled by all the crowds who set off with him from the Casa Oliván 5 miles and 1,500 feet below. There are climbs beyond Soaso over the crests into the valleys of Añisclo and of Pineta. And there is a particularly fine path running at 6,000 feet in *corniche* along the southern cliff of the Park, which is said to give wonderful views of the main range to the north. Even in these exotic regions one will be lucky to catch a glimpse of the rare ibex, the *cabra hispanica*. It is now protected, but over the years it has well learnt how to protect itself, and it is only the forest guards who know when and where to locate the last representatives of the species.

As I have never taken any of these wilder paths myself, I can only recommend those interested to make full inquiry in Ordesa before setting off along them, or better still, to get in touch with the authorities mentioned in the Appendix.

7. Sobrarbe

'para los siglos IX y X . . . de Sobrarbe no nos ha llegado docu-
mentación de ninguna clase. De aquí que haya sido campo
adecuado para toda clase de fantasías históricas'. Jose María
Lacarra *Aragón en el Pasado*, the historical section of *Aragón*,
published privately by the *Banco de Aragón*, Zaragoza 1960.

Again and again when reading accounts of the history of Spain
one is told that whilst the Asturians were rallying round Don
Pelayo and his family, the Christians of the Pyrenees were also
developing a centre of resistance in the kingdom of Sobrarbe, of
which the capital was Jaca, and which was the precursor of the
kingdom of Aragon. I have seen historical atlases, published under
perfectly reputable auspices, which on the map entitled 'Europe in
the year A.D. 800' show a 'Kingdom of Sobrarbe' in a distinctive
colour – like Guatemala or Bulgaria on a modern atlas – with Jaca
marked in heavy type and given a square dot like other ninth-
century 'capitals' such as Aix-la-Chapelle, Cordoba, and Constantinople! And my copy of the *Guide Bleu* refers to the grotto
of the Virgen de la Cueva on the Peña de Oroel, where *'d'après
la tradition, 300 gentilhommes proclamèrent en 724 l'indépendance
chrétienne et fondèrent le royaume de Sobrarbe, origine du royaume
d'Aragon'*.

As one gets to know the central Pyrenees more intimately, this
'tradition' becomes more and more puzzling, until one wonders
whether it is not simply historical hearsay which has been often
repeated and never examined.

The truth – as I see it – is that Sobrarbe as a geographical expression is quite distinct from Aragon. Whereas Aragon, in the
original restricted sense of the term, is the Canal de Berdún with its
adjoining valleys and sierras, Sobrarbe is the valley of the Cinca
with those of its affluents. And whereas the natural capital of

162

Sobrarbe

Aragon stands where the river Aragon reaches the Canal de Berdún at Jaca, the natural capital of Sobrarbe stands where the Cinca is joined by its most important tributary, the Ara, at Ainsa.

These combined streams offer a reasonable route up from the plains, and far from being the first part of the Pyrenees to be liberated from Moslem rule, Sobrarbe was almost certainly the last. The far north-eastern corner of Sobrarbe, the valley of Plan, seems to have come under the rule of the Counts of Toulouse at the beginning of the ninth century, and from then onwards was in contact with the bishops of Seo de Urgel. The mind boggles at the route which must have been followed by the ninth-century priests of Pan, San Juan, and Gistaín as they went to take charge of their parishes: from Urgel over one of those terrible tracks through San Juan de l'Herm or Les Llacunes, across that region around Laspaúles which until only a few years ago was still *incomunicado*, and finally from Benasque up the Val d'Estos and over the 8,200 foot Col de Gistaín!

But the rest of Sobrarbe was liberated neither by its own efforts, nor by the Counts of Toulouse, nor by the Aragonese, but by the kings of Navarre, and in particular by Sancho the Great (1004–35). Ruling all the way from Leon to Ribagorza, he deliberately aimed to prevent Aragon from expanding towards the south (although it too formed part of his dominions), and the stronghold which he established at Santa María de Buil, a few miles south of Ainsa, was held by the Navarrese and not by an Aragonese garrison.

Sancho the Great's death in 1035 marks a watershed in Spanish medieval history. For by dividing his territory amongst his four sons he not only set Castile, Navarre and Aragon on their individual and independent paths, but also gave them each a vigorous dynasty from his own loins. Saint Ferdinand of Castile, Sancho the Strong of Navarre, and Alfonso the Warrior of Aragon were all his descendants. The fourth dynasty, however, was short-lived, for Gonzalo, to whom had been given Sobrarbe and Ribagorza, died within two years, and these territories were at once incorporated into Aragon by his brother King Ramiro I. And from 1035 to 1037 was the only period of independence that Sobrarbe ever had. All the rest, from the 300 noblemen on the Peña de Oroel in 724 to the neat and tidy 'Kingdom of Sobrarbe' of the ninth century –

complete, no doubt, with civil service and adult male suffrage – are simply what Dr. Lacarra calls 'historical fantasies'.

Ainsa, the capital of Sobrarbe, should not therefore be approached with reverence for a past greatness which it never had. But it should be visited all the same, leaving the two good restaurants and a few shops beside the Cinca, and climbing up to the old citadel. The church, still technically ranked as a collegiate church, is pure Romanesque of the early-twelfth century, with a fine doorway. But the castle, away to one side of the huge *plaza mayor*, is in ruins, and there is little to see of a palace of the kings of Aragon which used to stand inside its walls. And if one is prepared to walk a mile and a half beyond the castle, along the plateau between the Cinca and the Ara, one can visit the so-called Cruz de Sobrarbe, a medieval cross said to mark the site of a battle.

Ainsa was no doubt the site of many different engagements. For it is at the junction of four important roads. Apart from the road down from Broto through Boltaña, and the road up from Barbastro, there is a good gravel road over the little pass of Foradada. This last leads from the valley of the Cinca into the valley of the Esera, or in other words from Sobrarbe into Ribagorza. Travelling along that road I had my only view of the Monastery of San Victorian, five miles away at the base of the Peña Montañesa. I was unable to visit it, for I was a lonely male amidst a coach-load of hearty girls from the *Consejo Superior de Investigaciones Científicas*, and they were in search not of monasteries but of mountains.

San Victorian was the religious centre of Sobrarbe, and although no documents earlier than Sancho the Great refer to it, one is assured that besides its re-built eighteenth-century church, containing sixteenth-century *retablos*, it shows traces of ninth-century construction. San Victorian himself is supposed to have arrived in this remote region from Italy in the first-third of the six century. We have the example of Fortunatus, who wandered around behind the sixth-century iron curtain before settling down as Bishop of Poitiers to prove that a few people could and did get around in the early Dark Ages. Nevertheless San Victorian's settlement in this inhospitable march between *Francia* and *Gotia*, and the ninth-century construction of the monastery named after him, remain in my own mind as not proven.

The fourth road from Ainsa is the road up the Cinca, deep into the complex of lonely valleys which make up Sobrarbe. It deteriorates after reaching a long *garganta* called the Desfiladero de las Devotas, and lurches from one side of the Cinca to the other across improvized bridges which are swept away each winter. But before we reach this *garganta* another road leads off to the left at Escalona, to follow the river Vellos. Where this is joined by a stream running down from the remote village of Fanlo it is best to leave car or coach, and to proceed on foot. For we are entering the valley of Añisclo, a long gorge cut like a knife in the soft rock. This little-visited valley of Añisclo is in fact one long *garganta*, and demonstrates as on a diagram the formation of those level terraces, left when the river has channelled out a lower bed, where in a warmer climate villages would automatically have been sited.

Just beyond the Desfiladero de las Devotas, on the other hand, we encounter the opposite phenomenon to Añisclo: a valley which throughout its length has been subject to glacial action. This is the valley of the Cinqueta, which is almost as big a stream as the Cinca into which it flows. Its valley, known as either Plan or Gistaín from its two most important villages, is to my own taste the most rewarding in eastern Aragon. And it is probably the most remote centre of population in the Spanish Pyrenees. For it is set too far back from the main range – here at its highest – for anyone to use it as a route to France. And although the gravel road along the Cinqueta has a good surface, it is narrow and winding and passes through a number of tunnels.

But once this road has been negotiated we find ourselves in the glacial 'bucket' formed by three smaller converging valleys, where at 4,000 feet – half as high again as Hecho or Ansó – three little villages have successfully practised a pastoral economy since before history in this part of the world began. Their inhabitants, the *chistavinos*, speak of declining population, and lovely old houses in San Juan which are falling to pieces seem to bear them out. But actual figures show a drop of not more than twenty per cent between 1900 and 1957; whereas there are villages within fifty miles which have lost up to half their numbers. Señor Violant y Simorra, in his lavish volume *El Pirineo Español*, wrote some undeservedly harsh words about the *chesos* (the inhabitants of Hecho), which brought down upon his head the wrath of my friend Don Veremundo Méndez. But his remarks about the *chistavinos*, by contrast, are kind indeed.

'Spending a few days in the pleasant company of that good-hearted people, one is borne back to the patriarchal life of the old times, almost legendary, of the Golden Age. Of the same make-up as the *chistavinos* are the *ansotanos*, in the other, the western extreme of the same Aragonese Pyrenees. Here, in the valley of Gistaín, one can say that the Aragonese race begins and the Catalan comes to an end.'

The Golden Age was no doubt a more technologically simple one than our own. Beyond the village of San Juan a group of us climbed a hillock, to see as far as we could in the direction of the Hospital of Gistaín before turning back. It was then that we caught sight of two women in a small field. Each had leaned a slab of slate against a wooden chair, and in the hot sun they were beating these slabs with the meagre sheafs of rye so that the grain fell to the ground. It was an even more primitive method of threshing than I was later to see at Bohí, where a pair of horses, harnessed to a rotating wooden bar, walked round and round treading the corn. For that was threshing with the horses' hooves, but this was threshing with the human arm. We talked with them for a while, and learnt that here too a Pyrenean dialect had survived. As we turned away a girl from Barcelona addressed me in a tone of Catalan superiority.

'To see them you would think that we are still in the Middle Ages! Surely the village could have combined to buy just one little machine, which could be taken round each of these little pocket handkerchiefs of fields in turn, to do in half an hour the work which it will take these women all day to finish? And if they must do it this primitive way, then why do they wear those heavy black clothes? At least they could have the sense to put on bikinis!'

Returning down the Cinqueta to where it ends its independent existence at Salina, where a little salt is still produced, and turning right to continue our journey up the Cinca, we find the road no better than it was lower down. It comes as a surprise when about four miles later we reach Bielsa, something of a metropolis with its seven hundred inhabitants, two hotels, and café. This inaccessibility of Bielsa enabled the Republicans to defend it for months on end during the Civil War, long after the Nationalists had overrun the rest of the region.

'We had plenty of supplies to start with,' I was told by a man who had been in the 'Bolsa de Bielsa' during its long siege. 'And when they had run out, we lived on the cattle. But we had to give up eventually, because we had run out of ammunition. So leaving everything behind us, we all of us – soldiers, women, children, and old people alike – struggled up the Puerto de Bielsa* and into France. When we at last reached the station of Arreau we saw a train in the sidings. It was full of ammunition destined for us, but los *c**ñ*s hadn't let it come through.'

'Did the French put you in a camp?' I asked him.

'Oh, no! We simply went round the other way, re-entering Republican Spain by Figueras.'

This siege explains why much of Bielsa was burnt, and why I was puzzled by the church, which is obviously modern outside, but seems ancient within. Another architectural aspect of the village which puzzled me was the roofs of many of the houses, which are covered with wooden tiles. I learnt that there are slates underneath, and that the layer of wood is designed simply as a protection against the cold.

Bielsa is not the last inhabited place before the tragic pass. There are Chisgües and Parzán; and two and a half hours' march farther on, at 5,300 feet, a mountain refuge at the foot of the crescent of mountains known as the Circo Barrosa.

And then there is the valley of Pineta. For many, this is the supreme experience of the central Pyrenees. Pineta is the name given to the upper valley of the Cinca, beyond Bielsa. A good gravel road climbs steeply as far as the hamlet of Javierre (yes! the Basques were here, too), and past a reservoir into a perfect, almost level glacial valley. Its broad 'U' stretches for eight miles into the mountains, past sanatoriums, and beyond Espierba, the last hamlet, with only seven households and twenty inhabitants. Where the road ends easy paths wind alongside the young stream as far as a few summer *bordas* beside an ancient chapel with a crudely carved window.

Here, where Harold Spender and his companions sheltered for a day and a night in 1897, there is always a detachment of Civil Guards, ready to go to the rescue of anyone lost on Mount Perdido, whose white slopes close in the end of the valley. We are only a few miles as the crow flies from Soaso over in the valley of Ordesa. But between lies some of the most uninviting country in the whole range, on the high, north facing slopes of the Marboré.

* 8,087 feet.

The Aragonese Pyrenees

'This corner of the Pyrenees appears Siberian rather than Aragonese,' writes Solé Sabaris, and Violant y Simorra describes it as the most snowy part of the Pyrenees, with a lake which is frozen all the year round.

But there is nothing inhospitable about the valley of Pineta below this kingdom of Jack Frost, as one picks one's way amongst the woods beyond the chapel on a summer's day. Indeed, so bright and strong is the light that the plants themselves sometimes have to seek protection. Looking down, one may be surprised to see as red a plant which one had thought was always coloured green. This is no optical illusion, but a development of red pigment against ultra-violet rays. It is a phenomenon found amongst many species in the high mountains, and varies with height, with the season of the year, and with the quality of the light.

8. Loarre and Alquézar

Nine hundred years ago the two most compact and exciting little states in Europe were deliberately planning the conquests to which their own efficiency so clearly entitled them. Their rulers had certain things in common. Both were illegitimate. Both had had a hard struggle to unify their states a generation earlier. And both were good churchmen, who did all they could to encourage the stricter Cluniac order in their monasteries. Moreover, the conquests which they both planned were successful. But there the resemblance ends. For it took Duke William of Normandy only four years to quench the last spark of Anglo-Saxon resistance in England. But fifty-five years elapsed before the great-grandson of Ramiro I of Aragon entered triumphantly into Saragossa.

Nevertheless it was the eventual capture of Saragossa which King Ramiro had firmly in mind when he called the Council of Jaca in 1063. For although summoned for the consecration of Jaca cathedral, the establishment of a see at Jaca was specifically regarded as provisional, until the occupation of the true capital of the diocese, Huesca, 'today overrun and destroyed by the pagans'. There were nine bishops and archbishops at the Council from all over southern France and northern Spain, together with the Abbot of San Juan de la Peña. But what was Paterno, the bishop of Saragossa, doing amongst them? Some historians have argued that he was a Mozarabic bishop, a Christian bishop under Moslem rule. But why, then, was no Mozarabic bishop of Huesca present? A more daring, and a more intriguing theory is that Paterno had been given the title because in due course the see of Saragossa would belong to the king of Aragon, to appoint whom he wished. King Ramiro, then, from his Pyrenean eyrie was lifting his gaze beyond the small mountain kingdom which he actually ruled to the major state over which his great grandson would preside.

His vision was justified. Since the death of the last Ommeyad Caliph of Cordoba in 1031, Moslem Spain had split into a score of small kingdoms called the *taifas*. But these *taifas* still had a certain common interest in opposing a Christian advance. The Castilians, it is true, faced little opposition at first as their columns moved south across the deserted lands of La Mancha and the Sierra Morena. But the Aragonese faced what amounted to a Moslem Maginot line. Deep in the rear were the two great cities of Lérida and Saragossa, on which depended a more advanced chain of towns: Tudela, Ejea, Huesca, and Barbastro. Protecting these, and at the same time supplied by them, were a series of strongholds in what we have already described as the sub-Pyrenean sierras. These strongholds had first to be taken before the Aragonese could ever break out from their mountains.

For Aragon had developed around the Canal de Berdún precisely because this was so easily defensible, and the same geographical reasons were going to make it difficult to launch an offensive from there against the south. Just as Sobrarbe had been so long under Moslem occupation because the Cinca valley lay more open to the south, so it was now the Cinca valley which offered most hope for Aragonese expansion. And thus it came about that King Ramiro lost his life in this same year 1063, whilst trying to capture Graus on the Cinca's tributary, the Esera.

Graus at last fell twenty years later, in 1083; but already in 1070 Ramiro's son, King Sancho Ramírez had secured two other vital positions, Loarre and Alquézar. With these two fortresses on the southernmost flanks of the Pyrenees in Aragonese hands instead of warding off the Aragonese, the conquest of the plains below was as inevitable as such things can ever be.

From the castle which he built at Loarre we can gaze down at those plains, stretching away beyond the Cinco Villas in one direction, and towards Lérida in the other, just as his garrison, and the College of Augustinian canons whom he established there in 1071 must also have gazed out over their promised land. And the Moslems down on those plains must have looked up with foreboding as the clean white walls and towers took shape.

As we ourselves drive up from Ayerbe we may find it harder to discern them. For not only is Loarre in ruins, but its walls, although as clean as ever, are no longer white. During nine centuries the castle has become such an organic part of the hillside that we are less than a mile away before it dissociates itself as a recognizable artefact from the dry green and grey sierra.

The road though steep is not impossible, and once up there we can walk all round the double curtain wall, thus seeing the castle at its best, with the whole mass of fortifications against the skyline, as in the photograph reproduced in this book. To see inside the Romanesque chapel, with its great nave, it is necessary to make enquiries in the village of Loarre below, and to pick up there not only the key, but the guide who has charge of it. One's first and last impression of Loarre must be wonder, not only wonder at its position, but wonder at its early date. None of the castles of King Stephen's robber barons, which Henry II pulled down so easily all over England seventy years later, can have been remotely as powerful as this.

This architectural advance obviously owed much to the experience gained in building Jaca cathedral and San Juan de la Peña. But there is a hint of other technical sources in the authorities who see Arab influences in the sculpture of the capitals of Loarre's chapel.

For in extending their kingdom, Sancho Ramirez and his descendants were altering its character. As we continue from Loarre towards Alquézar we shall pass near to the small town of Bolea, built on a hill which is crowned by a fifteenth-century collegiate church with a vast sculptured *retablo*. The guide is a heavy, swarthy man, agreeable, but unshaven, with an intense but materialistic – indeed, blood-curdling – devotion to Our Lady of the Pillar in Saragossa. He outlined to me in considerable anatomical detail just exactly what he would do to anyone who dared to harm *la Pilarica*. Neither his racial type nor his superstition would be found north of the great red basalt stacks called the Mallos de Riglos, where begins the climb to the cool clear air of upper Aragon.

On my way down from the church with him, we stopped to sample some of the wine and olives which are Bolea's main crops, and I reflected how the northern limit of the olive almost exactly corresponds to the northern limit of Moslem settlement. As that grand old lady Doña Sancha urged on the Aragonese rearguard at the gates of Huesca, she was fighting with history, but against geography.

And thinking of her made me realise a further difference between the rulers of Aragon and of Normandy in the eleventh century, whose positions in many respects were so similar. For William the Conqueror died alone, and his sons fought each other, imprisoned each other – and perhaps killed each other – for his inheritance. But the little that we know for certain of the royal family of Aragon tells us that they were a devoted team. Trouble with their nobles they had, like all other early medieval rulers. The Moslem danger was never more than a few miles away to the south. But the family itself, fathers, sons, sisters, and aunts, pulled together, and were prepared to surrender a monastic life, or themselves in marriage, for the future of Aragon.

A maze of country roads at last brings us to Alquézar, the southernmost place to be described in this book. Its very name is Arabic, its Roman origins as *Castrum Vigetum* being quite overlaid, and its houses too, huddled together on a hill amidst the olive groves, could easily belong to a village of Andalusia or North Africa. One wonders who first gave it the title 'the key of Sobrarbe'. For it was the key to a Moslem Sobrarbe for two or three centuries, but the key to a Christian Sobrarbe for only thirty years, until the fall of Barbastro in 1100.

It was one year earlier that Alquézar's collegiate church was consecrated under the rule of King Pedro I, Sancho Ramirez's son and successor. For like Loarre and Leire this was in the Spanish tradition of fortified palace-monasteries which was to culminate in the Escorial. The fortifications of the castle still date from the turn of the eleventh and twelfth centuries, and the entrance porch is a very early example of *mudéjar*, built, that is, by Moslem workmen under Christian rule. Of King Pedro's church, however, part of the cloister has alone survived, with just three Romanesque capitals.

Let it not be thought, however, that the sixteenth-century church which replaced it is without interest. On the contrary, Alquézar is one of the unknown treasures of Spain. It seems incredible that with thirteen million tourists crossing the Pyrenees in 1964, such a treasure should remain so little visited. It was almost lost during the Civil War; but although the Republican troops burned much of the extensive library of documents, their government sent Alquézar's most valuable contents to Geneva for protection. For the front line was not far away: Huesca remained in Nationalist hands throughout the war.

Loarre and Alquezar

The church is late Gothic, but the *retablo* of the high altar, although also of the sixteenth century, is Baroque. And an earlier and more unusual merging of styles is shown by a huge wooden crucifixion in a side chapel. It is a beautiful and a moving sight without any artistic or historical glosses, but this lovely sculpture of the early thirteenth century is also a unique example of the transition between Romanesque and Gothic in the plastic arts. It stands in a dark corner, and the priest of Alquézar illuminated it for me with a candle on a long holder, which brought out depths in the features with shadows such as no other light could have cast.

The sacristy of Alquézar deserves a chapter to itself. It contains all the finely worked vestments and all the plate – including a silver reliquary of the twelfth century – which a wealthy community collected over centuries. So I shall limit myself to the mention of two *retablos*. One was painted during the fourteenth century by an artist whose name is forgotten, but whose style can always be recognized. He is known as the Maestro de Arguis, and his happy colours and his delightful figures are reminiscent of the pictures of Fra Angelico in the Convent of San Marco in Florence.

The other retablo was painted in the fifteenth century by Juan de la Abadía, a disciple of the great Catalan *retablista* Jaume Huguet. Aragon and Catalonia had become united politically when Count Ramón Berenguer IV of Barcelona married Petronella, the only daughter of King Ramiro the Monk, the brother of Alfonso the Warrior, in 1151. It is satisfying to see that this marriage between two very different states, the Mediterranean, outward-looking Catalonia, and the unsophisticated, landlocked Aragon, produced artistic as well as political fruit, and that something of Aragon's prodigious outpouring in the eleventh and twelfth centuries returned after many days.

9. Ribagorza

The proposition that Aragon and Catalonia were very different states would be challenged up in the Pyrenees, which extend to both. And nowhere more so than in Ribagorza, which in many minds is associated with Catalonia, although in fact it lies almost wholly within Aragon.

There are two reasons why there should be confusion about the position of Ribagorza. In the first place it has given its name to a river, the Noguera Ribagorzana, of which the valley is therefore often regarded as the axis of the whole territory. But it was in reality the frontier rather than the axis, as it still is the boundary between Aragon and Catalonia, and it was given this name to distinguish it from the Noguera Pallaresa, a river which pursues a parallel course between ten and twenty miles to the east.

Both Nogueras are of similar force, and both empty themselves into the Segre, but there the resemblance between them ends. For the Noguera Pallaresa, with half a dozen lesser valleys dependent on it, and with long stretches of level land around Esterri de Aneu, around Sort, and above all in the Conca de Tremp was predestined to form the basis of a well-defined region – Pallars.

The very name Ribagorza, on the other hand, probably means 'craggy heights and chasms'. And the only considerable valley leading off the Noguera Ribagorzana, that of the Noguera de Tor, or of Bohí, never belonged to the counts of Ribagorza, but either to the counts of Pallars, or to the independent lords of Erill.

The two rivers which are more essentially 'Ribagorzano' than the one which bears the name are the Esera and the Isábena. But these are tributaries of the Cinca; and during the ninth, tenth and eleventh centuries, when Ribagorza was attempting to establish itself as a member of the Spanish 'heptarchy' alongside Galicia, Leon, Castile, Navarre, Aragon, and Barcelona, the Moslem lines ran from Graus on the Esera through Laguarres and Lascuarre on

Ribagorza

the Isábena. The Moslem positions therefore prevented easy communication between the three valleys of Ribagorza, which run like thin veins through a tangle of difficult country. Until the construction a few years ago of the road from Castejón de Sos on the Esera to Vilaller on the Noguera Ribagorzana there were a score of hamlets around Laspaúles, between the headwaters of the three valleys, which had never seen a wheel.

It is therefore not to be wondered at that Ribagorza, as a viable political entity, never really got off the ground. That it ever tried to lead an independent existence was due to two familiar factors. The first was the facts of geography. The second was that decisive Carolingian intervention which was both the most important and the most exciting event in the history of the Spanish Pyrenees.

The one made possible the other. Although the highest peak in all the Pyrenees, the Aneto, rears its 11,168 feet squarely within Ribagorza, the passes across the watershed are here very slightly lower than in Sobrarbe. They have certainly always been regarded as practicable, even if strenuous routes. This is shown by the existence of the now empty Hospital of Benasque at the headwaters of the Esera, below the 7,930-foot pass to Luchon, and of the still-functioning Hospital of Viella at the headwaters of the Noguera Ribagorzana, below the 7,500-foot pass over to the valley of Arán.

And so it came about that in that moment of awakening soon after the year 800 – some quarter of a century after the abortive expedition through Roncesvalles – Ribagorza took the same step as Aragon, Pallars, and Barcelona, and threw off Moslem domination with help from the Christian Empire to the north. This help in the case of Ribagorza, however, came not directly from the Emperor, but from his nephew Saint William, Count of Toulouse. This nuance meant that Ribagorza was never directly incorporated in the Spanish March which became the basis for the state of Catalonia.

In a way, it suffered all the disadvantages of being connected with the Franks, without any of the solid benefits derived by the territories farther east. As we shall see when we visit the cathedral of Roda, the counts had difficulty in establishing their independence, but little help from their would-be overlords when attacked by the Moslems of Huesca and Lérida. And Ribagorza never really recovered from the last of those attacks in 1006, led by the son of the great Almanzor – he who sacked the shrine of St. James at Compostela. The last act came in 1025, when on the excuse that his wife was a member of the ruling family, Sancho the Great of Navarre occupied Ribagorza, thus making it the far eastern province of his dominions. It has shared the political fate of Aragon ever since.

After Petronella of Aragon married Ramón Berenguer of Barcelona in 1151, Ribagorza became one of the most important feudal baronies in the enlarged kingdom of Aragon which resulted, and its sons played important parts in Aragonese history. None more so, perhaps, than Berenguer de Entenza, who if he had not been killed in Thrace in 1307 would today be better remembered than Roger de Flor as a leader of that fantastic Catalan expedition to the east, which shook the Empire of Constantinople. The men whom Berenguer's wise counsels had saved from destruction beside the Bosporus lived to found the Duchy of Athens, of all the 'Frankish' states in the eastern Mediterranean the most curious. For it violently juxtaposes two of our most cherished mythologies, the classical and the medieval: bold bad barons clanking in armour through Periclean temples.

Berenguer de Entenza belonged to the Catalan section of a family from Ribagorza which had divided into both an Aragonese and a Catalan branch. And this dual character of a border country is reflected in the *ribagorzano* dialect. Violant y Simorra says that this has only survived amongst the elderly, except in the hamlet of Bisaurri where it is spoken by young people too. So I brought the subject up over an earthenware jar of wine in *El Covarcho*, an attractive bar in Benasque which had only opened in the summer of 1964. Not only the earthenware jars and cups, but the wooden chairs and benches, the panelled walls, and the leather-bound cattle and sheep bells which decorated them were so 'primitive' that they could only have been thought up by a very up-to-date young man indeed.

The proprietor was in fact in his early thirties, and at once denied that there was any tendency for *ribagorzano* to die out. His own children could speak it; and to let us hear what it sounded like he called some instructions to his assistant. Someone from Barcelona told me that they could follow the gist of what he was saying, and *ribagorzano*, as might be expected, is the nearest of all the Pyrenean dialects to Catalan. They, all of them, whether from

19. Aynet de Besan, a village of the Valferrera in Pallars

18. Bonaigua Pass, looking south into Pallars

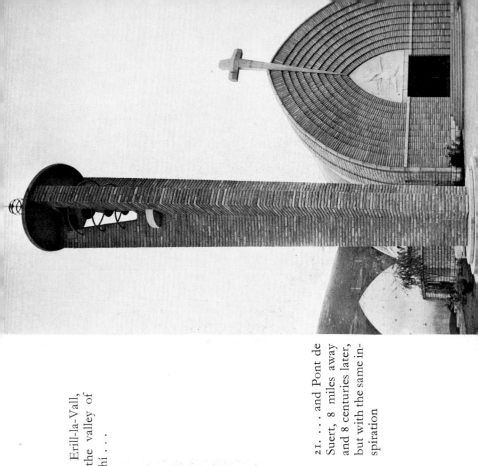

20. Erill-la-Vall, in the valley of Bohí . . . .

21. . . . and Pont de Suert, 8 miles away and 8 centuries later, but with the same inspiration

the north or the south of the range, have more in common with each other than with Castilian, that violent innovator, and one of the earliest troubadours could sing in provençal:

> *'Tota Basconn' et Aragons*
> *E l'encontrada delz Gascons*
> *Sabon quels es aquist canczons'**

though the people of his *Basconn'* were surely not speaking Basque! The traditional costume of Benasque, too, which was seen in 1787 by Ramond, first and greatest explorer and writer of the Pyrenees, seems to have been a cross between the French revolutionary fancy dress which occasionally appears at Sardana festivals, and the more sober appearance of the ancients of Ansó.

Benasque, the capital of upper Ribagorza, although its population now runs well into four figures, is the very last village at the head of the Esera valley. Its charm must have lain in its Shangri-la quality: a little world on its own after the 62 long miles up from Barbastro, through the narrow *garganta* called the Congosto de Ventamillo, or after the steep climb across the pass from Bagnères de Luchon. But it has been discovered by the French, and 75 number plates from Paris, and 31 number plates from Toulouse outnumber the HUs of Huesca during the summer months. Work is proceeding apace on a road to Luchon, due to be opened in 1966, and this will effectively deprive Benasque of such isolation as it still has.

Ten years ago, when Robin Fedden, encamped in the Val d'Estos or below the Maladeta, would drop down to Benasque to replenish his supplies, this isolation must have been almost complete. From now onwards until we leave the Noguera Pallaresa behind us, we are in the country which he has immortalized in *The Enchanted Mountains*. Whatever this book has to say about Ribagorza, Bohí, Arán, or Pallars is merely in the nature of footnotes on aspects of these districts which that wonderful book does not seek to cover. To read *The Enchanted Mountains* is to step through a magic casement into these loved highlands, whether we already know them or not. *Cras amet qui nunquam amavit: quique amavit cras amet.*

---

* 'All the Basque country and Aragon and the country of the Gascons know what that song is.' From *The Poem of Sainte Foy*, written in the second half of the eleventh century, probably near Narbonne.

Though Benasque today may be rather less likely to invite one to weaken and stay the night, the country around it is as lonely and as lovely as ever. There is as yet no road worth the name up the Val d'Estos, leading up towards the 11,047-foot Posets. It was somewhere in the shadow of that peak, so the proprietor of *El Covarcho* told me, that a bear found comfortable winter quarters for the winter of 1963–64. They never see a bear in this region nowadays, nor did they see this one. But passing that way in the spring, they could see where he had been, one of a dwindling race whom some number as few as forty, and no one numbers higher than a hundred.

Rather more frequented is the track up to the Baths of Benasque. This is best tackled on foot or (as I travelled myself) in the back of a lorry. Like Panticosa and Caldas de Bohí, Los Baños de Benasque are not quite as the Romans left them. But their modernization has been on a smaller and more tasteful scale, and purely as a holiday centre they would make a good base for exploration of the little-known valley of Valibierne to the south of the Maladeta massif; and right up the infant Esera, beyond the empty Hospital*, and behind the north face of the same massif to the Renclusa refuge hut.

A little way beyond the Renclusa lies one of the wonders of the Spanish Pyrenees. In the section on Ansó, we have seen that the valley of the Esera is unique in still possessing, though in attenuated form, the glacier which once carved it out. But the Aneto, highest peak of the entire range, on whose north face that glacier lies, gives birth to another and a greater river than the Esera, a river which empties itself into the Atlantic, after gathering into its waters at least three tributaries of greater volume than any stream we shall cross between Cabo Higuer and Cabo Creus. These other waters of the Aneto, gathering force south and east of the headwaters of the Esera, find abrupt tranquillity in a pool known as the Trou du Toro. From there they follow a subterranean passage longer than the man-made tunnel of Viella, to reappear two thousand feet lower down, and on the other side of the watershed. But we must await our visit to the valley of Arán before we attend this rebirth of the Garonne.

* Although the Hospital de Benasque is now empty, admirers of J. B. Morton's *Pyrenean* will still find the frontier guards there.

10. The Valley of the Isábena: Roda

There is one other spa in Ribagorza besides the Baths of Benasque. This is at Las Vilás de Turbo, beneath an almost perfect cone of a pre-Pyrenean mountain called Turbón. At one time it was approached up the valley of the Isábena, within whose catchment area it lies, but the road which now links this remote *balneario* to the outside world joins the main route along the Esera at Campo.

This means a few less visitors still to a valley which has at no time received many. But the peasants of the Isábena shrug their shoulders. They are inured to disappointment, for they have had a thousand years of it, from the great Moslem raids of 908 and 1006 right up to the depopulation of the present century. And beyond this stoicism they have the built-in fatality of dwellers in a dry land.

This aridity strikes the most casual traveller as he drives up from Graus, or from Benabarre over the red sierra of Laguarres, from whose heights the Moslem watchmen for three centuries looked towards the defiant white peaks of Christendom. The valley of the Isábena is almost treeless, and such few bushes as do grow are stunted. Even the blackberries bear only a wizened and horny fruit.

There is little need to ask whether any dialect has survived. The dialects – and I employ the plural deliberately – are in constant use. At Serradúy *'nem a diná'* will be an invitation to 'come to dinner'. But two miles down the road at Puebla de Roda the same injunction will vary to 'nem a disna'. And another two miles up the hill, at Roda itself, the *rotense* form of the same phrase will be 'nem a comé'. *Rotense*, if you please! A separate language for some sixty people whose only water supply is from the rain water drained into the cloister well by their cathedral's roof.

We are back at the water problem. Why should this valley be

179

so dry, when other valleys to east and west are worth damming to provide reservoirs and hydro-electric power? The answer is that the Isábena, alone amongst major Pyrenean rivers, rises not in the main chain, but in the pre-Pyrenees, where annual rainfall has already dropped below 1,000 millimetres – less than half that of the high peaks. As a result its *caudal* – that expressive word which can be used either of a man's fortune or of a river's volume – is a fraction of that of the Cinca or of the Nogueras.

This has always been true. But a millenium ago, before deforestation was complete, the valley may have been relatively a little richer than it is today. And situated as it was in the heart of their territory, it was here that the counts of Ribagorza chose to make their bid for ecclesiastical independence from the bishops of Seo de Urgel, and from the great metropolitan sees to the north of the Pyrenees.

The story of the diocese of Roda, a little-known by-way of early-medieval history, has recently been charted by a French scholar*. It divides neatly into two acts. In the first, the newly independent counts of Ribagorza were trying to set up their own bishopric – the status symbol of the Dark Ages – just as newly independent countries today insist on setting up their own airlines. The first bishops were itinerant, like the early Celtic bishops, and probably travelled from one to another of the big monasteries of Ribagorza: Ovarra, Alaón, and Lavaix. Then Count Ramón the Pious endowed a cathedral at Roda in 957.

The bishops of Seo de Urgel did everything possible to oppose this loss to their own diocese; and when Abd-el-Malek occupied Roda in 1006 and captured Bishop Aimerico, its independence seemed to be over. For leaving a nephew as hostage, poor Bishop Aimerico was reduced to trudging round France to beg the money for his own ransom. When he eventually returned to Ribagorza he made no attempt to re-establish himself at Roda, and accepted the fact that he was no more than a suffragan of Urgel.

But then in 1025 Ribagorza was occupied by Sancho the Great of Navarre, and soon after his death became part of his son Ramiro's dynamic new kingdom of Aragon. There began the second act in the story of Roda. For the kings of Aragon regarded suspiciously Roda's connexion with Seo de Urgel, as giving oppor-

* Jacques Ducos *Un diocèse espagnol des Pyrénées centrales: Roda de Isábena.* Imprimerie du Petit Commingeois. Luchon, 1964.

tunities for Catalan interference. The bishops therefore found their position almost as difficult as before, but for quite different reasons.

One of them, Bishop Ramón (1104–26), the most famous of all the bishops of Roda, evidently decided like many later clerics that the best way to get on with the top people was to join in their sports – especially when these mainly consisted in fighting the Moslems. So he joined in that light-hearted expedition with King Alfonso the Warrior which penetrated all the way to Malaga. Perhaps this was one reason why he was later canonized.

The solution to the problem of Roda, however, followed like so much else from the marriage of Princess Petronella to Count Ramón Berenguer. The interests of Aragon and of Catalonia were thenceforward no longer opposed, and their united forces could advance against the cities of the plains to the south. The question of a new city for the see may have been discussed at the Council of Jaca in 1063, at which Bishop Arnulfo of Roda was present, and three-quarters of a century later the wily Pope Pascal II suggested that Roda was simply the transferred see of Lérida. So when Lérida fell to the combined Aragonese and Catalan forces in 1149, the bishop of Roda moved there, and the 'problem of Roda' was over.

The Chapter of Roda, however, stayed on, and retained a one-third share in the election of the bishops of Lérida. It would have been a pity if they had not stayed on, for a fine new cathedral had just been built for them.

Here lies the glory of the Isábena. The Esera's only important relics from those early years are a few chapels: Vilanova, and Guayente near Sahún; and the pride of the Noguera Ribagorzana, the monastery of Lavaix, is now half-covered by the waters of the reservoir of Escales. But the superb twelfth-century cathedral of Roda stands intact, with a perfect twelfth-century cloister, whilst the tomb of Saint Ramón in the crypt dates from the same period of early Romanesque.

Perhaps it was Saint Ramón, himself a warrior, who saved this lovely building from destruction during the Civil War. It is to him, ever since the thirteenth century, that the people have climbed to pray for the rain to return to their ever more desiccated valley. And the Republican troops were only persuaded not to burn the cathedral when they learnt that the *rotenses* depended upon the catchment of its roof for their water supply.

A century before, Roda had suffered more seriously during an earlier civil war. Not from the Carlists, but from their enemy the liberal minister Mendizabal, who was responsible for that typically 'progressive' measure, the confiscation of church property. Some idea of the treasure which had accumulated in remote Roda is given by the fact that fourteen mules were required to take the gold and silver away down the Isábena, leaving the poor valley poorer still.

Some objects, however, were too bulky for such summary removal down stony tracks, and these now constitute the nucleus of a museum in the Romanesque cloister. There is a folding chair of Arab craftsmanship in an oriental wood. It is known as 'the chair of Saint Ramón', but it in fact belongs to three hundred years before his time, to the ninth century. There is another much larger chair, a bishop's throne of the thirteenth century. Then there are a number of paintings which show the weak but familiar features of Philip IV, and of various members of his family. They are so familiar that we wonder if they can be copies of those great originals in the Prado. But we learn that they are genuine enough, though from the workshop of Velázquez rather than by the great courtier-painter himself.

Roda must have had a moment of prosperity in the seventeenth century to acquire such paintings. For the portico in front of the main door (itself slightly later than the immense Romanesque interior) is also of seventeenth-century date. Standing there with the priest of Roda, a genial and highly cultured Friar Tuck in spectacles, I heard what the hard life of the dry Isábena valley did to its inhabitants.

'They are slaves to an ungrateful soil,' he said. 'It is the earth itself which anyone who lives here must fight, even if their work is not directly connected with the land. The schoolteachers, lively girls from nice homes in the towns, never stay in these *pueblos* for more than a year – their first after leaving training college. And even in that time a little of the drag of the soil begins to deaden their step and to sadden their features.'

I wanted to ask him how he, a man with an education far beyond theirs, could survive for years on end, without the schoolteachers' long holidays to look forward to. He evidently sensed this, for he went on:

'These girls, of course, have not chosen to come here. I myself used to be Principal of the Seminary in Lérida, and when I had to resign through ill-health, I deliberately chose to come up here because of the dry mountain air. The work is lighter, I am feeling better in health, and I am enjoying my researches into the cathedral's archives. But I took good care to buy a Citroen *dos caballos*, so that I can meet my fellow-priests up and down the valley two or three times a week, and we can keep our minds working with good conversation. By the way, although the cathedral may have nothing by Velázquez himself, it has a masterpiece by a much older Old Master.'

I followed him into the cathedral and past the steps leading down to Saint Ramón's tomb. He turned a key and we entered a long, narrow chapel which for some centuries had served as the treasury. He struck a match, and where the whitewash had been removed from the apse I saw for the first time the firm colours and masterly line of the greatest artist of the Spanish Pyrenees.

'The *Pantócrator*, Christ in glory, has disappeared, and these two paintings which stood on either side have only survived in part. If you've been up in the valley of Bohí you can imagine what the complete apse must have looked like.'

'I haven't yet. But I've seen slides. This isn't by . . .?'

'Yes, it is. The experts agree that they can only be ascribed to one man, whose name we can never hope to know. The Master of Tahull.'

The Isábena has yet another Romanesque monument in the ruins of the monastery of Ovarra, which stand across the river from where the road ends at the entrance to a gorge. Work is proceeding on a continuation of this road to link the valley of the Isábena up with that of the Noguera Ribagorzana near Vilaller. But at present anyone visiting Ovarra must make the twelve-mile journey from Roda on purpose, and afterwards return on his tracks.

The unsteady footbridge across the river is worth risking, for the Isábena, low though its *caudal*, is cold even in summer as one approaches its sources. Many of the monastery's walls are still high, and the eleventh-century church is still roofed over, with a Virgin of perhaps two hundred years later standing lonely on a dusty altar. And a hundred yards away from the main group of buildings a small, rectangular Romanesque chapel, locked up but evidently in perfect condition, could perhaps tell us of the very earliest moments of Christian resistance in Ribagorza.

Interlude at Hecho, a village of the Aragonese Pyrenees

The first important affluent received by the river Aragon after it turns right at Jaca is the Aragon Subordán. I have never been given any convincing explanation of this name. As the distance from its source to Puente de la Reina where the two streams join is little less than the distance from Puente de la Reina to the source of the Aragon itself, it may be that both streams were regarded as alternative beginnings of the Aragon, and that the suffix Subordán was added simply to distinguish one from the other.

Those who live in the valley of the Aragon Subordán would be the last to deny such a possibility. They claim that it was down their valley rather than over the Somport that the pilgrims used to travel to St. James of Compostela, and even that Charlemagne passed by Oza and Siresa instead of by Roncesvalles.

Agriculturally, certainly, it has every advantage over the narrow valley of Canfranc, with its succession of rather depressing villages squeezed out along the main road, or perched uncomfortably high up the sides of the circumscribing mountains. There is in contrast a note of cornucopic plenty about the whole valley of the Aragon Subordán, from the cornfields around Javierregay right up to the Selva de Oza, with its trees ever felled yet ever growing. Nor is there anything mean or straggling about its villages.

There is, however, a significant variation in the atmosphere of them as one proceeds up the valley. The first village one comes to, on a hill to the right, is Javierregay. Its name may be Basque, but in every other quality it is as drowsy and listless as the other villages of the Canal de Berdún. 'Yes, other tourists have told me that the name is Basque,' a woman will tell you, 'but there have never been any Basques here to my knowledge,' and the weedy cobbled *plaza* where she stands, and her tousled hair and burnt complexion prove her point. The next village, Embún, has a rather more withdrawn quality, corresponding to its position all by itself on the other side of a bridge. But to find a true mounttain village one must go right up to Siresa, the last inhabited locality of the valley, where the cold dark stone and the cold air can chill the bones even on a September evening.

Between Embún and Siresa lies Hecho itself. The valley is indeed generally known simply as the valley of Hecho, and its largest village is rightly regarded as something more than a mere *pueblo*. 'La villa de Hecho' is the twin of Ansó. But it is an unequal twin. Everything about the two corresponds, but nothing corresponds exactly. The dialect of Hecho, known as *cheso* – of which we shall have more to say later on – is, like *ansotano*, a relic of the ancient Aragonese. But although the two valleys understand each other perfectly, an inhabitant of one can never pass himself off as being from the other. And the dialects are not only different, but are in a different state of degeneration. This is an unhappy word, but it is the one used by the speakers themselves, and both would agree that the degeneration has proceeded further in the case of *ansotano*.

But whereas, as we have seen, more than a score of the older *ansotanos* still wear their traditional costume every day, the last *cheso* to do so died in 1960. And although sheep and timber are the principal wealth of both valleys, they are of unequal importance in the two economies. Ansó is best represented by its shepherds and their flocks, and the whole valley, joined to the outside world by only the narrow Foz de Biniés, shares some of the shepherd's isolation and reserve. The spirit of Hecho, on the other hand, can be seen in the lorries piled high with timber, squeezing their way down from Oza, or in the conversation of the driver of one of those lorries who has just returned from delivering a load. At the bar of *El Costero* or of *El Navarro* he will describe what the weather was like at Bilbao the previous day, and compare it with that of Valencia where his work took him only last week.

Perhaps it is merely accidental that I have met or heard of a number of *chesos* in other parts of Spain, but have never yet encountered an *ansotano* off his native heath – though official figures support this impression, showing a 25 per cent drop in Hecho's population during the first half of this century, against a mere 10 per cent in that of Ansó. And this more outgoing spirit is paralleled by a greater willingness to encourage visitors. Ansó, as we have seen, is now trying to induce outside interests to build a hotel. But Hecho's *Hospedaje de la Val*, conveniently situated on the edge of the village with a view up the valley, is already a going concern.

This contrast between the two valleys has a geographical foundation, as indicated in the section on Ansó. No narrow gorge like the Foz de Biniés separates Hecho from the outside world, and the *chesos*, proud as they are of their *patria chica*, are less tempted to regard themselves as a world apart. A form of the *cheso* dialect has survived in Urdués, in a subsidiary valley of the Aragon Subordán, and certain words are still in use as far down as Embún. Both these and the strange-sounding villages of Jasa and Aragüés del Puerto, however, are quite independent of Hecho, although Urdués has merged its timber interest with those of the larger centre in a *Mancomunidad Forestal*. The actual *municipio* of Hecho includes only Hecho and the hamlet of Siresa, whose dwindling numbers (today less than a hundred) send two councillors to the *ayuntamiento*.

Siresa, though humble today, was once the home of kings from whom perhaps came the name of *Camino Real* given to this particular route to Compostela, following an old Roman road from Aquitania to Caesaraugusta, and the name of Puente de la Reina given to the bridge over the Aragon where the valley of Hecho joins the Canal de Berdún. In the early ninth century, when the struggling county of Aragon consisted of no more than the two valleys of the Aragon and the Aragon Subordán, Siresa was its natural heart, sufficiently deep in the mountains to avoid Moslem attacks. And here rose one of those great monasteries which played so important a part in the Dark Ages.

In 848 it received an illustrious visitor in the person of Saint Eulogio. He was full of praise for its hundred monks who 'shone throughout the West for the exercise of regular discipline', for their virtue and their knowledge. And he bore away with him to Cordova a number of books unknown in Southern Spain, and joyfully received by the Mozarabic Christians. These included works of St. Augustine, Virgil, Juvenal, Horace, and Porphyry, together with a rich collection of Catholic hymns.

The monks of Siresa no doubt owed their 'regular discipline' to the movement for monastic reform initiated by Benedict the counsellor of the Emperor Louis the Pious (who achieved more in the Spanish Pyrenees than his father Charlemagne, for it was he who captured Barcelona in 801). Their learning, too, must be regarded like that of Leire as a gleam of that 'Carolingian Renaissance' on which some modern scholars have poured such scorn. A few other scholars, pre-eminent amongst whom is Mr. Wallace-Hadrill, have continued to argue that much of the real Rome survived in the West, and survived only in the West. Certainly the books taken by Saint Eulogio to Cordova show that cultural currents in medieval Spain were not all in one direction – as is claimed by those who seek to prove that the Provençal courts of love were hatched in the harems of *al-Andalus*.

Siresa in ninth-century Aragon corresponded therefore to Leire in ninth-century Navarre. Both were palace-monasteries enjoying strong connections with the empire of *Francia* to the north. But the very year of Saint Eulogio's visit, 848, was the year when the parish church of San Caprasio was built at Santa Cruz de la Serós. The Canal de Berdún was now incorporated into Aragon, and with this and every succeeding extension of territory Siresa would be left further and further from the centre of things.

The kings of Aragon did not forget Siresa, however, even when their cavalry was probing down the Cinca towards Barbastro, and when their garrison at Loarre was threatening the plain of Huesca. For the surviving monastery church of San Pedro was not built until 1082 on the orders of Sancho Ramirez. And the whole court must have continued to visit the valley, for at Hecho was born his grandson Alfonso the Warrior, the conqueror of Saragossa.

Despite this royal background, it is as proud republicans that one always thinks of the *chesos*, who in their devotion to Aragon and to the greater Spain lose none of their pride in their *patria chica*. Given that one valley in the Spanish Pyrenees was destined for independence, one wonders why the choice had to fall on Andorra, which shares a language with the adjoining provinces of France and Spain, which has no genuine regional costume, and which has no monument comparable to the great church of San Pedro de Siresa. For Hecho with its own language and its own dress has everything which Andorra lacks, and more besides. There perhaps lies the answer: apart from the fact that the *chesos* have never even dreamed of wanting independence, there would be a fundamental inequity in adding to all they already possess.

Andorra, with its villages at between 4,000 and 6,000 feet in the dry eastern Pyrenees, is essentially poor. It would today be facing a bleak future indeed if it were unable to cash in on the touristic and other advantages of its curious political status.

Hecho, at only 2,700 feet and with substantially greater rainfall, has been able to earn a good living in this century as in any century. And this is reflected in the *chesos'* open-handed hospitality and in their picturesque but solid and spacious houses.

Some years ago the Civil Governor of the province of Huesca was an Andalusian who – perhaps in nostalgia for the bright white streets and *patios* of his homeland – gave orders that every house of every village in the province should be whitewashed. His command was certainly not carried out to the letter. Presumably hamlets in remote districts which he was unlikely to visit turned a blind eye, although whitewash was just what some of those earthy little *pueblos* in lower Aragon needed. And in the years since he left new buildings have gone up and the coats of whitewash have often peeled away. In some villages, notably in Ansó, the idea was a misconceived disaster, hiding their true Pyrenean character. But many of the houses of Hecho must surely always have been white. At least it is hard now to imagine them otherwise; and it comes as a disappointment to leave the brilliantly white *plaza*, and the steep cobbled streets towards the river, whose houses are all white save for their great bare corner stones, and to find as one penetrates towards the main road at the back that there are still two or three lanes in their natural state. The stones of Siresa, too, are very much as they left the quarry, which perhaps helps to make it appear so run-down by comparison with its 'capital'.

Perhaps Hecho acquired this fresh face to the world when it was rebuilt after the French had burnt much of the village at the end of August, 1809. It has another striking architectural feature. For although the covered chimney with a little 'roof' of its own to keep out the snow is found in many villages of the high Pyrenees, and of mountain regions everywhere, in Hecho it seems to have assumed an independent life, sometimes almost dwarfing the house from which it grows. Wherever one looks one sees one or more of them, each with six or eight window-like vents under its beehive hat.

Like Ansó, and like other villages when they are sufficiently prosperous, Hecho has its own miniature welfare state. The doctor is appointed and paid by the *ayuntamiento*, just as are the schoolteachers, and medical treatment like education is a free service to all *vecinos*. The excellent new school, built after the same pleasing and traditional style as Ansó's cinema, contains, incidentally, something unusual in Spanish villages – a lending library. The chemist, too, is appointed by the village, and dispenses from a shop, scrupulously clean and well-equipped within, whose quaint exterior would serve as a set for a film of one of Jane Austen's novels. And as for the barber, not only is he obliged as in Ansó to give every *vecino* a free weekly shave, but his shop is itself in a corner of the ground floor of the town hall!

It is in the town hall that many of the traditional *cheso* costumes are now kept, although there are others still in the possession of the families who a generation or two ago wore them daily. Now they only come out at special times, and more especially when Hecho celebrates its fiestas of 'the Virgin of September' (to distinguish her from 'the Virgin of August', another manifestation of Our Lady celebrated three weeks earlier). The fiestas last for five days from 8th September, and include fireworks, music by local and imported bands, competitions of pelota, of clay-pigeon shooting, and sometimes even of chess, and a *novillada*, or bullfight using younger bulls not yet fully grown. It is as well that only young animals are employed, for, to quote a recent official programme of the fiestas, 'in this fight there can also take part local *aficionados* who have fulfilled the legal requirements and who ask the mayor's permission with twenty-four hours' notice'.

There is nothing second-rate about Hecho's bullfight in its particular category. But talking of bullfights in *pueblos* reminds me of a true story about a village much smaller than Hecho and much poorer. 'Four magnificent bulls have been purchased for our *corrida*', read the poster of its fiesta, 'but for reasons of economy the fourth bull will be a cow.'

The most simple and even childish game at the fiestas – which perhaps for that very reason I personally enjoy the most – consists in stretching a rope high across the *plaza*, from which hang a dozen or more earthenware pots of various sizes. One by one people are then blindfolded and given a cane some twenty feet long. With this they hit out, wildly or cautiously according to their temperament, in the hope of breaking one of the pots. Sometimes one of these – though no one knows which – is filled with coins. But even without this additional excitement the antics of the protagonist inspire immense enthusiasm and laughter.

As recently as 1952 according to an old programme in front of me, the competitions included dancing of the *jota*, but the only *jotas* which I saw in 1964 were performed by a professional team from Saragossa. I was told that very few *chesos* today know the steps of that great dance of Aragon, although at one time many of the valleys cherished their own individual variants, with corresponding tunes.

But of more modern dancing there is plenty. I was about to write ballroom dancing, but that is hardly the word, for the 'ballroom' is the central *plaza*, between the church and the town hall. I danced there one evening under the stars with a girl who proved to be the only *ansotana* at the fiestas of Hecho, and I was thus able to make some first-hand enquiries about the relations between the twin villages. They were not as strong as I anticipated. She herself had only scrambled over the hills with her brother and two of his friends because her sister lived in Hecho, having married a *cheso*. My partner's brother-in-law, she told me, had met his wife when a few years earlier he too had scrambled in the reverse direction to the fiestas of Ansó. But such marriages between the two villages were rare: she only knew of three others. However, with the population of each being a little over a thousand, and with no direct road over the six miles between them, four personal unions is perhaps about as many as one can expect. And I later discovered that the young man who taught at the little primary school at Siresa was an *ansotano*, who each weekend sped off on his moped to cover the forty miles by road to his home five miles away.

It is at the very beginning of the fiestas that the traditional costumes reappear. And since they are so little seen nowadays, let us at least rejoice at the excellence of their presentation. For they are worn by the Queen of the Fiesta and her four Maids of Honour, all chosen for their beauty. Beauty would be an inappropriate test for the *cheso* cavaliers who ride proudly on horseback beside her open carriage, but there is obviously a test of some kind, for they are manly figures, who yet seem proud to be going through some form of initiation. And this is the case, for the task of escorting the Queen is entrusted each September to the four or five young men who during the following year will leave Hecho for their military service.

Interlude at Hecho, a village of the Aragonese Pyrenees

There is no need to give a detailed account of the clothes of either the girls or the men, for a photograph is reproduced elsewhere in this book which give a clearer picture than a long description. One point of interest is that most of them were produced entirely within the valley. The men's white socks were knitted with wool spun from the fleeces of the *cheso* flocks, and the thick green dresses of the women were woven from yarn drawn from the same source. They were even dyed green on the spot with pigments which were at least partly of local origin. The most important article of clothing purchased from the outside world was the men's broad brimmed felt hat, and one of the difficulties faced by the ten old men of Ansó and Fago who still wear this daily is its replacement, now that this particular headgear is no longer in regular production.

The fiestas last for five days, and end with a *merienda típica de hermandad*, a traditional brotherly picnic in a field outside the village called Las eras del D'echo. There, *con pan y vino*, is consumed the meat of the bulls killed the previous day, *guisada a la pastora*, prepared as by the shepherds. As I shall later be inviting the reader to assist at a similar agape farther up the valley, I shall not enlarge on this happy occasion. The field where it takes place, however, besides being the theatre for the fiesta fireworks and clay-pigeon shoots, is of interest for two other reasons. For its name, Las eras del D'echo, allows us to see the derivation of that puzzling word *cheso* which describes anything to do with the valley or its inhabitants. From *echo* they began by calling themselves *echesos*, and from *echesos* the transition to *chesos* was a short one. As for *las eras*, these are the thrashing floors, which are still in use after harvest.

The very fact that one can speak of a harvest points to one of the great differences between this village and Ansó, whose economy is so pastoral that even the vocabulary of agriculture seems out of place there. Ansó is about a hundred feet higher, and there is perhaps slightly less level land in its valley, but the real difference is psychological and historical.

Historical? Ansó owns all the frontier pastures from the border with Navarre as far as the Somport – an '*ansotano* corridor' cutting Hecho off from France. Both villages assert that this is no accident; that 'a war' of some sort took place at some date in the past; that Ansó was 'loyal', whereas Hecho was 'with the rebels'; and that as a direct result Hecho's best pastures were taken from her and given to her rival.

The bare facts of this story are the same whether one hears them beside the Veral or beside the Aragon Subordán. But there is a delicate shift of emphasis. Whereas 'loyalty' on *ansotano* lips evokes almost Churchillian images of Cavaliers giving their all for their king, 'the rebels' with whom the *chesos* claim association seem to have combined a whole spectrum of noble nonconformities from Carlism to upholding the Rights of Man. There may be something in the story, for the parish of Ansó certainly looks a funny shape on the map. But at present I rather tend to put it in the same category as the assertion of the old lady with whom I once had digs in Fuenterrabía. Sweeping her arm out over the Bidassoa in the general direction of Bordeaux and Paris she used to proclaim: 'In the old days all that belonged to Spain.'

But although Hecho grows a certain amount of crops, they are all locally consumed: the valley's export trade lies elsewhere. And although Ansó has the better grazing lands, Hecho is not without its pastures, with flocks which provide a few shepherds with a full time living.

I met one of these, Isidro by name, up near the forest guard's refuge halfway between Siresa and Oza. He was not what one could call a natural shepherd, for it was three-quarters of an hour before I could get a word in edgeways. He was obviously starved of an audience, and even if I had not spoken Spanish I think that the flow of words would have been the same. He told me that at sixty-four he was beginning to feel in his bones the many damp nights he had slept in the open as a young man. He and his dog were obviously good friends, and he evidently felt his isolation, telling me that he only got to Jaca twice a year.

'Let alone Jaca, it's not so long ago since he only came down to Hecho twice a year,' they told me in the village. 'But he made the most of it when he did. One of his two visits used to be at the fiestas, and no one knew how to get as drunk as Isidro did when he wanted to!'

The wealth of Hecho, however, lies neither in its agriculture nor in its flocks, but in its timber. And the greatest concentration of timber lies twelve miles above the village, in Oza.

For the first two miles after Siresa the road up the valley is

Interlude at Hecho, a village of the Aragonese Pyrenees
surfaced with asphalt, and even when this gives out the going
remains fairly easy until beyond the *casa forestal* where I met
Isidro. Then the climbs become steeper and the corners sharper,
and presently the road passes under the first of three short tunnels
in the rock.

The Aragon Subordán has become a mountain torrent, cascad-
ing downwards over the stones, and the road has to climb in
order to keep its level above the water. And now, for more than
a quarter of a mile, it is a mere ledge between the torrent on the
right and the rocky cliff on the left. It is wide enough for two small
cars to pass each other, but one must hope on entering the defile
that a heavy lorry bearing tree trunks down to the sawmill is not
at the same time entering it in the opposite direction. This defile
is sometimes called the Boca del Infierno, the Mouth of Hell, and
we who have passed so many *desfiladeros* and *congostos* in our exploration of upper Aragon at once recognize it as the *garganta* of
the Aragon Subordán.

The defile once passed, however, we find ourselves, as at
Belagua and Zuriza, at the edge of a small plain surrounded by a
wide circle of mountains. And up the slopes of those mountains
in every direction stretch the trees of the *selva* or forest of Oza. Oza,
like so many other place-names in the Pyrenees, is of Basque
origin, but its significance for the *cheso* of today is as the hinter-
land of his *patria chica*. Oza stands in the same relationship to
Hecho as does Lapland to Stockholm, or as the American West of
a century ago to New York.

'I did enjoy my visit to Hecho,' you may remark, and you will
at once be asked, 'But did you get as far as Oza?'

'I haven't seen Javier this week. Is he in Jaca?' someone may
enquire at Hecho, to receive the reply, 'No. He's staying up in
Oza.'

For although it lies nine miles beyond the last permanent
habitation, at Siresa, Oza is not lacking in animation during the
summer months. Here, as in so many other lovely places in the
Pyrenees, is a children's camp, where boys from the towns enjoy
each year a taste of mountain peace and mountain air. Camp is an
inadequate description of this group of solid white buildings
completed by a flagstaff and a chapel.

There are other campers of a less-organized variety. The provincial tourist brochures state that there is a camping ground at

Oza for fifty tents. This is probably just about the number that the level stretch of ground between the road and the stream would take. But there are none of the toilet blocks, showers, and so on which go with a commercial camping site, and there are unlikely to be more than a dozen families at any time between late June and early September thriving on an open-air life beside the Aragon Subordán. Half of these, surprisingly enough, are usually Dutch. They are able to buy their supplies from two equally seasonal bars, the owners of which bring up groceries, bread and fruit by van. One of these bars has already received the pine panel, wine-cask-into-table treatment which has made *El Costero* the most attractive bar in Hecho, for the same man owns both. The other is more genuinely rustic, with trestle tables and benches on the green-sward, and is run by a friendly soul who has one of the two shops-cum-bars of Siresa. 'In the summer he practically lives up in Oza,' they say of him in Hecho.

His most regular customers are the *parejas* of Civil Guards, the only visitors to Oza who are not seasonal. Even in the summer time hangs heavily on their hands, and their winter vigils along this quiet frontier belt must be long indeed. They are generally only 'destined' to these more remote stations for their first eighteen months after training, and are then transferred to more populated and congenial areas. Some even achieve the ambition of every Civil Guard under thirty whom I have met: to join the mobile traffic police who patrol the main highways of Spain on powerful motor cycles.

The *parejas* are sent off on duty down to Oza for twenty-four hours at a time, but the barracks where they are based, the Refugio de la Mina, is a few miles farther up the Aragon Subordán. The road there, the continuation of the one we have already travelled, runs through dense woods until it comes to an end and 'dies' at a place called Guarrinza. Walking through these woods the traveller can remark a quality common to all Pyrenean forests: they are extremely silent. Such birds as there are are silent birds – the magpies nesting in chopped-off trunks, the ubiquitous rock swallows; and even the black-cock only utters his characteristic 'cok-cok-cok' at the mating season.

From Guarrinza one must proceed on foot up a now bare valley, although there are still trees halfway up the slopes to the right, with another *casa forestal* – the last building belonging to

Interlude at Hecho, a village of the Aragonese Pyrenees

Hecho – down beside the stream. From this *casa forestal* the barracks of La Mina are in sight some distance farther on but across the river. They are situated therefore not in Hecho but in Ansó, for from Guarrinza onwards all the land on the right bank of the Aragon Subordán belongs to the *ansotanos*, thus giving them that corridor already referred to, which cuts the *chesos* off from France.

Just as Isaba in Roncal wants to build a road to France from the Venta de Arraco, so also the long-term aim of the *ayuntamiento* of Hecho is to construct a similar road from La Mina. There are two possible routes. By driving a tunnel under the Palo pass above La Mina a road could be opened to Lescun. Or alternatively the new road might follow the old route to Compostela, running alongside the Aragon Subordán all the way to its source, and over a gentle watershed to Les Forges d'Abel in France, and so to Urdos and down the valley of Aspe. If one has the time, it is worth-while following this second route on foot, to enjoy the peace of this lovely bare valley, called Aguas Tuertas, before it is broken by motor traffic. One can follow a path all the way to the Ibón of Estanes, and the shepherds one encounters will be either from Ansó or from Fago, which share *mancomunidad* (commonwealth) of pasture, just as Hecho and Urdués share *mancomunidad* of timber.

The Selva de Oza celebrates its greatest day each year to the glory neither of its timber nor of its tourists, nor even of some battle long ago with the circumscribing *ansotanos*. It owes it instead to one of Hecho's greatest sons, Don Domingo Miral, who numbered amongst the achievements of his three score and ten busy years the foundation of the *Universidad de Verano* of Jaca. On 15th August the students of all nationalities following the courses pay their annual visit to Hecho. On arrival those who are Catholics cross the river to hear Mass at the chapel beside the cemetery where Don Domingo lies at rest in his family's vault. Then everyone steps back into the coaches, and the cavalcade continues up the valley.

Mine hostess of the *Fonda Concheta* has been up at Oza with her acolytes since before nine in the morning, and as the coaches emerge from the long defile and disgorge their passengers they are met with a sight which would have brought cheers from the throats of Robin Hood and his Merry Men. Sheltered from the wind in a narrow subsidiary valley great iron cauldrons are steaming away over a huge wood fire. The resinous aroma of the flaming logs would alone draw appreciative sniffs without the added savour of roast mutton at 4,000 feet, five hours after a light breakfast.

Other smells with less power of immediate association indicate that this is to be more than a one-plate menu. And a veritable pyramid of wicker-covered demijohns resting in a shady corner show that there will be no lack of liquid accompaniment to the feast ahead. The images which spring to mind as one contemplates the scene are all of Nordic origin: Valhalla, barbarian camps beyond the Rhine, even the Badger's kitchen in *The Wind in the Willows*. But the Latin location has contributed at least one important element. Oza may be at 4,000 feet, but it is fifty miles south of Nice. When they have collected their first course, *migas*, the Pyrenean shepherd's staff of life, which is best described as breadcrumbs toasted with coarse bacon, the students gratefully move under the trees to escape the full heat of the sun.

By the time that they are ready to return towards the fire to collect the second course they are already settled into the groups where they will spend the afternoon, on rocks beside the stream or stretched on the moss around the bole of some great tree. This course, like the first, appears regularly on the menu of the Pyrenean shepherds when they are up on the high pastures for months at a time, and have to prepare every dish with their own hands, preferably from ingredients which do not have to be carried a long distance. This is indicated by its name, *cordero asado a la pastora*: it is the roast mutton already smelt on arrival, and now done to a turn. Other dishes will follow, cheese and fruit, and all the while bottles of red wine will be circulating, ever and anon returning to the corner of the wicker-covered demijohns for replenishment. Those who are not already asleep will return towards the fire for the last time to collect coffee and *coñac*. And then for a long hour the spirits of the old Basque gods of Oza will receive the silent worship of their prostrate pilgrims, lost in the brief beatitude of a Pyrenean nirvana.

The trees which from the surrounding slopes look down on the proceedings are of three kinds: pine, beech and fir. To a certain extent the proportion of each varies with the height up the mountainside, but there are hundreds of acres where the three mingle on an equal footing, and there is so much room available that it seems unlikely that the beech will be ousted by the faster-growing coniferous species.

As at Arano, these forests are all common land. But the *Mancomunidad Forestal* of Hecho-Urdués is an altogether bigger enterprise than the plantations of the little Basque village. Not only is the 'territorial base' from which it operates much greater, but it has achieved a large measure of vertical integration. For the *servicio municipalizado* includes two factories, so that much of the timber from Oza can be processed before leaving the valley, and thus provide further work and prosperity for the industrious *chesos*. One of these factories prepares the larger pieces of wood for use as floorboards, scaffolding, pit-props, and so on. The other specializes in plyboard, and even assembles some of the slats thus produced into fruit boxes for transport to the consumers in Valencia.

Prominent amongst those whose enterprise distributes Hecho's timber all over the peninsula is the Aisa family. All its men are easily recognizable for their height, which would distinguish them in Scandinavia, let alone in Spain. But although the present head of the family and his two fine sons are all very tall men it was the grandfather, now dead, whose physique will for long remain a legend. Indeed, an earnest researcher from Barcelona, anxious to prove some anthropological or ethnological thesis in connexion with the settlement of the Pyrenees, found all his averages of the stature of *homo pirenaicus* upset when he came to measure the two metres-and-the-rest of this *cheso* giant.

It was his height amongst other qualities which earned him a career of which the Aisa family is still rightly proud. Whilst he was doing his military service his physique and his bearing led to the offer of a place in the royal bodyguard, where he spent exciting years accompanying the court from one to another of the vast palaces, now museums, but then living centres of government. Amongst other things he saw the end of the Regency when Alfonso XIII was declared of age; and he was with the royal cortège when that monarch's young bride, the English 'Queen Ena', suffered the terrifying experience of having her wedding dress spattered with blood in the assassination attempt against the King.

He is only one of many *chesos* who over the centuries have distinguished themselves outside their valley on the wider stages of Saragossa and even of Madrid. To give a brief idea of the type of men whom one Pyrenean *pueblo* can produce, I have selected just three from the *cheso* roll of honour: a churchman, a don, and an industrialist.

JUAN REGLA was born at Hecho in 1500, in a house of which the owners still bear the same surname. His family was old-established, but not, it seems, very well off at the time of his birth. Destined for the Church, he went to study – just like a *cheso* of today seeking higher learning – at Saragossa. He so distinguished himself in the humanities and in philosophy that even before he had left there his learning was already renowned beyond the boundaries of Aragon.

A man of his abilities could hardly have been born at a more propitious moment, when Aragon and Castile, only recently associated through the personal union of Ferdinand with Isabel, became merged in the far vaster empire of their grandson Charles V. The latter was a figure cast in the heroic mould required by his enormous task. Brought up amongst the Flemings, and transacting much of the business of state in Latin, Charles also had a fluent command of the other four languages of his dominions: Italian (for Naples and Milan), French (for Franche-Comté and the Walloon provinces), German (for the Holy Roman Empire), and Spanish. A famous quip has it that Charles-Quint – for the French had to invent a special ordinal to describe this *stupor mundi* who threatened them from every side – spoke Italian to his mistresses, French to his ministers, German to his horse . . . and Spanish to his God.

The quip at least enables us to appreciate the delicate position held by his Spanish confessor, who in his later years was none other than Fray Juan Regla, now a member of the Hieronimite order. And there is probably some truth in the saying, for when in 1557 Charles V of Germany and I of Spain decided like Diocletian to lay aside the burdens of empire, he chose as his retreat a remote monastery in the Spain which he had last visited thirteen years earlier. Fray Juan accompanied him, and remained with him at Yuste until his death the following year. It is significant that the patron of Yuste, like the patron of the Hieronimite order, was Saint Jerome.

The greatest task which faced Charles V, beyond even that of keeping his empire together, was that of preventing Christendom from falling apart. We know that he was unsuccessful. But the unity of the Church was still in the balance at his death, and there was still some hope that the Oecumenical Council which had been sitting on and off at Trent in northern Italy since 1545 might find some formula to paper over the cracks. For six important months, from September, 1551 to 18th March, 1552, Juan Regla was at the Council of Trent, sent there by his imperial master; and one wonders whether his experience there was translated later into advice to that master's son.

For on death of Charles V, Fray Juan Regla became confessor to Philip II, and remained so throughout those years, so critical for England, when the Spanish king could with ease have crushed his young sister-in-law, *Isabel de Inglaterra*, in the uncertain opening period of her reign.

This *cheso* who had played as a boy in the remains of the palace-monastery of Siresa, and who in middle-age had witnessed those macabre enactments of the imperial funeral before the still-living Charles V at the palace-monastery of Yuste, died as an old man at Philip II's newly-built palace-monastery of the Escorial on 16th August, 1574. His portrait hangs in the sacristy of the parish church of Hecho.

DOMINGO MIRAL was born at Hecho on 18th February, 1872. Like Juan Regla, he was destined for an ecclesiastical career, and as a youth spent some years at the seminary in Jaca. The 'leakage' during the twelve long years of training before ordination is much greater than critics outside Spain believe: no one with any doubts is encouraged to continue, and there was therefore nothing un-usual about Domingo Miral's decision to leave the seminary and to abandon the study of theology. He continued his studies at a school in Tarragona, and at the University of Barcelona, and completed them when he obtained the degree of Doctor in Philosophy and Letters of Madrid.

He began his academic career lecturing at the now closed University of Oñate in the interior of Guipuzcoa, moving in 1902 to the senior University of Spain, Salamanca, where he was elected to the Chair of Greek in open competition.

His heart remained in Aragon, however, and in November, 1913, he seized the opportunity of an exchange to take the Chair of Literary Theory and Fine Arts at Saragossa. There he remained for the rest of his life, becoming in succession Dean of the Faculty of Philosophy and Letters, Vice-Rector, and finally in 1931 Rector of the University. His other activities included the foundation of a *University Review*, and of the Language Institute in Saragossa. In Spain it is not unusual for men at the top of the academic world to take an active part in commerce or industry, and Domingo Miral was for a time associated in the management of *La Crónica*, a leading Aragonese newspaper.

But his most lasting monument, and the one by which he would most have wished to be remembered, is the *Universided de Verano* of Jaca. He would have felt that his dreams had been realized if he could have seen two of his old pupils, then army officers, talking happily together during the Second World War. For the German officer was a prisoner of the British officer, but they recognized each other from the golden days spent together beneath the Peña de Oroel a decade earlier. But he died when the issue of that war was still undecided, on 16th April, 1942, and was buried with his fathers at Hecho, the third *cheso* Rector of Saragossa University since 1586.

LUIS BISQUER was born at Hecho far more recently, for he is only now on the threshold of middle-age. Tragedy struck him early, for his father died when he was only a fortnight old, and at thirteen he set off for Barcelona to make his way in the world. Working in the capital of Catalonia he could soon speak Catalan in addition to Castilian. But he never forgot his own mother tongue – *cheso*.

The day came when he saw an opportunity for going into business for himself in Jaca. He had become skilled in many different branches of engineering during his years at Barcelona, and was at first prepared to turn his hand to whatever work presented itself. When I first met him, in 1951, he was carrying a metal statue of Christ which had been entrusted to him for repair by the priest of a remote country church. And this association with and interest in the countryside where he had grown up never left him, however deeply he was immersed in business. As we were gazing out over the Canal de Berdún one summer evening in 1952 he suddenly exclaimed: 'If only your English manufacturers knew the market awaiting them in Spain for their wonderful tractors! Just try to imagine the number which will be needed between here and Pamplona when our agriculture really begins to get mechanized!'

He then had it at the back of his mind that he might himself one day manufacture agricultural machinery. But as time went by his plans took a slightly different turn. It was six or seven years before I visited Jaca again, and I was as pleased as surprised to find that he had built a fine new factory, where amidst all the clatter and acetylene flames of a modern engineering shop more than a dozen men were busy assembling identical examples of a robust, beautifully finished machine which stood a little below shoulder height.

'I decided that if I was to organize a production line,' he said, 'my product must be something fairly small, of which one simple model could be adapted to a variety of uses, and with a market which was bound to grow within the foreseeable future. What one thing is in demand here in Spain, and indeed everywhere in the world, and increasingly in demand? The answer: housing. So I set about designing a small multi-purpose crane, easily moved from site to site, and from one part of a site to another, and not too heavily priced for the smaller contractors who are responsible for so much of our construction over here.'

During the winter which followed the Spanish government, under the inspired leadership of the brilliant finance minister Señor Ullastres, took a number of hard but brave decisions. The peseta, long pegged at the unrealistic exchange rate of 117 to the pound sterling, was devalued to the level at which it was already standing in the external currency markets. At the same time a ferocious credit squeeze was applied, and much of the paraphernalia of import quotas and even of protective tariffs was swept away at a few strokes of the pen. A healthy but a bitterly cold wind blew through Spanish industry and commerce. Spain's present prosperity, and the fact that the peseta is now one of the harder currencies, owe much to those reforms. But the immediate effects were painful.

When Don Luis greeted me with his usual smile the following summer I could see that he had successfully ridden the storm.

'It's true that orders are down. But overheads here in Jaca are low – I knew what I was doing when I chose upper Aragon to set up an industry. Presently business will pick up, and Spain will be all the better for this little shake-up. The government has done the right thing – the only right thing.'

'We've been much better off in England since we had a similar little shake-up. We all admire your Señor Ullastres. In fact, we call him the Spanish Mr. Thorneycroft.'

'I remember: he's the one who put your bank rate up to seven per cent. For the moment, of course, the Spanish building industry has taken a nasty toss.'

'I've seen the cartoons showing the half-finished skyscrapers in Madrid, which can't get beyond the fifteenth storey because the money's run out.'

'Not only the skyscrapers in Madrid.' He pulled down a large loose-leaf ledger from the shelf above his desk. 'Here we have a company in Valencia, which has gone bankrupt owing me this figure here.' He turned a few pages. 'And here's another one in Malaga, which has gone out of business still in debt to me to this amount.' So he went on. It was a long catalogue: the casualty list of a dramatic change of economic direction, which not even the most wary Trade Protection Society could have guarded against. At last Don Luis closed the last of the 'dead' accounts, and replaced the ledger.

'All told, those bankruptcies have cost me a good many tens of thousands of pesetas in bad debts. And there,' he added with a wry smile, 'you have my personal contribution towards *la estabilización de la peseta.*'

His customers are now no longer limited to Spain. It may be true that certain sectors of Spanish industry are uncompetitive, but Luis Bisquer at least has nothing to fear from any future association with the Common Market. Better still: I have even seen enquiries which he has received from Germany! British industry, as well as Spanish, could do with more men of his calibre.

But it is at Hecho that he is most truly himself, relaxing during a summer weekend on the terrace of the *caseta* which he has converted high above the Aragon Subordán. His wife, too, is a *chesa*, and he has brought up his three children to think of themselves as *chesos*. And during all his travels and experiences he has never forgotten the *cheso* dialect.

This is the nearest living speech to the ancient Aragonese. Like all the romance dialects on the periphery of the peninsula it is in some ways nearer to Latin than is modern Spanish, as in its use of *fablar* instead of the Castilian *hablar* for 'to speak'. It has been fortunate in having thrown up a *cheso* poet, Don Veremundo Méndez, who each year writes an Ode in celebration of Hecho's fiestas, and who regularly contributes a piece of *fabla chesa* to

Interlude at Hecho, a village of the Aragonese Pyrenees

Jaca's weekly paper, *El Pirineo Aragonés*. He and Luis Bisquer are old friends; and it is with the permission of both that I end this interlude with the first few lines of a poem in *cheso* written by Veremundo Méndez as long ago as 1942. Not only will it give the reader an idea of what *cheso* looks like in print, but its protagonist is none other than Luis Bisquer himself.

GUSARAPOS

Bisquer diciba una nuey
de lo diaple gusarapo.
!Qui no ha limpias las truferas,
ye lelo u ye meyo fato!
Yo vos faria la preba,
que so veníu prexinando
y ye remedio seguro,
pa que no'n quede ni rastro;
mas güeno que lo verano,
que ha que'star muito mas malo
y ha dar mas güén resultáu,
que a lo arroz li caye un gallo.
Li preguntemos qué yera,
por qu'hemos plagáus los campos
y lo nos dicié, amonico,
lo que vos digo vociando.
!Ah, lo diaple de Bisquer,
no vos penséz que ye fato!

(These lines were written at a time when the potato crop of Hecho had been attacked by grubs, to which the title Gusarapos refers. A free translation runs:

'Bisquer was talking one night about the devil of a grub. "Whoever hasn't kept clean his potato plants is stupid or half mad. I'll show you what I've thought up and it's a sure remedy, so that not a trace of the grubs remains; better than poison, it's bound to be much worse and to give a better result, just as the rice suits the chicken (in a *paella*)." We ask him what it was, for we had our fields full of the grubs, and he told us very gently what I am telling you out loud. Ah! that devil Bisquer, don't believe that he's a fool!' The poem goes on to explain the remedy, which was to apply the poisonous gossip of the *chesas* to kill off the grubs.)

Part Three

The Catalan Pyrenees

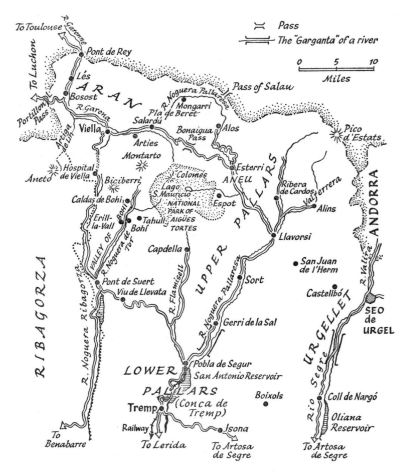

Map legend

⊃⊂ Pass
═╪═ The "Garganta" of a river

0   5   10
Miles

To Toulouse
R. Garonne
To Luchon
Portillon Pass
Pont de Rey
Lés
A R A N
Bosost
R. Garona
Artiga de Lliga
Viella
Aneto
Hospital de Viella
Biciberri
Caldas de Bohí
Erill-la-Vall
Bohí
Tahull
VALLEY OF BOHÍ
R. Noguera de Tor
Mongarri
Pla de Beret
Salardú
Arties
Montarto
Colomes
Lago S. Mauricio
NATIONAL PARK OF AIGÜES TORTES
Espot
R. Noguera Pallaresa
Pass of Salau
Bonaigua Pass
Alos
Esterri
ANEU
Pico d'Estats
Ribera de Cardos
Val Ferrera
Alins
U P P E R   P A L L A R S
Llavorsi
San Juan de l'Herm
Castellbó
Val Llosa
ANDORRA
SEO de URGEL
Capdella
R. Flamisell
Pont de Suert
Viu de Llevata
Sort
R. Noguera Pallaresa
Gerri de la Sal
R I B A G O R Z A
R. Noguera Ribagorza
U R G E L L E T
Río Segre
Pobla de Segur
San Antonio Reservoir
LOWER PALLARS
(Conca de Tremp)
Tremp
Boixols
Coll de Nargó
Oliana Reservoir
Railway
To Lerida
Isona
To Artosa de Segre
To Artosa de Segre
To Benabarre

VI ARAN AND PALLARS

1. The Valley of Bohí

The Noguera de Tor, the river of the valley of Bohí, is a tributary of the Noguera Ribagorzana, and many would describe the valley as belonging to upper Ribagorza. It would require some difficulty, however, to prove that it has ever been directly governed from Benasque or from Benabarre; and its situation to the east of the Noguera Ribagorzana means that for several centuries it has been firmly within Catalonia.

Linguistically, too, we have crossed a frontier. The dialect of Benasque may have some affinity with Catalan, but the people of Bohí talk Catalan pure and simple. 'We speak just the same language as they do in Barcelona or Lérida. Our accents may vary slightly, but there's never any question of them not understanding anything which we say.'

This valley suffers from none of the drought of the Isábena. The Noguera de Tor itself rises amongst the greatest concentration of lakes in the Pyrenees, forever replenished by a series of peaks which include Biciberri, Montarto and Colomés at over 9,000 feet. And its tributary, the Barranco de San Nicolas, rises in the National Park of Aigües Tortes, a green paradise of running waters in the dryest summer.

The track along the Barranco de San Nicolas is one of the best ways into this beautiful park, which in area is several times the size of Ordesa, the other National Park in the Spanish Pyrenees. In theory it is possible to drive right through it, from Bohí across the pass of Portarró, and down past the lake of San Mauricio to Espot, from where a metalled road zigzags down to the level of the main route along the Noguera Pallaresa. This track was opened up in 1959 in a great flurry for a special visit by the Head of State. Then, once Franco had passed through, it was neglected. Trees have fallen, and rain and frosts have worked for several winters unopposed. Parts are practicable enough, and I have heard that the occasional jeep still negotiates a passage, but until the authorities decide to establish this as a regular through route it would be unwise to plan any itinerary which included passing right through Aigües Tortes on four wheels.

We must hope that it is some time before the track becomes a highway, for it is those on two feet that Aigües Tortes would surely most welcome. It offers them three refuge huts: the José María Blanch in the south-eastern corner of the Park, another beside Lake Llong whence issues the Barranco de San Nicolas, and one – I in fact counted three when I was there – beside the Lake of San Mauricio. Outside the boundaries of the Park there is another hut beside the Lago Negro; and two others, beside Lake Clotes, and on the Valarties, lying as they do beyond the watershed belong strictly to Arán.

There is nothing more to be said about this lovely area of forests, lakes, and high peaks. Or, to be honest, everything there is to be said has been said already, and said for ever. I feel guilty of plagiarism merely in mentioning the Lago Negro. Anyone thinking of visiting the country between Bohí, Flamisell, Arán and the Nogueras must read, largely learn, and digest at length *The Enchanted Mountains*.

The author of that beautiful book rightly condemns the 'nastiness' of Caldas de Bohí, the spa at the head of the valley. Many of the smaller Spanish spas have an endearing rustic charm, and apart from their healing waters can offer some of the cheapest holidays in Spain, with the opportunity of mixing with 'genuine' Spaniards. Bohí also, before its two big hotels were built and the road was driven up from Pont de Suert, must have been a charming little backwater. The seventeenth-century spa remains, grouped around a patio of which one side is formed by the still-used chapel. And on the hillside behind are the ruins of the first baths at Bohí, built by the Romans. They are modest ruins and of no special archaeological interest, being very much after the standard pattern of the early Empire, but like Hadrian's Wall or the Alcántara bridge they impress simply by their remote situation. The waters of these Roman baths, with a temperature of 45° centigrade, are still one of the thirty-seven sources in use at Bohí. Another source with a temperature of 26° centigrade has been utilized to create a heated open-air swimming pool – a pleasant feature at 5,000 feet above sea-level.

The Valley of Bohí

The main architectural interest of the valley of Bohí is not Roman, however, but Romanesque. In seeking to describe its quality one is tempted to contradict oneself in speaking of 'classical Romanesque', such is the purity of line of the four beautiful churches in the three villages which crowd together at the head of the valley. Four churches for only three villages? Yes, for one village – the highest and most remote of all – has the two largest churches all to itself. In search of an explanation we are driven once again to postulate a period in the early Middle Ages when the Spanish Pyrenees were at once much more prosperous and much more populous than they are today. For it is only when there are hands to spare from the necessary tasks of daily living that communities can afford to build beautiful buildings – or to decorate them with beautiful paintings.

Bohí, the central village of the three, and the one which has given its name to the valley, lies three miles below the Baths. Its two quaint streets, which tunnel their way in low arches under two of the houses, number barely a hundred souls. Bohí, however, has the only *fonda* of the three villages, and its church, although the simplest of the four, is for that very reason the 'standard' by relation to which we can examine them all. Its tower is the only one with less than six storeys.

It is on the towers that all attention is focused in these churches. They could exist quite independently of the simple naves and apses which they dominate, and it is the subtle variations on a very simple theme which constitute the differences between them and their individual charm. Whereas Erill-la-Vall across the valley, and San Clemente up in Tahull have five of their six storeys perforated with arches, Santa María, the other church in Tahull, has only three so opened up. On the other hand the perforations of both the Tahull towers are of double arches, whilst Erill-la-Vall's are appreciably narrower. It is this which helps to make the tower of Erill-la-Vall the slenderest and most elegant of all: it is also distinguished by the decorations worked in limestone between each storey, of a type common in Languedoc.

The interior of Erill-la-Vall, however, has no murals, unlike Bohí, where a fabulous animal stares down from each of its side-chapels. But for the treasures of this side of the valley's artistic heritage we must set off on foot – cars occasionally do make the journey but ought not to! – up the steep path to Tahull. When we emerge half an hour later at over 5,000 feet we find ourselves beside the church of San Clemente at one extremity of a long village, most of whose three hundred inhabitants live around Santa María a quarter of a mile away. It is Santa María who is now the patroness of the village, and an old man told me that once there had been more houses both around San Clemente and between San Clemente and the present *casco urbano*. But the wonder is that as many as three hundred people should still remain at such a height and in such isolation, and that throughout the growing poverty of the high Pyrenees since the Reconquest they should have succeeded in preserving intact both their magnificent churches.

It is in part this very poverty which has preserved so many Romanesque churches in the Pyrenees. There were the resources to build them eight hundred to a thousand years ago, but there have fortunately never since been the resources to rebuild them. Many of the Romanesque churches of Norman England have been rebuilt not once, but three or four times, as the advance in wealth has enabled their patrons to keep up with the architectural fashions of the day. But this poverty must not go beyond a certain point, or village, and church with it, will disappear altogether. And whatever the present 'nastiness' of the *balneario* of Bohí, we owe to the Baths the survival of Tahull. For until the construction of the road up the valley twenty years ago, those taking the waters travelled by mule, and over quite a different route. They followed the valley of the Flamisell as far as Capdella, and then the track over the hills which descended to the Noguera de Tor through Tahull. The good folk of Tahull kept body and soul together by hiring out mules to these wealthy Catalans in search of a cure – people whom one would never normally have seen except in a carriage on the Ramblas, or being driven in their Hispano-Suizas down the Paseo de Gracia.

It is time to enter San Clemente, which was built in 1128. As soon as we do so we realize how just is the title Romanesque, whether applied to architecture or to painting. For we recognize at once the archetype of this rural basilica, and the ancestors of this hieratic face whose eyes command us from the apse before we are past the threshold. Fashions travelled more slowly and lasted longer in those days. For almost six centuries separated the architects and mosaicists carrying out the exarch's orders in

The Valley of Bohi

Byzantine Ravenna from the unknown Master who painted the *Pantócrator* of San Clemente of Tahull. Santa María is of a less regular plan, and its uneven series of roofs culminates in a curious octagonal dome. With its tower leaning quite as much as that of Pisa, it is a unique building which no one can fail to recognize. There is less regularity of design, too, in the fresco which the Master has left us here. The Virgin, whose church this is, holds the infant Jesus in her arms, worshipped by the three wise men.*

We emerge into the *alta soledad* of Tahull, free of traffic because the metalled road has already 'died' hundreds of feet below. Contrasting its present poverty with the level of culture which it must have known when these frescoes were painted, the witty comment has been made: 'What shepherd in the valley of Bohí today could imagine a sheep like the one with seven eyes depicted by the Master of Tahull?'

Returning down the valley, those with time to spare can visit the churches of Durro and Barruera, which would have been worthy of further mention were they not so much in the shadow of Tahull and of Erill-la-Vall. Then less than two miles after the road down the Noguera de Tor has joined the main road down the Noguera Ribagorzana we enter Pont de Suert. The squat arcades of its old quarter down by the river show that it was not founded yesterday. But it has grown to displace Vilaller as the main centre on the Noguera Ribagorzana only because of the hydro-electric developments evidenced by the huge reservoir of Escales below the town. The immigrant workers needed not only new housing estates but a new church, and seeing it as we do now, after a day amongst the Romanesque glories of Bohí, we must agree that Señor Torroja and Señor Mijares, the architects who completed it in 1955, did not travel far to seek inspiration. For they have successfully translated into a modern idiom the spirit of those who built Erill-la-Vall and her sisters.

* The original murals of Tahull, like those of most of the churches in the Catalan Pyrenees, including Andorra, have been moved to the *Museo de Arte de Cataluña* at Montjuich, Barcelona. In Tahull and Bohí, however, exact reproductions have been left in their place.

2. Arán

Mention the valley of Arán to a group of Spaniards in Saragossa or Barcelona, and a dreamy pre-Raphaelite look will come into the eyes even of those – indeed, especially of those – who have never been there.

'They say it is beautiful – *pero precioso*.'

'They call it the Spanish Switzerland.'

'And the houses are tiny, and the villages are so quaint, and it is all so green.'

They choose almost the same words as sentimental Americans describing the English countryside.

A casual glance at the average uncoloured map gives little clue to the reasons for this attitude. As with most of the Spanish Pyrenees, there seem to be mountains both to the north and to the south. The names of the villages would not seem out of place in adjoining parts of Catalonia. And although Arán is remote in distance from any provincial capital, it has the unparalleled advantage of two main roads linking it to the rest of Spain, and two other main roads linking it to France. So what is so special about it?

The answer is to go and see.

Then the special character of Arán becomes obvious, whichever approach is chosen. The French signs at Bagnères de Luchon indicating the road across the easy 4,350-foot Portillon pass to Bosost, only eighteen kilometres away, have a more domestic flavour than the Spanish signs at Pobla de Segur towards the Viella tunnel or the Bonaigua pass at five times the distance. And although the main road from France into Arán crosses the frontier at a narrow defile which precisely marks the end of the valley, the Pont de Rey – itself altogether in Spain – reveals by its very presence an unaccustomed intimacy between this corner of Spain and the land to the north. For the river which it bridges is the Garona, and as one proceeds up it through Lés and Bosost towards Viella one realizes that the tumbling stream which drains the valley, and the mountain torrents (here called *artigas*) which swell it are on their way neither to the Mediterranean nor even to the Spanish Atlantic coast but to the Gironde.

For the valley of Arán is on the 'wrong' side of the Pyrenees, the north side, the French side. Politically, however, it became part of the kingdom of Aragon in 1192, having previously belonged to the county of Comminges. Ecclesiastically, the old tie persisted until the see of St. Bertrand-de-Comminges was suppressed along with so many of the smaller French bishoprics at the time of the Revolution. Since then it has been attached to the distant Seo de Urgel. Going to see the bishop can be quite a problem, and the priest of Aubert told me his own solution. He and a group of fellow priests took the daily bus from Lés to Barcelona as far as Sort, where they clubbed together to hire a jeep. This took them to Seo de Urgel over hair-raising muletracks by the most direct but bumpiest route of all.

It might have been expected that the valley would have changed hands at the Peace of the Pyrenees in 1659, when so much other Spanish territory to the north of the watershed was surrendered to France. One of the anecdotes associated with the picturesque conferences which led up to that treaty relates that a Spanish negotiator remarked casually 'And of course the valley of Arán will remain Spanish', to which his French opposite number, who had never even heard of it, as casually agreed.

It is not really necessary, however, to invoke this story to explain Arán's unique position. For amongst the valleys to the north of the main watershed it is unique. It is the longest, it has the most villages, and it is the only one to run from east to west. Yet although it runs thus horizontally, it has peaks of over 9,000 feet limiting it both to north and to south.

It was Charpentier who first made the point that the Pyrenees are composed not of one chain of mountains but of two chains, one beginning at the Atlantic in Cabo Higuer, and one originating in the Mediterranean at Cabo Creus. In the centre these fail to meet, being connected by the ridge over which runs the Bonaigua pass. They instead overlap for some thirty miles, and the depression between them is the Valle de Arán.

Whether French or Spanish, Arán would always have been a little world apart. It is the perfect example of that lovely Spanish word *comarca,* which is used to describe a natural geographical area somewhere in size between a *pueblo* and a province. Its sense is very nearly that of the French *pays,* but simply because it is a Spanish word and not a French word the associations which it brings to mind are of a totally different order: steeper hills, darker villages, browner skins, stronger wine, and harsher, warmer speech.

The speech of Arán is not in fact as harsh as that of the Catalonia of which technically it forms part (it is in the province of Lérida). Many Catalans say that *aranés* is a dialect of Catalan, but this is even less true than the Castilian claim that Catalan is itself no more than a dialect of Spanish. *Aranés* is rather a variety of the Gascon of south-west France, and more specifically of the *commingeois* patois still spoken throughout the old county of Comminges to which Arán belonged until 1192.

'We speak exactly the same dialect as they do at Luchon or Montréjeau. But we speak it better, because we don't mix in a lot of French words as they do.'

The Catalans may have made their mistake because most *araneses* obligingly learn Catalan as well as Castilian, so as to be able to welcome their compatriots whether they come from the south-east or the south-west. And they also, of course, learn French for the benefit of their visitors from the north, who in their scores drive up into the valley every summer weekend.

It is not of this facility in languages, however, that Spaniards are thinking when they describe Arán as the Spanish Switzerland. They are thinking of its cool, fresh climate, of its small tidy fields, of its often cloudy skies, of its neat slate-roofed houses. Even a visitor liked Robin Fedden, with experience of many mountain systems, can describe it as 'almost an Alpine valley'.

Its 6,500 inhabitants are spread evenly throughout its length in seven *villas* or big villages and twenty-three hamlets, some on one side of the river and some on the other. Only Artiés and Lés extend to both banks of the Garonne, and a few of the hamlets, such as Uña, Casau, or Caneján right against the frontier, are set back some distance on the hillsides. The seven *villas,* going down the valley, are Salardú, Artiés, Viella, Vilach, Vilamós, Bosost, and Lés. Bosost, with just over a thousand inhabitants, is the largest of these, but Viella with just under a thousand is the capital of the whole valley. Vilach and Vilamós, today only small, were relatively more important during the Middle Ages, Vilamós being by tradition the oldest settlement in Arán.

Again like Switzerland, Arán holds a great deal in a small area, and the best way to give a concise account of what the visitor should look out for is to travel slowly in imagination down the valley. We shall approach it therefore from Pallars over the Bonaaigua pass by the only road connecting it to the rest of Spain until the opening of the Viella tunnel in 1955.

All the *artigas* or tributary streams of Arán like to consider themselves the original Garonne, but the one which presently appears sparkling far down on our left has the most claim to the title. Called the Garona de Ruda, its source is in the lakes of Saburedo, on the northern edge of the Park of Aigües Tortes. At the first pueblo of Arán, Tredós, it is joined by another stream, Aiguamoix, bubbling under an ancient bridge. The fine twelfth-century church, known from its position at 4,500 feet at the head of the valley as the church of Cap d'Arán, stands beside the main road, a little apart from Tredós. Then a mile farther on, after we have dropped a further three hundred feet, river and road come together at Salardú, the capital of upper Arán, with a thirteenth-century gateway and a church whose plan owes something to that of San Clemente de Tahull.

On foot or by jeep we could have reached Salardú from Pallars by another route, which would have involved a climb lower by 700 feet than that over the Bonaigua. This secondary route continues to follow the Noguera Pallaresa when the main road leaves it to assault the Bonaigua, and I mention it for three reasons. In the first place its opening twenty miles from Esterri de Aneu may one day form the Spanish section of a main international road across the pass of Salau and down to St. Girons. I hope – and with a certain amount of confidence – that many years will pass before this remote area is thus desecrated. For as long ago as 1909 Hilaire Belloc could write of 'the pass of Salau where the French have made, and the Spanish are making, a high road'. The 'high road' has still got no farther than Alos, the last inhabited village.

If we follow the track along the river for another thirteen miles beyond Alos, however, we reach that unusual curiosity, an uninhabited village. This is the second reason why I mention this secondary route, for Montgarri is not only of interest for its shuttered houses, deserted only a few years ago when its inhabitants at last tired of fetching their winter supplies on skis. One wonders for how many millenia some of those families had been living in that isolated hamlet at 5,500 feet; for Montgarri is an obviously Basque place-name. And one building a few hundred yards beyond the village is still in use: the Sanctuary of Montgarri. Although mainly of an unremarkable Renaissance style, it was founded as long ago as 1117. With its dependencies, which include a hospital in the Pyrenean sense, it is a striking ensemble to find in so remote a situation beside the Noguera Pallaresa.

For we are still in the valley of the Noguera Pallaresa, and therefore still geographically in Pallars, although the inhabitants of Montgarri regarded themselves as *araneses* and retired to the valley of Arán when they left their village. And to my mind this is one reason why Arán has remained Spanish, although it stands on the French side of the watershed. For although it may seem illogical and untidy for the upper Garonne to flow through Spain, it would be at least equally illogical and untidy for the upper Noguera Pallaresa to flow through France.

The two rivers practically meet in the Pla de Beret, at 6,200 feet, the highest point of this secondary route, and the third reason for mentioning it. Strictly speaking this is not the main Garonne running down to Salardú past Bagergue, but the fact remains that only a very short distance separates the Noguera Pallaresa on the start of its journey to the Mediterranean from waters which will eventually flow through the Gironde into the Atlantic. Around the Pla de Beret are the most extensive ski slopes of the Spanish Pyrenees; but those called Baqueira, immediately behind Salardú, are more accessible, and were being equipped with a ski-lift in the summer of 1964.

Artiés, two miles beyond Salardú, is of greater importance than its two hundred inhabitants alone would warrant. Artiés in Basque means 'between two waters', and this well describes the position of the main village around the twelfth and thirteenth century parish church, between the Garonne and its tributary or *artiga* of Valarties. From the main road the view up the Valarties, whose sides perfectly frame that lop-sided Fujiyama the 9,273-foot Montarto, is one to bring a smile of recognition to any lover of Arán. From the main road, too, can be seen two buildings which stand on the nearer, the right bank of the Garonne, away from the main village. One is the disaffected thirteenth-century church of San Juan, which once belonged to the Templars. The other is the Casa Portolá, a fortified manor house of the sixteenth century.

The Baths of Artiés, half a mile downstream, stand all by themselves on the other side of the river. They are one of those forgotten little spas, with an endearing rustic charm, to be found in the most unexpected corners of Spain. In the summer of 1964 their all-in terms, for board, lodging, and as many baths as one wished, were only eighteen shillings a day.

We are now in the central section of the valley, which the *araneses* call Mig Aran (pronounced *meech*). But less than a mile before we reach Viella we must stop briefly at Betrén, whose Romanesque church of San Esteban, enlarged in the fifteenth century, has a fascinating tympanum over the main door.

And so we enter the capital. Oh! blessed capital, with but one petrol pump and a population which does not reach four figures. All one's memories of Viella are happy memories: the minute but so courteous post office behind its grille, the charming young *aranesa* who presides over the bright new Tourist Information Office, the helpful and generous Señor Porras to whom this book owes some of its loveliest photographs, the white waters of the *artiga* of Nere splashing down under its bridges, the good restaurants and the homely little bars where every drink, whether a *copita* of *coñac* or *anis*, or a deep glass of full-bodied wine, seemed to cost the same standard one peseta. It is a fitting capital for 'the Valley of Arán, which was made for man's happiness' to echo J. B. Morton. And it is a real capital, for through its isolation Arán still retains some of its *fueros*. The land register for the valley, for example, is here in Viella instead of in distant Lérida.

Viella has a number of seventeenth-century houses, built as the homes of leading *aranés* families such as Burgarol or Rodés. And the Romanesque church, besides a fine tympanum over the north-west door, now contains that lovely twelfth-century torso of Christ known as the 'Ecce homo of Mig Arán'.

The actual chapel of Mig Arán, less than a mile from Viella on the main road to France, was destroyed in 1936. Near its ruins stands a much older landmark, a menhir nearly eight feet high called the Peira de Mig Arán. For in every age the geographical centre of the valley seems to have acquired a religious significance. And at approximately the same distance from Viella but on the other side of the river stands Gausach, remarkable as having the only wholly Gothic church in this valley of the Romanesque.

The hamlets of central Arán follow each other every few hundred yeards as we proceed down the narrowing valley. Soon after Aubert we cross the Barradós, which can be followed up a track for five miles to a lovely spot called the Salto del Pix. Then just before the Garonne takes a wide wheel to the north we reach Las Bordas, a village of humble origins as its name suggests, whose comparatively modern growth was only thought to warrant a church as recently as 1806. Here the river receives its most interesting tributary, the Jueu. Its valley is known as the Artiga de Lin, and can be followed by car for seven steep miles of gravel road all the way to the Pla de la Artiga, a plateau at 6,000 feet beyond which rise the peaks of the Forcanada and the Escalette marking the frontiers with Aragon and with France.

A little way below the Pla a *parador* is being built near an old chapel, and a little farther down still is the source of the stream: the Guell del Jueu. Here the waters of the Aneto which we saw disappearing into the Trou du Toro burst above ground once again to flow towards the Atlantic. Myself, I feel inclined to honour the old tradition and to name this abrupt cascade the main source of the Garonne.

There must be a wealth of other unknown springs beneath the beechwoods of the Artiga de Lin. One has been tapped to provide a fountain beside the track, which bears the following inscription in *aranés*: HONT DET GRESILLUN ETAM AIGUARDEN ENCARA SOMULMILLU. I was told in Viella that the translation runs: 'Fountain of the Gresillun. Made with firewater it is better still', a sentiment with which it would be churlish to disagree.

Bosost is the largest place in Arán, and the best shopping centre. For this reason many of the French weekend trippers get no farther into Spain. They can reach Bosost not only up the Garonne, but also over the 4,350-foot Portillon pass from Bagnères de Luchon, a mere eleven miles away. From Belloc onwards, travellers have been at once surprised and dismayed that so civilized a resort as Luchon, 'the noisy and wealthy capital of luxury', should have grown up so deep in the heart of the Pyrenees. But it is a tidy, concentrated town, without spreading suburbs, and has in no way spoilt the countryside around.

Indeed, the area of about ten miles around Luchon probably holds as many members of the dwindling race of Pyrenean bears as any other of its size. Some authorities say that the few who remain have become degenerate through inbreeding. But there was little sign of degeneracy in Ursula, taken as a cub by some frontier guards, and for several years cruelly but necessarily confined in a subterranean cage in San Sebastian's zoo on Mount Igueldo. We all became very sorry for Ursula and very fond of her, and it was with sadness as well as joy that we said goodbye to the powerful snarling girl when she left for Barcelona, where a mate had been found for her from the closely related and more numerous race of Cantabrian bears.

A few paces away from Bosost's tree-shaded boulevard beside the foaming Garonne – which here already boasts a substantial *caudal* by Spanish Pyrenean standards – lies its Romanesque church. There is no hint of any later style in its ancient stones, and the tympanum of its main door is as fine as that of Betrén. Legend has it that Bosost vowed to erect seven chapels if it was spared by the Black Death, and it is certainly true that the parish contains no less than eight of these tiny *ermitas*.

The last village on the main road to France is Lés, straddled across the Garonne with another of those forgotten little spas of Spain on the farther bank. These healing waters were known to the Romans, and traces of their presence include an inscription referring to the god Lex, after whom the place is perhaps named. Here takes place the customs examination before the frontier, which is crossed four miles farther on at the lonely Pont de Rey, its very name a marriage of tongues.

The traveller who has followed the route which we have now completed in imagination from the Bonaigua to Pont de Rey will not only agree with the description of Arán as the Spanish Switzerland, but will add a further reason for this resemblance. Nowhere else in Spain (except Minorca, where they were introduced by the English during the eighteenth century) will he have seen as many cows. There is a Swiss abundance of milk at all the restaurants and hotels, and butter is only half the normal Spanish price. Many of these cows are in fact of Swiss stock, for the same 'alpine' conditions have been found suitable for the same race of cattle. As I walked round the cattle show of the *comarca*, in a field outside Viella, the *aranés* farmers in their black corduroy suits told me that the first *suizo-pardo* bulls were imported about ten years ago; and I could see from the labels of the beasts exhibited that the native strain was being crossed and recrossed with the newcomers.

It is about ten years, too, since the tunnel of Viella was opened to the upper valley of the Noguera Ribagorzana, so ending the valley's winter isolation from the rest of Spain. But the *araneses* have never allowed the snows of the Bonaigua to cut them off from their countrymen. During the Civil War the young men would enter France without passports to re-enter Spain by another route, and they were recognized as the best guerilla fighters on either side. And the hospital of Sant Nicolau dels Pontells, at the southern end of the tunnel, where those crossing the steep pass to Arán could find refreshment, is known as the Hospital de Viella because it was the people of Viella who established it to secure their communications with the farther slopes of the watershed.

The reader may wonder why I have called this section simply 'Arán'. I have done so because to speak of the valley of Arán is in a strict sense tautological. For *arán* in Basque means a valley.

3. Pallars

A purist would enter Pallars from the Pla de Beret, following from its source the Noguera Pallaresa to which the *comarca* gave its name. Even our own route across the Bonaigua pass will involve a little discomfort. For from Salardú all the way up and down again to Esterri de Aneu the road is untarred, and now that the tunnel of Viella has been opened it may never be made up.

In the bare lonely pass itself one almost welcomes the presence beside an iron cross and a ruined house of electric cables and of the neo-Gothic refuge of the electricity company. And pausing there one can compare the vistas to north and south, well contrasted by José María Espinás in *Viatge al Pirineu de Lleida*:

'Pallars is a country of sun, the valley of Arán is a country of mist; Pallars is heroic, the valley of Arán is mellow; Pallars is mineral, Arán vegetable; Pallars throbs, Arán breathes; Pallars is manly, Arán feminine,'

The descent from the pass is one of the great drives of the Spanish Pyrenees. A couple of miles of twisting road and nine hundred feet below stands another of the Pyrenean 'hospitals', Nuestra Señora de los Ares, often abbreviated in Catalan to *la Mare de Déu*. 'A priest told me that *Ares* means altars,' said a servant there, and certainly the chapel still stands on one side of the road. It does not seem very ancient, but then the hospital opposite was built only forty or fifty years ago, on the site where previous ones had fallen into ruins. Full board there in the summer of 1964 was only fifteen shillings a day, and no doubt included from time to time the rich sausage called *xolis* for which Pallars is renowned.

From the hospital can be seen the waterfall in which the Bonaigua river which has given its name to the pass leaves the lake of Gerbé, high up on the edge of the National Park of Aigües Tortes. And there are many smaller cascades as we descend through fir forests whose trees are noted for their height. At last signposts mark turnings off – to the first village of Pallars, Sorpe, and to the beautifully named Son del Pino. We pass through Valencia de Aneu, recalling an eleventh-century Countess Valencia of Pallars, and two miles later we are on a metalled road, and, as so often at the very head of the long central valleys, in a village of considerable importance. For like Bielsa and Benasque, Esterri de Aneu is almost a small town, and the effective capital of Aneu, the name given to the broad level valley of the upper Noguera Pallaresa from here to beyond the summer resort of La Guingeta.

Aneu was dominated by a castle of the Counts of Pallars, the most powerful vassals of the kingdom established by the marriage of Petronella of Aragon to Ramón Berenguer of Barcelona. And this castle, today in ruins, was the last stronghold of the last Count, Hugo Roger III, before he was driven to France, to die at last tragically in Sicily, where he had been fighting his own Catalan countrymen.

The spiritual centre of Aneu, however, remains intact. Santa María de Aneu stands at the heart of this broad level basin, between the road and the river. It was probably founded soon after A.D. 800, and although the present building appears to date from the eleventh and twelfth centuries it contains mural paintings which some authorities regard as earlier in date than Almanzor, the last Moslem leader who penetrated deep into the fastnesses of Christian Spain. If so, they were executed before the year 1000.

The Noguera Pallaresa is the axis of Pallars in a sense in which the Noguera Ribagorzana has never been the axis of Ribagorza. One of its characteristics is the number and importance of its subsidiary valleys. From Esterri one can reach the valley of Unarre with its three small villages; and at the other extremity of Aneu, where the valley narrows again to permit the construction of a dam, a well-surfaced road climbs steeply above the bed of a torrent called the Escrito to the village of Espot.

Espot's deep isolation amidst wild country makes it the ideal base for the exploration of the National Park of Aigues Tortes, to which we have already referred in the section on the valley of Bohí. It is well equipped with two *fondas*, and with the Hotel Saurat, a family-run establishment which combines the up-to-date and comfortable with the personal and intimate.

The road to Espot is continued beyond by a gravel track through delicious deserted woods. Anyone not too particular about their springs should be able to drive the first four and a half miles, although the last steep climb past the chapel of San Mauricio may be too much for less-powerful engines. In any case it seems a much shorter journey on foot than it in fact is. I set off after tea when a rainy day had at last turned bright, and was surprised to find myself back at Espot for dinner after covering nearly twelve miles without conscious haste. One is recharged by the champagne-like air, and constantly inspired by the views.

The most famous of these is that of the twin peaks of the Encantados across the lake of San Mauricio. The legend explaining their name implies that the little chapel of San Mauricio is of greater age than they are. It tells how the inhabitants of the valley of Espot were gathered in *romería* up at the *ermita* when two of them, anxious to commence their day's hunting, stole away from Mass to clamber up the single mountain which then rose beside the lake. The priest invoked Heaven to punish such impiety, and a flash of lightning answered him. The ensuing thunderbolt struck the mountain top which the two hunters had just attained, and when the smoke cleared away it was seen that it had been cleft in twain, leaving the two impious figures for ever turned to stone. A happy sequel to this grim legend is that it was a priest, Jaime Oliveras, who was the first Spaniard to climb both peaks; and he is said to have granted the Sabbath breakers absolution.

Continuing our route down the main Noguera Pallaresa, we pass on the left soon after Escaló the ruins of the monastery of San Pedro del Burgal, another spiritual centre which sprang up in the exciting ninth century. Here again murals have been found, and moved for protection to Barcelona. Five miles on is the sizeable village of Llavorsí. It is a pretty spot, noted for the skill of its woodcutters and for the excellence of its fishing, and things have changed since Belloc could write of it as an 'unpleasing village' where he 'would not recommend sleeping'.

Trout abound in the streams of the Spanish Pyrenees because their waters are exceptionally well oxygenated; but Llavorsí can offer the angler not one river but three. For here the Noguera Pallaresa is increased by the combined waters of the Noguera de Cardós and of the Valferrera, the valleys of which are of interest not only to fishermen but to the less-specialized traveller.

Near the southern end of Aneu, beside the road which we have just travelled, stand the hammer of an old forge. Known traditionally as the hammer of Roland, we can reasonably treat it as symbolically marking the point where two Pyrenean pasts overlap. To the west of the *Mall de Rotllan* is a legendary past of high chivalry and of superhuman heroes. To the east is a less-aristocratic legendary past, more suited to the prosaic Catalan spirit, a past of small-scale industries of wood and metal, which lacking the resources or the communications of Barcelona have vanished as utterly as the paladins of Charlemagne.

We first encounter this other past in the Valferrera, the very name of which recalls the iron once produced by its eighteen forges. Another old iron hammer stands in the plaza of Alins, the capital of this valley. A recently opened track leads from Alins to the remote hamlet of Tor, at 5,500 feet and in the shadow of the peaks which mark the frontiers of Andorra and of France. The main Valferrera continues beyond Alins to Areu, whose present population is less than a third what it was in the days of the iron industry. With two *fondas*, it would make a good base from which to reach the frontier peak of Estats, at 10,302 feet the highest in Catalonia, and from which to explore the surrounding region, where even today a few bears may survive.

An alternative base from which to reach this unspoilt area would be Tabescán, with one *posada*, at the head of the valley of Cardós, or as it is generally called here, the *ribera* of Cardós. For a hotel with all 'mod. cons.', however, one must descend as far as the capital of the valley, which bears the same name: Ribera de Cardós. I am not speaking of 'mod. cons.' in any pejorative sense: to be remote and yet comfortable is a worthy but an elusive and all too often a self-defeating aim. Ribera de Cardós, however, where a café terrace gives straight on to green fields, the willow-lined river, and the mountains, is less remote than Espot, but more remote than Caldas de Bohí – just the happy medium that many seek.

For those simply passing through, Ribera de Cardós has a magnificent Romanesque church standing in isolation from the village. Its tower has four unequal storeys, of which only the uppermost has more than the plainest opening. It is obviously closely related to the churches of the valley of Bohí, though it belongs to a distinct sub-species.

Even greater comfort, at the cost of a loss in isolation, will be

22. Bonaigua river, Pallars

23. Son del Pino,
Pallars

provided by a big new hotel going up near Rialp – another Basque place-name – which we pass through five miles after rejoining the main road down the Noguera Pallaresa at Llavorsí. The promoting company bears the ominous name of *Urbanizadora Pirenaica,* and is also responsible for the chalets being built nearby.

Three miles after Rialp we pass on our right the road up to the little-known valley of Assua, and enter Sort, the capital of upper Pallars, or of Pallars Sobirá as it is called in Catalan. Although its population is slightly less than that of Esterri d'Aneu, it presides over the whole valley north of the Desfiladero de Collegats. It illustrates in a particularly marked form the division common to so many smaller Spanish towns into a 'modern' front along the main road, and an 'old town' up the hill at the back. Where a miniature park beside the Noguera faces three or four cafés across the road a traveller who has crossed the frontier at Lés meets the nearest approach to urban living since he has entered Spain. And walking through the squat arcades of the old quarter, where the upper storeys almost meet above the narrow streets, he will come upon a section of fortifications with a doorway belonging to the castle of the Counts of Pallars. From here the last Count, Hugo Roger III, had first to be dislodged before his enemies could drive him from his last stronghold up in Aneu.

From Sort there is an appalling road through Vilamur – once the seat of powerful viscounts – and Les Llacunes over into the Urgellet. I would not recommend it any more than that other track to Seo de Urgel from Pallars, through San Juan d l'Herm and Castellbó, the difficulties of which have been described in the reverse direction both by Belloc and by J. B. Morton. A tough Yorkshire cyclist told me that even he had to start pushing his machine long before he had travelled half the distance from Seo to Sort.

These and other tracks throughout the Spanish Pyrenees are being at once opened up and churned up by the lorries of the prospering timber industry. But the improvement of the main roads along the principal valleys, combined with the construction of hydro-electric dams, has led to the disappearance of a colourful way of life for long associated with the timber trade. The Noguera Pallaresa in particular was the ready-made conveyor belt by which the great trunks used to be floated downstream under the direction of a *raier,* whose occupation was as specialized and as hered-

itary as that of the English bargee. The attitude of this vanished
figure has been caught in the Catalan of Jacinto Verdaguer:

> Soc fill del Noguera,
> dins un rai nasquí;
> ma esposa és raiera,
> raier vull morir.

The *raier* must have needed all his skill when negotiating the
long *garganta* called the Desfiladero de Collegats. Just before its
entrance stands Gerri de la Sal, which owes the first word of its
name to the Basques, and the last to a salt-water spring from
which the mineral is extracted by evaporation in rectangular beds.
The first to exploit this wealth were the monks of the monastery
of Santa María on the opposite bank of the river. Its twelfth-
century ruins are probably on the site of a ninth-century foundation, and a hint of that heroic age remains in the dance of La
Morisca, still performed every 3rd August, the third day of Gerri's
fiesta. Each couple are said to represent a Moslem king and a
Christian Queen enslaved by him: who made her escape by the
subterfuge of a dance.

Neither Gerri nor Sort are mountain villages in the same degree
as the *pueblos* farther north: already whitewashed walls have begun
to replace untouched stone, and slates are giving way to tiles.
Once through the Desfiladero de Collegats the transformation is
complete. Not only are the villages more Mediterranean in appearance, but the predominant colour of the countryside is brown
rather than green. And we have in fact entered another *comarca*,
that of lower Pallars or Pallars Jussá. Up a track to the right as we
leave the *garganta* are the ruins of a convent dedicated to San
Pedro, and three miles later we enter the friendly little town of
Pobla de Segur.

It is a good place to arrive in whether from the north, when it
appears as an oasis of civilization, or from the south, when it earns
its proudly claimed title 'The Gateway of the Pyrenees'. For from
Pobla run the roads both to Pallars Sobirá and to Ribagorza, and
thus up the two Nogueras along the alternative routes to Arán.
It is an exciting moment for the traveller north to see the two
signposts with their detachable suffixes: 'PUERTO DE LA BON-
AIGUA 74 – ABIERTO', and a few yards away but at right angles
'TUNEL DE VIELLA 69 – ABIERTO'. The Tourist Office of Pobla

de Segur is equal to its opportunities. Its folders on the Pyrenees of the province of Lérida have been well translated into English, and are the best and the most beautifully illustrated of any which I have seen in Spain.

Pobla is the gateway to yet another valley, that of the Flamisell, which here joins the Noguera Pallaresa. I personally find it delightful yet disappointing; a quiet suave green landscape which simply does not belong between Tahull and Espot, at the very foot of the wild wilderness of Aigües Tortes. It owes something of this tamed quality to the hydro-electric company which has established itself at Capdella at the head of the valley, specifically with a view to harnessing the waters of Aigües Tortes. Capdella, at 4,750 feet and with two hotels, would for this very reason make a good base for the exploration of the National Park. Thanks to the hydro-electric company there is even a *fonda* beside the remote lake of Estangento, high up beyond the cliff-like sierra which closes the end of the valley.

Despite its growing importance and its numerous hotels and *fondas* Pobla de Segur, like all places bearing the prefix *Pobla*, is of comparatively recent growth. Older, larger, and the traditional capital of Pallars Jussá is Tremp, ten miles farther down the river. It presides over a widening of the valley called the Conca de Tremp, a dry zone protected – like the Canal de Berdún and the Cerdaña – by the pre-Pyrenean sierras. And just as the reservoir of Yesa is a welcome sight amidst the arid Bardenas, so the reservoir of San Antonio, which occupies all the upper part of the Conca, is a refreshing spectacle beneath the parched hills. Tremp itself is a smaller and inferior Jaca, with a church which has suffered less from the Civil War than most other churches of Pallars below Sort.

The Conca has its widest extension where the Noguera Pallaresa is joined by the Rio de Conques, and along this subsidiary valley runs the first practicable road between Pallars and the Urgellet. It is now possible to travel from Jaca to the Gallego, up over Cotefablo, down the Ara to Ainsa, straight across to the Esera, and from Castejón de Sos over to Pont de Suert and through to Pobla de Segur on practicable roads, yet never more then twenty-five miles from the valley heads. But a long deviation becomes necessary when we seek to pass from the Noguera Pallaresa to the Segre. The shortest route without risking a broken neck is via Artesa de Segre, more than fifty miles south of Seo de Urgel.

At all costs eschew that so tempting short cut from Isona to Coll de Nargo, over the infernal red sierra of San Juan. 'Mala, mala', said the man whose advice I had sought on this road. Would that I had had the wisdom to take it! The only possible reason for travelling the seven or eight miles to the east of Boixols is to see just how desolate life can be in the wrong part of the Spanish Pyrenees.

4. Urgellet and Cerdaña

Its undeveloped road system, of which we have had a taste as we sought to cross from Pallars, is one of the characteristics of the upper and middle reaches of the valley of the Segre. This is the more surprising because they lie sandwiched between bustling industrial Catalonia to the south, prospering Andorra to the north, and the excellent roads of the French Cerdagne to the east. Nor does any watershed here divide the two nations. The Segre, like the Aragon, runs from east to west during part of its early course, and these fifty miles before it turns south at Seo de Urgel have always been an important natural highway. They have been no less so since the Peace of the Pyrenees in 1659 divided the Catalan-speaking Spaniards of the Cerdaña from the Catalan-speaking Frenchmen of the Cerdagne. But now the traveller on the French part of that highway, from Mont-Louis as far as Bourg-Madame, finds himself amidst a whole network of good roads, whilst once past Puigcerdá, leaving aside the international route to Andorra, he will have to proceed more than thirty miles beyond Seo before he finds another reasonable road to left or right.

Their dependence thus on one road and one river enables us to treat in a single section two distinct *comarcas*, the Urgellet of which the capital is the ancient episcopal city of Seo de Urgel, and the Spanish Cerdaña based on the growing town of Puigcerdá. One's first impression is that the Urgellet is a darker, poorer area looking towards the past, whereas Cerdaña is a brighter, prospering region with its eye on the future.

In fact, however, the Counts of Cerdaña were as important in the Middle Ages as the Counts and the Bishops of Urgel, and at Alp near Puigcerdá there still stands a Roman temple. And as for comparative wealth, the balance is tilted in favour of the Urgellet. Seo stands at 2,350 feet, Puigcerdá at almost 4,000, and though the Cerdaña offers wonderful pasture, it is beneath the arcades of Seo that one can buy fruit and vegetables almost as tasty as those of Jaca.

First impressions, however, are never wholly misleading. To its height the Cerdaña owes a rare quality of light and clear sunny skies which have made Font-Romeu, a few miles across the frontier, the winter sports resort *le plus ensoleillé* of France. There is something liberating about the great clear vistas, just as there

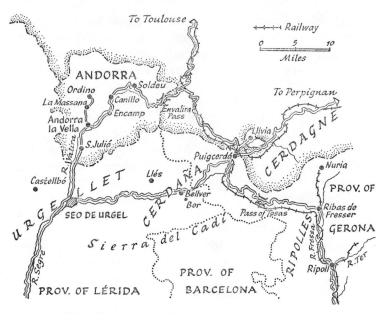

VII   Urgellet, Cerdaña, and Andorra

is something dispiriting about the more circumscribed if milder air of the Urgellet. There can be occasions when the herdsman's more primitive task seems at once more free, more noble, and more rewarding than that of the husbandman, and Violant y Simorra, catching sight of the first 'rickety vineyards' on entering the Urgellet from Cerdaña, exclaims 'A fragment of soil more desperately made use of and more watered with bitter sweat is not to be found in all the Pyrenees'.

We shall notice this prevailing depression as we drive up the Segre in the reverse direction past the castle of Oliana at the entrance to a long reservoir, and leaving on our left the 'short cut' which we wisely declined to take from Isona to Coll de Nargo. Only a few hundred yards up that 'short cut' stands a neglected but obviously ancient Romanesque church – my own guess would be early eleventh century – to which I have been unable to find any reference anywhere. We feel it in the listless little town of Orgaña, which has given its name to the *garganta* of the Segre. But the depression is most evident in the dwindling little villages away from the main road. For the tracks which wind up to them from the Segre never connect up with highways to Pallars or to Berga. Yet their inhabitants are Catalans, conscious of themselves as members of the same progressive race which has established in Barcelona the largest port and industrial centre in the peninsula.

I was particularly struck by this depression when I visited Castellbó, six miles from the Segre along a narrow track which wound round a mountainside. Sixty years ago Belloc could declare that 'the hospitality of the place is so great that you will wish to stay there', for it had 'a most delicious inn, with an old innkeeper of the very best'; and even a score of years later J. B. Morton's traveller could find there 'an enormous plate of reeking soup and a large hunk of bread'.

There is still a baker's in Castellbó – the last before Pallars – but when at nine in the evening I went in search of a glass of wine and a little convivial chatter the bar had to be specially opened for me, and its mistress stood exchanging glum monosyllables while I drank up, for all the world as if I was downing my monthly ration in some liquor store of eastern Canada or of Scandinavia. The one event of the day seemed to be the passage of the milk lorry, which clattering through the remote *pueblos* in the early hours had drained the valley of every litre before six in the morning. As I squeezed a few drops from a tube of condensed milk into my breakfast coffee I gazed up at the bramble-covered stones atop the rock which rose in the centre of the village. Even if their ruinous condition had not been evidence enough of their antiquity, this could have been presumed from their very situation. For the valley was minute, shut in on every side by heights which towered over the fortified rock. To find the age when a castle sited there could have been of military use, it is necessary to go back not merely to before gunpowder but to before the crossbow.

But in that distant period of the early Middle Ages the Counts of Castellbó were powers in the land, useful allies to the lords on both sides of the Pyrenees, and often thorns in the flesh of the bishops of Seo de Urgel. For they inherited or were granted – the evidence is conflicting, like so much in the early history of Andorra – the rights over the Valleys of Andorra which had once been held, and never finally renounced, by the counts of Urgel. The bishops for their part claimed that they had become the sole lords of the Valleys, and as the counts of Castellbó were less powerful than the counts of Urgel had been, and were subject, like all temporal authorities, to accidents of death and inheritance from which the Church is immune, it is possible that in time the bishops would have had their way. Then poor, bare Andorra, which only communicated with the rest of the world down the narrow valley of the Valira which flowed beneath the bishop's palace, would in due course have been absorbed in the Urgellet to become less visited and more hopeless than Castellbó today.

A subtle variation in this pattern was introduced when Count Arnaud of Castellbó married his only daughter Ermessenda to Roger Bernard, Count of Foix. For when he died without a male heir, his rights over Andorra passed to the house of Foix beyond the watershed. I say a 'subtle' variation because its significance was hidden in the days before nation states, when the kings of England were the greatest feudal lords south of the Dordogne, and when only a couple of centuries earlier the Holy Roman Empire had stretched as far as Barcelona. But when the Pyrenees came to form a true national frontier, the fact that one of Andorra's princes was on one side of that frontier, and one on the other, became the guarantee of her independence.

Of all this the present inhabitants of Castellbó know little. But they are dimly aware that their past state was greater than their present, although the past to which they look back with greater nostalgia is distant thirty years rather than eight centuries. They tell of when there were constant visitors to the shrine of San Juan de l'Herm, ten miles farther up in the mountains, on the very threshold of Pallars. There is still a great annual pilgrimage, but it seems that before the Civil War it was never deserted, with people in the guest house beside the chapel for days or weeks together, and with one or more priests always in attendance.

In contrast to the depression of the country districts of the Urgellet is the prosperity of Seo de Urgel itself. This prosperity has done nothing to alter the centre of the city, where the maze of deeply arcaded streets are like a vaster edition of the old quarters of Sort or of Pont de Suert. But on the outskirts are factories for processing the milk brought in from the subsidiary valleys, and new apartment houses for the growing population seeking to share in the reflected prosperity of Andorra. It is now about the same size as Jaca, although it was only about two-thirds as large before the Civil War.

Although there is no bustle in Seo, everything there seems wide-awake – even the Cathedral, which I had fully expected to recognize as one of Spain's medieval backwaters, like Sigüenza or Albarracín. Instead, the priests who officiated at Mass were spruce figures moving in swift precise steps at the end of the austere and lofty nave. The cathedral was finished in 1175, but had been begun in the previous century by Saint Ermengol, the most famous of all its bishops, and for all his sanctity a great defender and extender of the rights of his see – as the poor bishops of Roda learnt to their cost. Two of the finest views of the cathedral are from without: that of the main façade, and that of the apse, which from outside is seen to have a charming open gallery of Romanesque arches running above it.

Also outside the main building, but of the same date, is the cloister, of which three sides survive intact. We must in any case pass through it if we are to reach the diocesan museum, and if we are lucky in our day we may have the opportunity of attending there a *son et lumière* performance based on the life of Saint Ermengol. The accompanying *son* is chosen to give an idea of what people in the Middle Ages thought appropriate music to the scenes described: such pieces as the *Laudes Hincmari* of the coronation of Charlemagne, the sixteenth-century *Absolta del Maestro Brudieu*, or a twelfth-century lament for the death of a count.

The word *seo* means cathedral, and Urgel was already the seat of a bishopric in Visigothic times. It was the first Spanish cathedral city to be freed from the Moslems after these had first been driven from their trans-pyrenean bridgehead of Septimania – or *Gotia* as the Franks for long called it – around Narbonne. The act of consecration of the cathedral in 839 is only one of an extraordinary wealth and variety of documents which have survived in the archives of the prince-bishops, and a selection of these, with other treasures, is beautifully displayed in the diocesan museum.

Out of such a selection, any visitor will inevitably again make his own personal choice, preferring to file in his memory those particular exhibits which most appeal to him. My own first choice was an illuminated manuscript of about the year A.D. 1000, a *Commentary on the Apocalypse* of the Blessed One of Liebana. It was written in Visigothic characters, but its fascination lay in the illustrations of its 93 folios. Had anyone shown them to me without a clue as to their date I would at once have exclaimed 'Hieronymus Bosch'. For the world which his brush created almost five hundred years later was no stranger, no more filled with horrors, and no more troubling to the profounder depths of the mind than the fantasies depicted by this disciple of the Beato de Liebana about the time when men were expecting the world itself to end with the millenium.

The exotic culture of al-Andalus, when the caliphs still reigned in Cordova, must have been partly responsible for such wilder flights of imagination of scribes in the bleak Christian fringe. It was in wonder at the intimacies, as well as at the struggles between the two religions which made my second choice the *Dialogues of Saint Gregory*. My interest here was not in the almost running hand in which it was written, nor its early date of 938, but in the way in which this date was expressed: 'In the second year of Abderrahman, King of Cordova.'

As I like the Spanish Pyrenees as much as anywhere on earth, and as one of my favourite characters in history is Gerbert, the Auvergnat wandering scholar of the Dark Ages who 'made good' as Pope Silvester II, my final choice made itself. It was a papal bull which he had issued. For Gerbert as a simple monk had studied in the schools of the Spanish March, and as Pope he showed his gratitude by defining and confirming all the rights and possessions of the diocese of Urgel, '*ita ut nullus Rex, nullus Princeps, nullus Comes, nullus Marchio, nullus judex, neque ulla magna parvaque persona*' should in any way infringe them. I can almost hear the wily Silvester dictating that bull himself: no doubt he could have put a name to every King, Prince, Count, Marquis, judge, and greater or smaller person whom he was so impersonally warning off Seo de Urgel. His fantastic career had only made him more of a realist, and he well knew that the sources of power were fragmented indeed in the early medieval Spanish Pyrenees.

Picking up the tiny 'parish magazine' of the cathedral, I found that a sea-change can come over one's moral priorities at the gates of Andorra. For next to a cautionary quotation from Saint Francis of Sales: 'If once you should happen to dance, think while you are dancing of the souls who are in hell for having danced,' was a more reassuring little article entitled 'I am a smuggler'. This told how St. Anthony once miraculously turned into beans some tobacco which a poor man was seeking to take into Barcelona past the city's customs officers, and comfortingly concluded that 'smuggling – on a small scale, at least – cannot be considered a sin'.

It is perhaps the proximity of Andorra, where Catalan is the official language, which has also led to an addition to – or should one say the completion of? – a notice on the cathedral's main door. For underneath the printed warnings: 'ATENCION A LA ESCALERA – ATTENTION AUX MARCHES – MIND THE STEPS', someone has added in pencil: 'Vigilen l'escala'.

From the references which have been made to them here and elsewhere it will be obvious that the bishops of Seo de Urgel have always been, and remain today, perhaps the most important single figures in the area covered by this book. So that the reader will understand that when in a remote valley of upper Aragon the girl with whom I was catching toads and salamanders for the Pyrenean Centre for Experimental Biology told me in a sudden burst of confidence that her best friend's grandmother's brother was the Bishop of Seo de Urgel, I felt that I was as near as I was ever likely to reach to the heart of the Spanish Pyrenees.

Continuing our journey up the Segre, the dominant geographical feature is the cliff-like Sierra del Cadí, which towers up on our right and is responsible for the eccentric course of the Segre and hence for the existence of the Cerdaña – just as the Sierra de la Peña is responsible for the course of the Aragon and hence for the Canal de Berdún. Like the Sierra de la Peña, the Sierra del Cadí is a sub-Pyrenean formation standing apart from the main chain, but at more than twice the height and 150 miles farther east, it is very much drier. San Juan de la Peña has little water to spare: the Sierra del Cadí, as befits a massif which still retains the name bestowed on it by the Moslem invaders from north Africa, is practically waterless.

It is also practically roadless. Some maps mark an uncertain track from Seo south through Fornols, but this is on the western edge of the massif, and I was assured that it was totally unsuitable for wheeled traffic. There is also a road which penetrates a certain distance beyond Montella, halfway between Seo and Puigcerdá, but this 'dies' at the remote sanctuary of Our Lady of Bastanist. And how indeed could any useful road be driven across this wall, only two or three hundred feet below the main chain opposite, and far steeper? As indicated near the beginning of this book, it is a wall which effectively marks the frontier of the Pyrenean system: other mountains lie beyond, but to describe them is outside the scope of a general account of the Spanish Pyrenees.

'No hills in Europe look so marvellously high,' wrote Belloc of the Sierra del Cadí as seen from beyond Castellbó. And a view at least as fine can be had from the slopes of the main range. Fortunately one good road does climb these for a few miles. It was built to serve the little spa of Sanillés, set amidst well-wooded, well-watered grounds which turn a pleasant hotel into a very pleasant hotel indeed. But although the *Hotel Balneario* of Sanillés is endearing, rustic, and charming, it is not cheap, and more economic waters can be taken at the Baños de San Vicente down on the main road, or at the Baños de Musa about a mile away. No doubt the springs of all three draw on the same deep mineral sources.

Alternatively, if the visitor seeks good air rather than good waters, he can continue up the road beyond Sanillés, through Travaseras to Llés. Here the aptly named *Hotel Mirador*, although only graded as third category, has a swimming pool, a friendly atmosphere, and a breathtaking view of the *muralla* of the Sierra del Cadí. And there is a gravel track for some miles beyond Llés to a refuge hut set in high woods.

Fishermen would prefer to base themselves on one of the hotels in Martinet, or possibly at the recently opened luxury camping site beside the Segre at Bellver. There seems little lack of water here, and when the valley broadens out soon after to become the Cerdaña, it is surprising to note that the farms lying beneath the Sierra del Cadí are at least as green as those opposite, five miles away on the foothills of the Pyrenees proper.

'The reason for that is quite simple. Here beneath the Sierra del Cadí we face due north. Over there on the other side of the Cerdaña they face due south.'

I had forgotten the Segre's unusual course from east to west.

Urgellet and Cerdaña

But I could not have chosen a better informant, for the lady speaking to me was none other than the wife of Professor Solé Sabaris, the greatest geographer in Spain, and the author of that definitive and fascinating work, *Los Pirineos*. His own love of the mountains to which he has devoted so much study is shown by his choice of a summer home at the hamlet of Bor, in the south-west corner of the Cerdaña. Here, in an old mill house beside a stream, surrounded by his eleven children he leads that cultured rural family life of which many Englishmen dream, but which few achieve.

Little Gidding, Kelmscot Manor, the country rectory at its best: they were so delightful – why are they so hard to recapture? Partly, perhaps, because there is so little deep country left in England, and partly because there dominates here another, louder country tradition, with fashion and mammon on its side. Between the horn of the Jag' and the cry of Squire Western's hounds the quiet voice of Nicholas Ferrer is hushed, and even the loud laughter of William Morris is hardly heard.

The country scholar, enjoying 'sound sleep by night; study and ease together mixed' has never been a model for Spaniards in quite the same way. Yet without trying surprising numbers of them achieve it. In white cottages a mile or two behind the Mediterranean, or even in the unexpected glimpse of a book-lined study amidst the monotonous plains of Castile, we thrill in recognition of the reality which eludes us. And although the doyen of Pyrenean studies was himself away from home, conducting a postgraduate course in the Canary Islands, I carried away with me from Bor the memory of a happy home, where learning was no less prized for being lightly worn. Don Luis Solé Sabaris not only best knows how to write about the Pyrenees: he best knows how to live there.

Soon after Bellver the main road crosses into Gerona, the last of Spain's five northern frontier provinces, which throws a long salient over the pass of Tosas to within a few hundred yards of Andorra. One wonders what that rational eighteenth-century ruler Charles III was doing, in drawing such an illogical boundary when he divided the old kingdoms of Spain into the modern administrative provinces. He was not unmindful of the interests of the Pyreneans, for it was he who handed many of the private, feudally held forests over to the municipalities within which they stood, and thereby endowed them with the wealth which those forests have brought them in the past thirty years. Besides following older boundaries of county and *comarca*, he perhaps wished to retain a reminder of lands lost, just as the French, after the Franco-Prussian war of 1870, retained in the territory of Belfort, the rump of the department of Haut Rhin, a testimony of their unwillingness to acknowledge the permanent loss of Alsace and Lorraine.

But it is hard to credit such romantic motives to the most enlightened of all the enlightened despots; especially as just such a testimony to an older order already existed, and had existed ever since the Peace of the Pyrenees turned the Spanish Rosellón into the French Roussillon, and half the Cerdaña into the Cerdagne. The loss of the second territory followed on the loss of the first, for the Roussillon would have been a barren gain had it been united to France only by one vulnerable highway between the Corbière hills and the Mediterranean. So the French insisted on – and Spain in 1659 was in no position to refuse – the cession of just as many villages of the Cerdaña as would give them control of the route from Perpignan up the Conflent, over the Puymorens pass, and down into the Ariège valley. They thereby achieved not merely their Pyrenean frontier, but those extra square miles which gave them the means to defend it.

The Spanish negotiators, however, in the desperation of the defeated, clung to the straw provided by the word 'village'. Llivia might be in the area to be surrendered, but Llivia, which as Julia Livia had been the Roman capital of the Cerdaña, was in law a town.

So Llivia remained Spanish, along with its surrounding twelve square kilometres, and to reach it one must leave Spain, showing one's passport at a Civil Guards' checkpoint, and must proceed, feeling a little unreal and out of this world, along a neutral road through France. There is no French customs or passport examination, for although one has left Spain one never technically enters France. But at the point where the neutral road crosses the highway which led to all this trouble, a silent but watchful French police officer sits in a small wooden box, keeping an eye on everyone who enters or leaves the enclave of Llivia by the only official route.

Llivia, when reached, proves to be the most rural 'town' one is ever likely to see. But although it is sleepy, silent, and slow, there are generally plenty of people about the streets sloping down from the fortified church, for it has a population which just touches four figures. And many French families now spend their summer holidays there, enjoying the clear skies and pure air of the French Cerdagne, with greater peace and at Spanish prices.

The road to Llivia leaves Spain very near Rigolisa, which with a chapel, a *fuente*, and a *mirador* overlooking both nations, is one of the favourite points for a walk from Puigcerdá. Standing on a hill a mile back from the frontier, Puigcerdá is the only inland town in Spain with two 'seasons': one during its cool but sunny summer, and one during its snowy but equally sunny winter, with ice-hockey tournaments, and the ski-slopes of La Molina within easy reach.

Puigcerdá might be said to have started life as a resort, for it was founded in 1177 by King Alfonso of Aragon – the son of Petronella and Ramón Berenguer – who decided to build a summer home there while staying in his palace at the much older Hix, two miles away across the present frontier. And the artificial lake on the edge of the town, which with its willows and its swans is almost the trademark of Puigcerdá, was created as long ago as 1310. Of all this medieval past the present town has little to show, for the good reason that it has not been granted that supreme happiness of escaping history. Its situation, on the contrary, has in every century invited attack, right up to the second Carlist War, in which the unsuccessful siege of Puigcerdá by the Carlists was one of their early reverses, just as their own unsuccessful defence of Seo de Urgel finally extinguished their hopes in Catalonia. As recently as the Civil War of thirty years ago, Puigcerdá lost the body of its church of Santa María, begun in the year after the town's foundation, although the seventeenth-century tower still stands.

Personally I find Puigcerdá a disappointing and an uninteresting town, a little Sitges without the sea, with its menus all priced in francs – and in almost as many francs as at Bourg Madame. But there is no disappointment as we travel away across the wide fields of the Cerdaña, over which we have gazed from the 140 feet height of Santa María's tower. In those fields will be grazing some of the Cerdana's horses, who are one of the great breeds of Spain. The *ceretana* mare when sired by the French *percheron* gave birth to a most powerful carthorse. When sired by a Breton stallion she produced the animal which artillery commanders used to seek for their gun carriages. And when crossed with the Vich donkey she gave Spain that splendid mule which over the steep and cobbled *caminos de herradura* carried most of the peninsula's merchandise before the age of Primo de Rivera.

There are few gun carriages in the Spanish army since the Spanish-American Treaty of 1953; and even in the Pyrenees we have noticed as unusual those valleys which still have no tracks fit for wheeled traffic. So there are less horses than there used to be in the flat, rich meadows of the Cerdaña, and more cows, for which their grazing is equally well suited. And here the *comarca* has an advantage over most other parts of the Spanish Pyrenees. For when the butchers of Barcelona and Madrid raise the prices of veal and beef, and every one asks: 'Why can't our mountains provide us with more meat?' the only answer which the shepherds of Ansó or of Bohí can make is: 'Because Spanish housewives won't buy mutton.'

Most of the 2,000-foot climb out of the Cerdaña is accomplished in the first six miles after we leave the plain, and for six more miles the road coasts along mountainsides until it passes through the barely perceptible 6,000-foot pass of Tosas. At the top of the steep climb a road runs off to the right down to La Molina, the winter sports resort. The modern hotels of Super-Molina, with the *téléphériques* connecting the two places, suddenly face the traveller across a profound valley as he comes through the Puerto de Tosas in the reverse direction. Their clear white functional pattern, utterly modern yet utterly appropriate, is a not unfitting prelude to – or last impression of – the Cerdaña.

24. Tahull in the valley of Bohí: at over 5,000 feet yet with two churches
(San Clemente in the foreground)

25. Viu de Llevata at over 4,000 feet

26. Ruins of Ampurias, looking over Mediterranean towards Sierra de Rosas

27. Cadaqués

5. Andorra

Entire books have been written about Andorra, some of them very recently. So there is no point in trying to compress all that they have said into a few pages, especially as in a strictly political sense the co-principality forms no part of the Spanish Pyrenees. Geographically, however, it is no less Spanish than Sobrarbe or Bohí, and a good deal more Spanish than Arán.

The French co-sovereignty is indeed the only reason for Andorra's independence, and the Andorrans themselves have long realized this. Far from being grateful for liberty when the French Revolutionary government declined to assume the royal co-dominion inherited from the counts of Foix, they went on clamouring for the restitution of the old order, until in 1806 the new Charlemagne, Napoleon, graciously agreed to play his part as joint protector of the last vestige of the Spanish March.

It is Charlemagne whom the French invoke as they send their good things over the ludicrously high road which they have built over the Envalira pass, which at almost 8,000 feet is the only possible route from France into Andorra. Thanks to their double allegiance the Andorran parents now have the choice between French schools with French schoolteachers, and Spanish schools with Spanish schoolteachers, for neither of which Andorra pays a penny. And nowhere else is it possible to send a letter from a Spanish post office at the inland postage rate to anywhere in Spain, and a letter from a French post office a couple of hundred yards away at the inland postage rate to anywhere in France. Andorra thus always has two sets of stamps; and significantly the most frequently used French stamp when I was last there showed 'Charlemagne crossing Andorra'. Unable to believe that after Roncesvalles he would have led an army over the Envalira I found myself humming that rather irreverent French pop-song: 'Sacré Charlemagne!'

The Catalan Pyrenees

This nostalgia for a heroic Carolingian past, here adroitly exploited, is only typical of most of the valleys we have already visited. Typical, too, is the Romanesque architecture. As we gaze at Sant Joan de Caselles, Sant Miquel d'Engolasters, or Santa Coloma, we feel ourselves back in the valley of Bohí, but deprived of the crowning glories of Tahull.

For in essentials the valleys of Andorra are even poorer than Bohí. Tahull may stand at over 5,000 feet, but Soldeu, the highest Andorran hamlet, is set at over 6,000. The air can be raw even on summer evenings beside the two tumbling torrents which unite at Andorra la Vella to form the Valira. Four of the country's six parishes lie along these two torrents, and their strip of cultivable land alongside the water is sometimes no more than twenty yards wide.

The contrast between the inborn frugality of these outlying parishes, and the strident prosperity of the booming mushroom town which now extends from Andorra la Vella all the way to Les Escaldes should serve not as a basis for moral reflexion, but as a phenomenon to be savoured and enjoyed. As beside the rushing waters of the Valira we read the only English newspaper that we are likely to find between Fuenterrabía and Figueras, we can delight in the contradictory atmosphere of the most unusual, yet in certain senses the most representative corner of the Spanish Pyrenees.

6. Ripollés

Since Puigcerdá the signposts have uncompromisingly proclaimed the distances to Barcelona, and as we descend from the pass of Tosas we sense that we have moved much closer to the heartland of Catalonia. Lérida, in every respect the outlier of the four Catalan provinces, is now well behind us, and we are deep into Gerona. When the kings of Majorca ruled in Perpignan, and when Montpellier and Alghero took orders from Barcelona, Gerona lay in the centre of the Catalan dominions, and nowhere else today do we find in the same degree that peculiarly Catalan combination of a primitive peasant agriculture cheek-by-jowl with a flourishing industry and commerce.

The first place of any size is Ribas de Fresser, which takes its name from the valley into which the road has at last descended. One can follow the Fresser on foot beyond the 8,300 foot pass of La Marrana to the Ull de Ter refuge hut, which lies at 7,700 feet amongst the last high mountains of the Spanish Pyrenees.

The road up the Fresser 'dies' at Caralps, itself at 4,300 feet a minor winter sports resort. From Caralps another path follows a subsidiary torrent of the Fesser up to a more important winter sports centre.

It is not as a winter sports resort, however, that one first thinks of Nuria. For there has been a sanctuary of Our Lady there ever since the eleventh century, although there is now no church older than the seventeenth. Here beneath the Puigmal, at 9,542 feet the highest peak before the Mediterranean, lies the home of the second most popular Virgin in Catalonia. And although she comes a long way behind Our Lady of Montserrat in the 'christening league', she makes up for this in the quality of her followers. For the Catalans can hardly be said to produce the most beautiful women in Spain. But I have yet to meet a plain girl with the lovely name of Nuria.

243

The Catalan Pyrenees

Although no proper road climbs the 3,500 feet from Ribas de Fresser up to Nuria, they are connected by a mountain railway. At the height of the summer, and again during the winter sports season, there is a frequent service; but there are several months of the year when anyone proposing to visit Nuria, except on foot, will have to organize a little way ahead.

Nine miles down the valley from Ribas the Fresser empties itself into the Ter, the first river we have met which empties itself directly into the Mediterranean, instead of via the Ebro. In the angle between the two rivers stands Ripoll. This position has made it at all periods the capital of the area formed by these two valleys and the region depending on them, a *comarca* therefore known quite simply as the Ripollés.

A monastery was founded here at the end of the sixth century by Reccared, the first king of the Arian Visigoths to become Catholic. This, however, does not seem to have survived the fighting between Moslems and Christians in these marchlands; and the great Benedictine house of Santa María, which became one of the most learned communities in Spain during the early Middle Ages, was founded by Count Wilfred the Hairy in 888, in the days when the ruler of the Spanish March was still nominally appointed by the Carolingians who had conquered it.

The abbey church as it stands is largely the work of late nineteenth century restorers. But it is nonetheless impressive. The twelfth-century sculptures of the main door would look better still if the church stood in isolation, instead of at the end of a short street, but once inside the five aisles of its 200-foot nave awe us just as they must have awed when first built in the years before 1032. More unusual, and less restored, is the beautiful cloister. Its 440 columns are in two storeys, a fifteenth-century gallery in granite superposed on a twelfth-century Romanesque cloister in violet jasper.

In a neighbouring building is one of those all-embracing local museums which has never learnt how to say no to the exhibits thrust upon it. But it is worth visiting if only to see the collection of pistols and shotguns for which Ripoll was once famous throughout Europe. This industry grew up because Ripoll was the natural centre for many of the small ironworks of the Catalan Pyrenees, and it declined as these gave way to the greater industrial concentrations of modern times. The museum also shows models of these forges, which perfected what became generally known as the 'Catalan method' of producing iron, which was everywhere the most commonly used process from the fifteenth to the nineteenth centuries. *Farga* which described both this process and the forges where it was carried out, still occurs in place-names, and for the first time I realized the significance of Farga de Moles, where stands the Spanish checkpoint at the Andorran frontier.

Ripoll, for all its antiquity and importance, is a somewhat gloomy town. San Juan de las Abadesas, six miles up the Ter valley, is a much brighter place, although with about 5,000 inhabitants it is only a little over half the size. It owes this partly to its prosperity, for it has the factory which makes all the sausage skins of Spain – a growth industry if ever there was one! But I feel that it also owes its brighter atmosphere to the feminine touch. For here too Count Wilfred the Hairy founded a religious house, but for nuns instead of for monks. And the first of its abbesses or *abadesas*, who are still remembered in the town's name, was his own daughter, Doña Emma.

When the present church was built in the twelfth century, the foundation had been taken over by Augustinian canons. Some Romanesque work also survives in the mainly fifteenth century cloister, but San Juan's greatest treasures are sculptural rather than architectural: the fourteenth-century tomb of the Blessed Miró, and more important, the group depicting the Descent from the Cross which is known locally as the *Santísimo Misterio*. Gazing up at this thirteenth-century work in wood, of Romanesque inspiration in spite of its date, I was reminded of the Christ of Alquézar.

Nine miles farther up the Ter is Camprodón, a fresh summer resort with a shell of a monastery church, and a Virgin *dolorosa* in the parish church who has become the object of a strong local cult. From Camprodón a road has just been completed over the 5,300-foot pass of Arras into the French valley of the Tech – the lovely Vallespir: it forms a really useful addition to the number of transpyrenean links. The last place in Spain is Mollo. The first in France is Prats-de-Mollo. Such connections are only to be expected when a national frontier has only divided villages for a mere three hundred years.

Continuing up the Ter valley we pass through Llanás, with a

curious church to which I have been unable to find any references. Its doorway has a Renaissance tympanum supported on Romanesque capitals, and within the obviously ancient interior a framed medieval painting hangs beside the altar.

Seven miles beyond Camprodón, along a road which steadily deteriorates after Llanás, is the last village on the Ter, Setcasas. A path can be followed beyond to the headwaters of the Ter and to the Ull de Ter refuge hut, and so over to the upper valley of the Fresser.

It is not only the dirty white of its houses – now many more than seven – which makes us feel a little sad as we stand beside the stream outside Setcasas. It is also the realization that for the last time we have reached the head of a typically Pyrenean valley. There are more hills to come before the Mediterranean. But the last great height, the 9,135-foot Canigou, lies over in France. Never again during what remains of our journey will there rise sublimely above us, as here, a whole circle of peaks to between 8,000 and 9,000 feet.

7. Ampurdán

The roads east from Ripoll and from San Juan de las Abadesas both climb to drop once again to the small industrial town of Olot, lying in a basin surrounded by some thirty long extinct volcanoes. These may perhaps have some influence on the climate or the soil of the surrounding countryside, causing it to produce apples, pears, and maize rather than wine and olives: in this respect the little *comarca* of Olot resembles an Atlantic island set down in the Mediterranean.

The villages as we continue east all shelter small textile factories, and remind one of the smaller hosiery towns of Leicestershire, by the way in which no family is without one or more members at work. A café owner in San Jaime de la Llierca pointed with pride at the Seat 600 garaged right inside his bar amongst the chairs and tables: the fruit of his night shifts at the factory when his customers had gone home to bed. But they preserve a pre-industrial devotion to the various sanctuaries in the neighbouring hills, and in particular to Santa Julia to the south, and to Nuestra Señora del Monte to the north-east.

This last shrine belongs really to Ampurdán, the wide *comarca* into which the road is now descending. Besalú, where it divides into a road to Bañolas and a road to Figueras, is our last town lying deep in the hills. Though a small place of under 2,000 inhabitants, it was once the seat of a separate county; and after absorbing it the early Catalan rulers were proud to style themselves 'Counts of Barcelona and of Besalú'. From those days date the Romanesque church of San Vicente, the abbey church of San Pedro, and the ruined church of Santa María; and there is a beautiful garden amidst yet other ruins on top of the hill up which clamber the streets.

Bañolas, nine miles south of Besalú, is a restful market town around an arcaded *plaza*, with a small spa beside the lake which

VIII AMPURDAN

bears its name. It has two large churches, Santa María at the centre, and San Esteban set unaccountably right on the edge of the present town; but the church which must be seen is far smaller and over a mile away round the lake at Porqueras. This Romanesque jewel, with a fine doorway and capitals, was consecrated in 1182 on the site of an early ninth-century foundation. Beside it stands an ancient stone monument which was once functional, for it is called a *conminador*, or literally, a threatener. From here curses were pronounced against any who should damage the village's crops.

East from Besalú, after a few more twisting miles the road becomes almost level, whilst the country opens out on both sides. We are approaching the heart of Ampurdán, the *comarca* which has taken its name from Ampurias, and hence from Emporion, the leading Greek colony on the Spanish coast. We have several times during our journey noticed comparisons between the administrations of certain Pyrenean valleys and the constitutions of some of the cities of ancient Greece. Here in Ampurdán we are dealing less with comparisons than with survivals. Reference has already been made to the classical appearance of the *alpargata catalana*, here the everyday footwear; and some claim that the *sardana*, the national dance of Catalonia – so different both in steps and in spirit from any other dance in the peninsula – owes its wide rings and its measured pace to the Phocaean settlers from distant Ionia. But I have also read that the *sardana* originated in the Cerdaña, and took its name from there. And perhaps the truest, and the least contentious way to describe Ampurdán is not as a land of classical survivals, but as a land which is classical, pure and simple, like Provence or Campagna: a land where Greeks rejoiced to settle, but which would still have classical characteristics in a Greek city had never arisen in the bay of Rosas: a land 'naturally' classical in the sense that medieval scholars thought of Virgil as 'naturally' Christian.

> '*What little town by river or sea-shore,*
> *Or mountain-built with peaceful citadel*'

Ampurdán offers all these characteristically classical sites. But the founders of Emporion were too busy to think about how best to be classical. Their purpose was trade, and the very name of their city meant market. It was set where first a reasonable harbour after the long, flat, sandy shore from the Camargue to Collioure stood also within easy reach of the main route across the Perthus, at under 1,000 feet the lowest of Pyrenean passes.

And right across that route stands the modern capital of Ampurdán, Figueras. Coming to it as we do now, after traversing the entire Pyrenees, we are better able to assess its qualities than those who enter it immediately after crossing the frontier, for whom it is their first Spanish town, and who therefore see only what is obvious and general throughout Spain rather than what is particular and confined to Catalonia, let alone what is subtle and special to Ampurdán. We shall therefore recognize it as one of the pleasantest small towns of the peninsula: near the mountains, as near the frontier as is San Sebastián, and near the sea, which here means the lovely Rosas and the lovelier Cadaqués.

And coming from those noble but lonely highlands where man, because alone, can learn to know himself, we are as surprised as enraptured by the Mediterranean provision for man as a social animal which awaits us down in this Catalan Capua. There are a score or more of cafés, but the four largest lie together along one and a half sides of the central agora formed by the Ramblas. The only word to describe these four is 'profound'. Their pavement terraces alone hold six rows of tables, and there are unplummeted nooky depths in the maze of lounges behind.

Here, with a single *café cortado* one can spend entire mornings or afternoons, reading, writing, and staring, as in a quieter Paris the artists and writers used to sit in St. Germain-des-Près. Scattered over the wide terraces – for they are even wider than they are deep – will be a variety of characters who might have stepped straight from the pages of Henri-François Rey: men and girls in blue jeans, in for a day's shopping from one of the coastal resorts where they are spending the summer; older, more formally clad Germans and Dutch halting for their first Spanish refreshment on the way to Barcelona and the south; well-dressed women; and groups of business like businessmen, talking urgently in harsh Catalan.

This excellence of the cafés has a reverse side. I have wandered the narrow side streets for a long hour in search of a dark bar, with sawdust on the floor and paunchy barrels in the corner, where, as in Sobrarbe or Pallars I could munch a *bocadillo* of mountain ham to the accompaniment of half a litre of inky wine. The smallest *pueblo* of upper Aragon has two or three such bars, but Figueras appears to have none.

It has little in the way of monuments, either; in part because it was not always as large or as important as it is today. Indeed, with 30,000 inhabitants, it has more than doubled in size since before the Civil War, and only a fraction of this growth has been by natural increase. Figueras now has two factories producing bicycles and motor-cycles, and wherever in Catalonia there is industry there too one finds immigrants from the poorer provinces of southern Spain, where the mechanisation of the great estates has in the last few years deprived tens of thousands of their already irregular and ill-paid employment. I was told that the entire population of one *pueblo* in the province of Almería had moved up to Figueras, complete with its *alcalde!*

It is in Ampurdán that the purest Catalan is said to be spoken, and Pompeu Fabra, the Malherbe or Samuel Johnson of Catalonia, used the Ampurdán dialect more than any others for his dictionaries and grammars. That it thus speaks the classical Catalan can hardly be ascribed to Greek influence, but it may perhaps be some lingering tradition from Emporion which has given Figueras the best market along the whole belt of the Spanish Pyrenees.

Roussillon, the French Catalan province across the frontier, is in many respects the twin of Ampurdán, and Roussillon is known throughout France for the quality, excellence, and earliness of its fruit and vegetables. But Roussillon is the southernmost corner of France, and the Halles of Paris stand ready to welcome its products. The soil of Ampurdán is no poorer, nor the sun less warm, but it lies right in the north of Spain. So the best of what grows in its *huertas* gets no farther than the market of Figueras. 'They are from the mountains: they were picked early this morning up at Massanet' a vendor will tell you as she weighs out a kilo of juicy strawberries.

The mountains to which she refers are little more than hills, alongside those we have recently left behind us. Neulos, the highest point of the Albères, as the frontier chain is called betwen the Perthus and Mediterranean, rises to only 4,150 feet. But their actual descent into the sea is abrupt, and the coast road from Cerbère through Port-Bou to Colera is in every sense a *parcours difficile et dangereux*. Inland a few miles, and practically on the frontier, the twelfth-century Romanesque monastery of San Quirico de Colera lies in a remote site amidst this very Mediterranean countryside where the olives and vines of the plain have given place to an aromatic *maquis* and the occasional umbrella pine.

Massanet, where the strawberries were picked, lies on the other side of the main road, the 'A 2' of Spain, which enters France at El Perthus, where for a quarter of a mile one side of the street is in one country and one side in another. Here one or two of the frontier peaks are slightly higher than Neulos. But as hills they have three advantages over the Albères proper. They start earlier and stretch farther. They are thickly covered with pines mixed in certain places with deciduous trees. And they are deeply penetrated by the valleys of two small but genuine rivers, the Muga and the Manol, which contribute the sound of cool waters rippling over stones to the delights of Mediterranean warmth in the shade of resin-scented pinewoods.

This lovely area, only twenty miles by road from the Costa Brava, is still undiscovered either by those who crowd its mushroom resorts, or by those other millions who race down through Figueras on their way south. One September evening of 1964 at the fiesta of Lladó on the Manol, a week or so after the twelve-millionth tourist that year had entered Spain, I was the only foreigner watching the circling *sardana* dancers in the shady *plaza*. Yet it was in early June that after showing me the Romanesque façade of the parish church, and the burnt-out shell of the eighteenth-century priory, a friend there had taken me on to the first-floor terrace behind his house. Lladó stands only a little over two hundred feet above sea-level, yet so flat is the plain of Ampurdán that nothing obstructed our view of the bay of Rosas, glinting in the last rays of the setting sun. To the left of the bay rose the stark mass of the Sierra de Rosas. It was towards this that my friend pointed.

'Did you see that light flash for a moment between the two summits? And do you see that one now? And that one?'

'What are they?' I asked.

'They are the cars driving up from Cadaqués. Here we catch the beam of their headlights for a moment as they come over the top of the Sierra. In two months' time those flashes will be continuous.'

Ampurdan

Yet while the bay of Rosas was an Anglo-French lake, and while Spanish was but rarely heard in the synthetic horror of Playa de Aro, I have wandered a whole day in the woods behind Lladó without meeting a soul, and have picked my way around a deserted house in a bend of the Manol which will stand intact in the milder climate for many years after Descarga at Arano has disintegrated.

It is the proximity of the booming coast and of the industrial centres which has accelerated such depopulation in this part of the Pyrenees. It is particularly noticeable on the higher, poorer ground between the two rivers, as at Vilaritg, where only eighty people now occupy a fortified village built for several hundred. Down again in the other valley, that of the Muga, the land is more easily worked, and some of the villages, such as San Lorenzo, have been chosen by Barcelona families for their summer homes.

The natives of Figueras often drive up the Muga for a quiet picnic. Foreigners like ourselves may stop at Las Escaulas, where an enterprising farmer not only has a waterfall which he can turn on and off – 'on' to entertain visitors, 'off' to irrigate his land – but has established beside it a restaurant where his family serve delicious meals, prepared from his own produce. I particularly recommend the chickens, and the great dishes of snails. These are prepared in the Spanish way, which although slightly less refined than the French means that the consumer gets about sixty snails instead of merely six.

If we do not feel like eating quite so much we can take our *bocadillos* and wine farther up the valley. Halfway between San Lorenzo de la Muga and the last village, Albaña, there is a small chapel beside a farmhouse, and just across the river from there stone seats have been built in the shade of great trees beside a crystal-clear spring. The Fuente Palau is one of the coolest and most inviting of all the many Pyrenean springs. Chosen and prepared as they are by those who know the area and who esteem shade and water, they are always preferred places for picnics.

The road up the Muga, never a good one, 'dies' at Albaña, but a track continues beyond up to the remote chapel of Bassagoda. However, near Terradas, the village before San Lorenzo, stands a more accessible sanctuary. Nuestra Señora de la Salud has always been well loved in Ampurdán, and there were already several chapels dedicated to her when the priest, Felip Olivet, determined to build one on this hill looking over the Muga valley towards his native Massanet. He celebrated the inaugural Mass on Our Lady's day, 1681, and the shrine continued to grow in popularity after his own death at the age of 80 in 1710. Nuestra Señora de la Salud is now the patron saint of Ampurdán, and here at Terradas is her seat.

Although of no great antiquity, the chapel with its guest house, alone on its wooded hill, is in every sense good for the spirit. And though facing away from the sea it enjoys a superb view. For beyond the frontier range, to which cling Massanet and La Bajol, there rises from a soil which is no longer Spanish yet is still Catalan the white mass of Canigou.

Epilogue at Cadaqués

Solé Sabaris has plainly stated in the passage quoted at the very beginning of this book that Cabo Creus, at the eastern tip of the Sierra de Rosas, rather than Port-Bou, where the Albères meet the sea, should be regarded as the Mediterranean terminus of the Pyrenees. And the Sierra de Rosas, rising in isolation from the main chain, corresponds to Jaizquibel just as Cabo Creus corresponds to Cabo Higuer.

Leaving on the right the fishing village of Rosas, its ever more numerous hotels and bungalows now spreading across the marshlands where the Muga and the Manol empty themselves into the bay, the road climbs for five miles, and then for two miles more coasts along a plateau. A road leads away down to the left, to Puerto de la Selva, and on up the coast to Port-Bou. It is this route which must be followed if one wishes to climb on foot to the belvedere occupied by the ruins of the fortified Romanesque monastery of San Pedro de Roda. But our own road continues straight on, and almost at once begins to drop, falling more steeply than it climbed. To left and right uncultivated terraces of land are occasionally relieved by a single unpruned olive tree run wild, the mute witness to an economic tragedy which some might regard as a social tragedy, too.

For a century before 1956 olives were the greatest single source of wealth in Cadaqués. Earlier still, before the steamship had replaced the sailing vessel, and before the *phylloxera* plague had killed the vines in 1870, this semi-autonomous republic had three stout strings to its bow. Its stony soil, better suited than the rich earth of the plain of Ampurdán to the local grape, produced a wine of up to sixteen degrees, comparable in quality to the *priorato* of Tarragona. And its olive oil, though strong and crude, was highly palatable, and found a ready market.

This wine and oil formed the foundation for a lively commerce, carried out in locally-owned ships of from 200 to 800 tons, which traded with Italy, with other Spanish ports, with Spanish-America, and even with the distant Philippines. At its height all the men of Cadaqués – whose population then numbered 4,000 as against only 1,500 today – were sailors, and the land was cultivated by labour brought in from the interior of Ampurdán.

They were sailors by necessity as well as by choice. Until this road was built across the Sierra de Rosas some fifty years ago a steep mule track was their only land link with the outside world. It was only to be expected that smuggling became one of the regular occupations of a people more isolated than many islanders. And here, at the end of a promontory that countless Phocaean triremes had rounded on their way from Massilia, there flourished for three centuries perhaps the most perfect of our Pyrenean city-states. From the reign of Ferdinand and Isabella to that of Charles III it enjoyed *fueros* far greater than those of Navarre today; and in the old *plaza mayor* the entire adult male population would assemble to pass laws and to take decisions, as no doubt the assembly once deliberated in Hellenic Ampurias.

Today's *ayuntamiento* is more conventionally constituted. The *alcade* is advised by six councillors, two of whom are elected by the heads of families, two by the trade unions, and two by the professional and business community. Each presides over a particular committee, dealing perhaps with the harbour, or with the water supply; and it is to be regretted that the public expenditure which these public services require cannot be met, as in the central Pyrenees, from inexhaustible public funds. Cadaqués has no common lands, and here the *vecinos* have to pay rates.

The bitter winter which killed the olive trees ten years ago could therefore have spelt economic disaster for the village. It coincided, however, with the great upsurge of the Spanish tourist industry in the mid-1950's. Three busy months in a small shop will now bring a greater cash income than a year's hard work in the fields, and the land on which the olives grew is now in some cases worth more than the crops of several centuries. But Cadaqués has not been ruined, as so much of the Spanish Mediterranean coast has now been ruined, although it lies at only twenty-two miles from the frontier. It owes this in the first place to its situation.

This becomes apparent as the road bends round on itself for

perhaps the twentieth time, and the gleaming white village suddenly comes into view far below us. There is clearly no space between sea and sierra for *urbanizaciones* such as have transformed Lloret de Mar. And this mountain road, a trial of nerves despite its excellent surface, in itself acts as a deterrent to many tourists. The ones who get to Cadaqués are the ones who really want to get there.

This, the last road of the Spanish Pyrenees, 'dies' in the square by the sea, the village's only stretch of level ground, and its natural heart. Round this square are some half-dozen cafés, and sitting in one of these – the luxurious *Hostal*, for example, or the more personal bar of Melitón – we shall soon realize the second reason why Cadaqués has not been ruined, or is only being ruined in a delectable and civilized way. For the visitors around us, who have filtered here across the Sierra de Rosas, are of a rather special kind. International set? Intellectuals? Bohemian artist colony, clinging to the extremities of the Dalí moustache? Some of all these, with some of the *mores* and perversions characteristic of such groups. They are particularly in evidence during July and August, when Cadaqués becomes the Catalan St. Tropez.

It is a St. Tropez which has found its Sagan. Take heed of the eyes of that handsome Frenchman in his early forties, seated only a few tables away. Little escapes them, as Cadaqués discovered when it found itself reflected as Caldeya in *Les Pianos Mécaniques* of Henri-François Rey. He has caught in print a particular aspect of Cadaqués in its summer fever, when the cafés never close, and when the sea is always warm. His beautifully-written book contains incidentally a number of set pieces which lend themselves naturally to cinematographic treatment, and it was being filmed on the spot during the summer of 1964.

Its author would agree that there are other aspects of Cadaqués. He himself notes the sad 'English of September' in their plastic raincoats, having their late holidays when the weather has already broken. And the character who eventually emerges as the hero – or anti-hero? – finally decides to stay on for a winter in Caldeya, the joys of which are lyrically evoked by the highly competent heroine.

It is during these other seasons that much serious work gets done in Cadaqués – not least by M. Rey himself, to whom I have done a great deal less than justice in describing him as the Sagan of the Spanish Riviera. Here the English writer, John Lodwick, was spending more and more of each year until his tragic death in a motor accident in Barcelona. Here his friend, Luis Romero the novelist, creates such works as *El Cacique*, which won him the Planeta literary prize in 1963. Here Margarita Lozano, the actress, can often be found resting between roles such as that of Ramona in Buñuel's brilliant film *Viridiana*.

These and others are attracted to Cadaqués as 'an end of the world', as Luis Romero described it to me. Here they can create a congenial society amongst themselves, visiting each others' homes or talking for long hours in the cafés. Here, above all, they have the leisure to think denied them in the bustle of Barcelona and Madrid.

There is one artist, however, who would have made his home at Cadaqués whether he had found society there or not – or even if there had not been one human soul on all the thirty winding miles of coastline between Puerto de la Selva and Rosas. For he is a man of Ampurdán, for whom this promontory, rather than a retreat, 'an end of the world', is the world's natural centre. The view from his home, which he has built not at Cadaqués itself, but on a tiny bay a short mile away, appears again and again in his work as the background to the most diverse subjects.

Port Lligat, which Salvador Dalí has thus immortalized, will remain even more unspoilt than Cadaqués itself. For it is protected by a body called the Patronato de Port Lligat, of which the artist is a member. And the five wild, treeless, waterless, and wonderful miles beyond, on to Cabo Creus, are not yet in need of protection.

The cape itself is given a surrealist touch by the holiday village of the Club Méditerranée, an almost organic cellular complex of white buildings clinging to the bare rock, and offering every facility for the enjoyment of the pagan Mediterranean life in a nice blend of Gallic and Hispanic mood. If any of the Phocaeans were disciples of the more imaginative Ionian philosophers, they would surely have approved of this new colony upon what was their coast 2,500 years ago.

Even at this unspoilt 'end of the world', however, the problems of the twentieth century can never be forgotten. Whenever one looks up from Cadaqués one sees two gleaming metal domes on the summit of the Sierra de Rosas. Here, as near Elizondo, the

Epilogue at Cadaques

Americans have built a radar station. For even in this day and age the Pyrenees remain *una muralla rigida y apenas franqueable*, an almost impassable barrier for those who take the right measures to hold it. From 406 to 409, whilst half the tribes of Germany were milling around Gaul unopposed, a few odd detachments of Roman troops sufficed to hold the Pyrenean passes, until treason alone let the Sueve and the Alan and the Vandal into Spain. And as recently as ten years ago, when the Fourth Republic was tottering in Paris, the Americans planned to make the Pyrenees, rather than the Rhine, their main line of defence in the event of an attack from the east.

At Cadaqués, however, as we think back over 270 green or dusty miles to Cabo Higuer, we think not of a barrier against barbarians to the north, or against Moslems to the south. We think rather of a many-sided friend, appearing here as a quiet *pueblo*, here as a foaming river, here as a shady forest, here as a high mountain, here as a trackless valley: a friend who whenever we meet him brings us health and happiness, and whom we have named – because we have to call friends by a name – the Spanish Pyrenees.

Appendix

1. COMMUNICATIONS

Apart from the two great highways at either end: the National One from Irún through Barcelona, and the National Two from Le Perthus through Figueras, there are no roads in the Spanish Pyrenees approaching motorway standard. It will be many years before any are required, for this is one corner of the globe still mercifully free of traffic congestion. Nevertheless, driving requires as much care here as anywhere else.

For, in the first place, the roads are almost invariably narrow. When they are also international through-routes they therefore demand especial wariness, as on the road from Irún up the Bidassoa valley, or on the road from Andorra through Seo de Urgel and on down the valley of the Segre.

In the second place they show great variation in surface, not only from one road to another, but between different sections of the same road. The motorist will encounter recently-laid asphalt, good gravel roads – excellent provided that he keeps half a mile between himself and the dust cloud raised by the car in front – and occasionally the worst surface of all: asphalt which has been allowed to deteriorate until it is pock-marked by potholes.

This variety is due to their being constantly up-graded, as time and funds permit; and it means that there is little point in giving any exact summary of their condition, for it would be out of date as soon as published. Besides, the assessment of road conditions is largely subjective. Many roads unsuitable for a low-slung shiny sports car present no problems to the author's high-clearance motor caravan, with its commercial engine. But the latter vehicle's height, coupled with its driver's distaste for sheer drops into the sea, would make him avoid the coast road from Cerbère to Colera, a road which would present the sports car's owner, on the other hand, with a superb opportunity for demonstrating his skill.

Appendix

Subject to these severe limitations of time and temperament, the following is a minimal short list of roads over which I personally would not willingly have driven a motor vehicle during the summer of 1965:

Ansó to the valley of Roncal, via Garde.

Escalona to Bielsa, through the Desfiladero de las Devotas.

From a couple of miles beyond Benasque up to the Baths of Benasque.

None of the roads joining the valleys of the Segre and the Noguera Pallaresa north of the road from Artesa de Segre to Tremp via Isona.

Llers to Terradas. It is better to avoid this pock-marked stretch by approaching the valley of the Muga via either Viure or Cistella, although neither alternative is brilliant.

Cerbère to Colera via Port-Bou.

The forest tracks, known as *pistas forestales*, are sometimes better than they sound: the mule tracks, known as *caminos de herradura*, are often even worse. The motorist who wishes to penetrate deeply into the wilder countryside without damaging his car may choose to leave this at a village, and to make arrangements locally for a lift on a timber lorry or a milk lorry. Generally leaving at incredibly early hours, these reach incredibly remote areas, and are always prepared to give a bone-shaking lift – for a consideration. Even if no bargain has been struck beforehand, the passenger must always offer to pay. The charge will be reasonable, but the principle of paying for such lifts is universally accepted.

When in your turn you give a shepherd a lift down from the head of a valley, or drop a young conscript on leave at his village fiesta, he will ask how much he owes you. You will, of course, refuse payment, but he will then insist on buying you a drink. In accepting this you will both make him feel that he has done something to repay you, and you will learn something more about him and his *pueblo*. And if you make the drink a simple glass of wine with soda water, *un vino con sifón*, you will not only spare his purse, but you will still be fit to drive on refreshed after a pleasant interlude.

The timber lorries and milk lorries will be even more useful, of course, to travellers on foot. These should also note that even

Appendix

those villages which are not served by the occasional bus have a carrier, or *recadero*, glad to take passengers as well as goods and parcels.

Belloc rightly dismissed the railway system in the Spanish Pyrenees as being of little practical use to the tourist. But there have been certain extensions in the last sixty years. The range is now crossed by two lines apart from the main Paris/Madrid and Paris/Barcelona lines at either end. One runs from Pau to Jaca, under the Somport and down the valley of Canfranc. The other runs from Barcelona up the Ter and the Fresser, and under the pass of Tosas to Puigcerdá. From Puigcerdá French lines climb out of the Cerdagne to run down the Ariège in one direction and down the Conflent in another. And although Barbastro still remains the terminus on the Cinca, there is now a line up the Noguera Pallaresa as far as Pobla de Segur, 'The Gateway of the Pyrenees'.

Exploring the area covered by this book, one sometimes finds oneself spending one night at only five hundred feet above sea-level in the hot plains, and the next at over six thousand in a high valley. A heavy pullover can be useful even at the height of summer in the Spanish Pyrenees.

2. ACCOMMODATION

Here again, timing and temperament are all important. The Spanish government is generous in its grants to the foreign exchange earning hotel industry, and establishments which today are 'simple', may tomorrow have grown annexes with all 'mod. cons', and replaced unvarnished oak with Formica.

As a general rule, I have never eaten badly in a Pyrenean village, and I have never drunk badly – and with drinking I include the appetizing *tapas*, those savoury morsels on cocktail sticks – in a Pyrenean town. As much ordinary red wine as one can comfortably drink is invariably included in the meals at the village *fondas*, and although the general themes of their menus are similar to those of other parts of Spain, the Pyreneans have more mutton, more fresh vegetables and occasionally more butter to

make the same dishes more acceptable to northern palates. The
best Pyrenean cooking is very good indeed.

Prices of hotels and (if one sticks to the table d'hôte) of meals
are rigidly controlled. Details of these prices, with lists of hotels,
restaurants, and *fondas*, together with much helpful information,
can be obtained by writing to the *Oficina de Información y Turismo*
at:

Behobia (Guipuzcoa)
Canfranc (Huesca)
Gerona
Huesca
Irún (Guipuzcoa)
Jaca (Huesca)
La Junquera (Gerona)
Lérida
Pamplona (Navarra)
Port-Bou (Gerona)
San Sebastian (Guipuzcoa)
Pobla de Segur (Lérida)
Viella (Lérida)

I have included in this list every office in or near the Pyrenees,
but the two which are likely to be most directly helpful for the
central valleys are those at Jaca and at Pobla de Segur. Some of
the offices are agencies of the central tourist department, some are
provincial, some municipal, and one is at least partly under the
patronage of its *comarca*. But the title of *Oficina de Información y
Turismo*, the name of the town, and the name of the province in
brackets (except when it is the same) will find them all.

3. MAPS

The one series of maps which covers the whole area in detail,
that of the official *Instituto Geográfico y Catastral*, is at 1/50,000 on
too large a scale for any but the specialist or mountaineer. On the
few occasions when the normal traveller may find it useful, he will
probably be able to consult it free. For I have found the sheet or
sheets covering the surrounding district hanging in many *ayunta-
mientos*, educational institutions, or those hotels which are deliberately catering for the walker, fisherman, or climber.

Appendix

Of road maps, one has the choice of Michelin 42 and 43 at 1/400,000 and Firestone Hispania 2 and 3 at 1/500,000. Besides giving slightly greater detail, Michelin at least has a try at assessing the conditions of roads. Firestone, on the other hand, marks a number of villages of whose existence Michelin seems unaware. Large sections of the Spanish Pyrenees, including all the Basque Pyrenees, Arán, upper Pallars, and Andorra, appear at 1/200,000 in Michelin 85 and 86, the two southernmost maps of their French series.

4. SHOOTING AND FISHING

There is more game in the Spanish countryside, and there are more fish in the Spanish rivers, than perhaps anywhere else in western Europe. Nor are shooting and fishing the perquisites of the privileged or the wealthy. Nevertheless licenses, seasons, and protected birds and animals do exist. The responsible authority, the Servicio Nacional de Pesca Fluvial y Caza, operates through nine regional headquarters, and it is these which the intending sportsman should approach for further details.

The Spanish Pyrenees are divided between two of these regions. Guipuzcoa and Navarre come under the 1st Region, and the address of its headquarters is:

Jefatura Regional del Servicio Nacional de Pesca Fluvial y Caza.
Alfonso VIII, 7, San Sebastian (Guipuzcoa).

Huesca, Lérida, and Gerona come under the 7th Region:
Jefatura . . . , etc., Plaza Doctor Letamendi 5, Barcelona.

However, as the 7th Region is so large, it has set up a sub-headquarters for the province of Huesca alone:

Delegacion Provincial del Servico Nacional de Pesca Fluvial y Caza.
Distrito Forestal, General Las Heras, Huesca.

BIBLIOGRAPHY

Of the two comprehensive works in Spanish, *Los Pirineos* of Luis Solé Sabaris (Martín, Barcelona, 1951) covers both sides of the range with scholarly detail and illuminating generalizations; whilst *El Pirineo Español* of Violant y Simorra (Madrid 1949) is a more popular volume whose hundreds of photographs and as many pages of text fascinate by their greater emphasis on the human aspects of Spanish Pyrenean life. Of local guides the *Guía del Pirineo de Lérida* of José María Espinás (Aries, Barcelona, 1958), specially commissioned by the *Oficina de Turismo* of Pobla de Segur, is especially helpful when visiting the valley of Bohí, Arán, and upper Pallars.

In English the reader will particularly enjoy:

The Pyrenees, by Hilaire Belloc. Methuen, 1909.

Pyrenean, by J. B. Morton. Longmans, 1938.

A Book of the Basques, by Rodney Gallop. Macmillan, 1940.

Navarre, by Nina Epton. Cassell, 1957.

The Enchanted Mountains, by Robin Fedden. John Murray, 1962.

Index

Index

Index

Index

Index

Index